Discovering Psychology
Study Guide

to accompany

Zimbardo • Gerrig
PSYCHOLOGY and LIFE
Fourteenth Edition

Prepared by

**Rose McDermott
and Ellie Goldberg**

HarperCollins*CollegePublishers*

The Annenberg/CPB Project

Discovering Psychology Study Guide to accompany PSYCHOLOGY AND LIFE, FOURTEENTH EDITION

ISBN: 0-673-98202-5

Copyright © 1996 by WGBH Educational Foundation and the Corporation for Public Broadcasting

Requests for permission to make copies of any part of the work should be mailed to the Copyrights and Permissions Department, HarperCollins College Publishers, 10 East 53rd Street, New York, NY 10022-5299, (212) 207-7133. Address for orders: HarperCollins College Publishers, 10 East 53rd Street, New York, NY 10022–5299, 1-800-782-2665. *For information about any HarperCollins title, product, or resource, please visit the World Wide Web site at* ***http://www.harpercollins.com/college***

PRINTED IN THE UNITED STATES OF AMERICA

96 97 98 99 00 9 8 7 6 5 4 3 2 1

This book was developed for use by students enrolled in the *Discovering Psychology* telecourse. The telecourse consists of 26 half-hour public television programs, the Study Guide, Faculty Guide, and an introductory psychology textbook selected by the instructor. Selected short portions of the programs have been excerpted and are available as video modules. *Discovering Psychology* was produced by WGBH-TV, Boston, Massachusetts. Major funding was provided by the Annenberg/CPB Project. This series is closed captioned for the hearing impaired.

To order the study guide, contact:

HarperCollins College Publishers
10 East 53rd Street
New York, New York 10022-5299
       Orders: 1-800-782-2665

To purchase *Discovering Psychology* videocassettes and/or other video series from The Annenberg/CPB Collection, contact:

Discovering Psychology
The Annenberg/CPB Collection
P. 0. Box 2345
South Burlington, Vermont 05407-2345
1-800-LEARNER

For more information about telecourse licenses, contact:

Discovering Psychology
PBS Adult Learning Service
1320 Braddock Place
Alexandria, Virginia 22314-1698
1-800-ALS-ALS-8

ACKNOWLEDGMENTS

The distinguished members of our Advisory Board, listed below, provided invaluable assistance in developing both the programs and the print materials for this telecourse.

Philip Zimbardo
Chief Academic Advisor
Professor of Psychology
Stanford University

W. Curtis Banks
Professor of Psychology
Howard University

Ludy T. Benjamin, Jr.
Professor of Psychology
Texas A & M University

Tom Bond
Professor of Psychology
Thomas Nelson Community College

Freda Rebelsky
Professor of Psychology
Boston University

Daniel Goleman
Science Writer
New York Times

James B. Maas
Professor of Psychology
Cornell University

Margaret S. Martin
Associate Professor of Professional Development and Health Services Administration
Medical University of South Carolina

Joe L. Martinez, Jr.
Professor of Psychology
University of California, Berkeley

Wilbert J. McKeachie
Professor of Psychology
University of Michigan

Fay-Tyler M. Norton
President
Colleague Consultants in Higher Education

Michael Wertheimer
Professor of Psychology
University of Colorado, Boulder

Special thanks also go to Robert Arkin, Dean of Undergraduate Studies at Ohio State University and the project's chief print advisor, who carefully reviewed the manuscript at several stages in its development and suggested many valuable improvements. The print materials also benefited greatly from the editing and fine-tuning provided by Naomi Angoff. Winifred Dunn deserves considerable credit for developing the faculty test bank as well as review questions for students. Researchers Tamra Pearson and Susan Kopman spent many hours in the library to locate anthology readings, citations for studies, additional resources, and other information necessary to complete the project. Patricia Crotty was the editorial assistant for the project and, with Deborah Paddock, oversaw photo research. Karen Barss was the permissions editor; the manuscript was copyedited by Margo Shearman.

WGBH Educational Foundation
Boston, Massachusetts

Project Directors

Brigid Sullivan
Manager of Special Telecommunications

Kim Storey
Project Director

Print Development

Ann Strunk
Director of Print Projects

Beth Kirsch
Coordinator of Print Projects

Production Team

Thomas Friedman
Executive-in-Charge/Executive Editor

William C. Brennan
Executive Producer

Tug Yourgrau
Senior Producer

CONTENTS

COURSE OVERVIEW AND GOALS

The first psychology laboratory was established in Leipzig, Germany, just 100 years ago. Yet despite its relative youth as an empirical science, psychology has made an indelible mark on our culture. We have become a psychology-oriented society, especially in the last half-century. Psychological research has changed many of our views on mental illness, learning, perception, motivation, sex and gender, aging, decision making, and health. Today, researchers and clinicians worldwide continue to investigate the puzzles of human behavior, studying questions of great interest not only to psychologists but to all of us as we strive to unravel the mysteries of mind and body—why we think, act, and feel as we do.

Discovering Psychology, an introductory psychology course consisting of 26 half-hour programs and corresponding curriculum materials, will help students understand the variety of approaches to the study of human nature. Each program is designed to stand alone as well as to fit into the overall focus and scope of the course, which begins with psychology's basic conceptual frameworks and progresses to more complex extensions and applications.

Discovering Psychology will expose students to leading researchers and the latest developments in the field, from new ways of treating anxiety and depression to the psychological factors involved in space travel. The course explains the scientific method of gathering and evaluating evidence as well as how psychological knowledge can improve the quality of life. Important psychological concepts and principles are brought to life by documentary footage, interviews, demonstrations, classic experiments, simulations, computer graphics, and animation. The course encourages open-minded curiosity and critical thinking.

Goals

Discovering Psychology

- × Explores the major psychological approaches to the study of behavior, including their history, contributors, methods, research findings, terminology, and current directions

- × Promotes the development of scientific values and skills, a recognition of individual bias in experimentation, and the ability to evaluate generalizations

- × Encourages personal development through increased understanding and tolerance of the behavior of others and a curiosity about the forces that make us behave as we do

- × Integrates new developments with classic research findings

- × Challenges some traditional perspectives in light of new knowledge

× Illuminates the decision-making processes used by researchers

× Interweaves the theme of psychology as a scientific enterprise with that of psychology as a course of knowledge and practice that can improve the quality of life

The Host

Philip Zimbardo is Professor of Psychology at Stanford University. Internationally applauded for his vibrant teaching talent, he is the recipient of distinguished teaching awards from New York University, Stanford University, and the American Psychological Association. He has published more than a dozen books and more than 100 articles on a wide range of topics, including aggression, shyness, animal and human behavior, individuals, groups, and culture. The chief academic advisor for the *Discovering Psychology* television course, Professor Zimbardo has been teaching introductory psychology for more than 30 years.

COURSE COMPONENTS

Discovering Psychology includes five components:

1. Twenty-six half-hour television programs
2. Introductory psychology textbook (chosen by the instructor)
3. Faculty Guide
4. Study Guide
5. Video modules

The Television Programs

1. Past, Present, and Promise

An introduction to psychology as a science at the crossroads of many fields of knowledge, from philosophy and anthropology to biochemistry and artificial intelligence.

2. Understanding Research

An examination of the scientific method and the ways in which data are collected and analyzed-in the lab and in the field—with an emphasis on sharpening critical thinking regarding research findings.

3. The Behaving Brain

The structure and composition of the brain: how neurons function; how information is collected and transmitted; and how chemical reactions determine every thought, feeling, and action.

4. The Responsive Brain

How the brain controls behavior, and, conversely, how behavior and environment influence the brain's structure and functioning.

5. The Developing Child

The nature versus nurture debate, and how developmental psychologists study the contributions of both heredity and environment to the development of children.

6. Language Development

The development of language, and how psychologists hope to discover truths about the human mind, society, and culture by studying how children use language in social communication.

7. Sensation and Perception

How visual information is gathered and processed, and how our culture, previous experiences, and interests influence our perceptions.

8. Learning

The basic principles of classical and operant conditioning, and how renowned researchers—Pavlov, Thorndike, Watson, and Skinner—have influenced today's thinking about the nature of animal and human learning.

9. Remembering and Forgetting

A look at the complex process called memory: how images, ideas, language, even physical actions, sounds, and smells, are translated into codes, represented in the memory, and retrieved when needed.

10. Cognitive Processes

An exploration into the higher mental processes—reasoning, planning, and problem solving—and why the "cognitive revolution" is attracting such diverse investigators, from philosophers to computer scientists.

11. Judgment and Decision Making

A look at the process of making judgments and decisions, how and why people make good and bad judgments, and the psychology of risk taking.

12. Motivation and Emotion

A review of what researchers are discovering about why we act and feel as we do, from the exhilaration of love to the agony of failure.

13. The Mind Awake and Asleep

The nature of sleeping, dreaming, and altered states of consciousness, and how consciousness empowers us to interpret, analyze, and direct our behavior in adaptive, flexible ways.

14. The Mind Hidden and Divided

How the events and experiences that take place below the level of consciousness alter our moods, bias our actions, and affect our health, as demonstrated in multiple personality, hypnosis, and split-brain patients.

15. The Self

How psychologists systematically study the origins of self-identity and self-esteem, social determinants of self-concepts, and the emotional and motivational consequences of beliefs about oneself.

16. Testing and Intelligence

The field of psychological assessment and the efforts of psychologists and other professionals to assign values to different abilities, behaviors, and personalities.

17. Sex and Gender

The ways in which males and females are similar and different, and how sex roles reflect social values and psychological knowledge.

18. Maturing and Aging

What really happens, physically and psychologically, as we age, and how society reacts to the last stages of life.

19. The Power of the Situation

How social psychologists attempt to understand human behavior within its broader social context, and how our beliefs and behavior can be influenced and manipulated by other people and by subtle situational forces.

20. Constructing Social Reality

The factors that contribute to our interpretation of reality and how understanding the psychological processes that govern our behavior can help us to become more empathetic and independent members of society.

21. Psychopathology

The major types of mental illness, including schizophrenia, anxiety, affective and manic-depressive disorders, and the major factors that influence them, both biological and psychological.

22. Psychotherapy

The relationships among theory, research, and practice, and how treatment of psychological disorders has been influenced by historical, cultural, and social forces.

23. Health, Mind, and Behavior

How research is forcing a profound rethinking of the relationship between mind and body—a new biopsychosocial model is replacing the traditional biomedical model.

24. In Space, Toward Peace

New horizons in psychology, including the ways in which psychologists are preparing astronauts for space travel and insight into the psychology of peace, from the complexity of arms negotiations to our responses to the possibility of nuclear war.

25. A Union of Opposites

A review of some of the most significant insights and principles regarding human nature and animal behavior, and how a yin–yang set of opposites has contributed to our understanding of them.

26. New Directions

The speculations of prominent psychologists on the future of the field, new directions in research, theory, and application, and how psychology can contribute to improving the quality of our lives.

Textbook

A variety of introductory psychology textbooks can be used with this telecourse, but this Study Guide has been developed for use with the textbook PSYCHOLOGY AND LIFE, 14TH EDITION by Philip Zimbardo and Richard Gerrig, HarperCollins, 1996. The textbook is an integral part of this television course. The assigned textbook readings for each unit will expand upon the television programs and present new information. The review questions and tests for this course will include questions from both the programs and the textbook readings.

You may find that the television programs present certain concepts or topics somewhat differently from the way the textbook does. Sometimes the information is presented in a different order, or the textbook may provide different examples and illustrations. The Study Guide will help you link the programs with the textbook.

Study Guide

The 26 units of the Study Guide correspond directly to the 26 television programs. The Study Guide previews, reviews, and applies the concepts and information from the television program. It also integrates program themes and concepts with the textbook. Each unit of the Study Guide includes the following elements:

- Objectives—concepts, facts, and themes from both the program and textbook that you should be able to define, identify, explain, or apply

- Reading Assignment—identifies the page numbers in the textbook PSYCHOLOGY AND LIFE that correspond to the themes and topics of the television program.

- Key People and Terms—lists important terms, concepts, and people introduced in the textbook reading and programs, and defines new terminology from the programs. Textbook page numbers are given for key people and terms, referring to the assigned reading or to other, related sections of the text.

- Program Summary—a narrative description of the themes and highlights of the corresponding television program

- Review Questions—self-test items that enable you to evaluate your understanding of the program and textbook reading to prepare for exams (answers are included in the Appendix)

- Questions to Consider—open-ended questions to promote critical thinking (suggested answers are included in the Appendix)

- Optional Activities—a variety of optional projects, writing assignments, or experiences to help you gather evidence, raise issues, apply basic concepts, and review important information

- Additional Resources—an annotated bibliography of related books, articles, and films

Taking *Discovering Psychology* as a Telecourse

Find out the following information as soon after registration as possible:

- What books are required for the course

- If and when an orientation session has been scheduled

- When *Discovering Psychology* will be broadcast in your area

- When examinations are scheduled for the course (mark these in your calendar)

- Whether any additional on-campus meetings have been scheduled (plan to attend as many review, sessions, seminars, and other meetings as possible)

To learn the most from each unit:

1. Before viewing the television program, read the corresponding unit in the Study Guide, paying particular attention to the Objectives, Key People and Terms, and Program Summary.

2. View the program, keeping the Objectives in mind. *Be an active watcher.* Some students find that taking notes while viewing the programs is helpful. If your area has more than one public television station there may be several opportunities for you to watch the program. Many public television stations repeat a program at least once during the week it is first shown. The programs may also be available on videocassettes at your school, or you can tape them at home if you own a VCR. If you don't have a VCR, you can make an audiocassette of the program for review.

3. Read the textbook sections listed in the Study Guide. As you read, pay particular attention to the Key People and Terms identified in the Study Guide. In addition, chapter outlines, headings, summaries, and terms in bold type will help you identify the important information.

4. Do the Review Questions and any other questions, activities, essays, or experiments assigned by your instructor.

5. Keep up with the course on a weekly basis. Each unit of the Study Guide builds on knowledge gained in previous units. Stay current with the programs and readings. Make a daily checklist, and keep weekly and term calendars, noting your scheduled activities such as meetings or examinations as well as blocks of time for viewing programs, reading, and doing assignments.

6. Keep in touch with your instructor. If possible, get to know him or her. You should have your instructor's mailing address, phone number, and call-in hours. Your instructor would like to hear from you and to know how you are doing. He or she will be eager to answer any questions you have about the course.

A NOTE FROM PHILIP ZIMBARDO

Welcome to the start of an exciting and challenging adventure in *Discovering Psychology*. I am delighted that you are about to join in this unique exploration into the nature of human nature. Through the medium of television, we will leave the confines of the traditional classroom to go where the action is, has been, or soon will be in psychology's scientific study of behavior and mental processes.

Our journey will take us to research laboratories throughout the United States to observe experiments in progress that are unraveling the mysteries of how the brain works, how animals and humans develop and change, and how the mind guides us through life's mazes. We will also visit mental hospitals, clinics, and therapists' offices where the pathologies of human functioning are studied, diagnosed, and treated. And we will venture out into the field where other researchers observe behavior in its natural habitat, whether it is stress among African baboons, shyness among chimpanzees, healing practices of Native Americans, competition in the classroom, or the destructive power of cult leaders over their followers.

This introduction to the state of the art of psychological knowledge is shaped by interviews with many of its most distinguished contributors. We will meet more than 70 researchers, theorists, and practitioners, all offering their individual perspectives on why they have devoted their talents to trying to solve the puzzles that brain, mind, and behavior continually present to the curious explorer. In addition to new interviews with Nobel Prize–winners David Hubel and Herbert Simon, we will hear from psychology's most prominent figures, among them B. F. Skinner, Neal Miller, Noam Chomsky, Carl Rogers, Erik Erikson, Albert Bandura, and Eleanor Maccoby. To get an inside view of the "cutting edge" in psychological knowledge, we will turn to the new generation of psychologists who present ideas that are influencing the directions psychology is taking and charting the course it is likely to follow in the future.

We will do more than just talk about psychology. We will show it in action—through documentary footage, laboratory re-creations of experiments, case studies, and live demonstrations of perceptual illusions, hypnosis, memory, biofeedback, lie detection, and many other topics of vital concern to today's, and tomorrow's, psychologists.

We shall travel back in time to see the actual archival footage of some of the most significant experiments and demonstrations in the history of psychology: Ivan Pavlov's monumental discovery of the laws of conditioning, John Watson's research on infant emotional reactions, Kurt Lewin's study of democratic and fascist leaders, and Stanley Milgram's provocative look into the conditions that foster blind obedience to authority.

Throughout our series, we will discover that *what* we know about the content of psychological inquiry is influenced by *how* we know it. So we shall look behind the facts and principles to examine the methodology used to collect the data on which our conclusions are based.

For the most part, the selection of the programs and their sequence of presentation follow what has become traditional in introductory psychology courses. The flow is from the areas considered to be the "hard core" or foundation disciplines of psychology—such as brain processes, development, perception, learning, memory, cognition, motivation, and emotion—to those that are somewhat more complex, broader in scope, or more recent, or that involve applications of basic psychological knowledge. The latter topics include consciousness, the self, testing and assessment, sex and gender, social psychology, psychopathology, therapies, and health psychology. Finally, our journey, which started by looking inside a single nerve cell in the brain, ventures up and outward to travel in outer space and toward emerging research on the prevention of nuclear war and the maintenance of peace.

An important goal of this series is an increased understanding and tolerance of the behavior of others, along with a idler appreciation of the complex set of influences that determine our own actions, from the genetic, cultural, and environmental to the political and economic. just as we as individuals are always part of a broader array of overlapping contexts, so We will see that psychology too is at the crossroads of many other disciplines.

Psychology is a unique field of study, a social science that draws from sociology, anthropology, economics, and political science. But it is ever more akin to the biological sciences, especially to the neurosciences, the study of brain processes. For many, the new core of psychology is what it shares with the cognitive sciences, artificial intelligence, computer science, and applied mathematics. And because one of the distinguishing features of psychology is its concern for improving the quality of individual and collective existence, it is also a health science, brimming with ties to education, law, medicine, and the environment.

While this remarkable breadth and depth of modern psychology is a source of attraction to those who become psychologists, it is also what makes the field a difficult challenge for the first-time explorer. As an undergraduate, I certainly found it tough to integrate all that diverse information in my Psych I course; my only college C grade in that course represents an enduring testimonial to that difficulty. But the excitement of being able to contribute to our understanding of human nature as a researcher and to communicate it to others as a teacher has since been a continual source of joy to me. I have taught introductory psychology for more than 30 years now, in seminars as small as 10 students and in lectures at more than 700 colleges. With equal delight I have also shared psychology with high school students, ghetto kids, elders, and teachers and professionals in other disciplines.

Discovering Psychology presents the best of contemporary psychology in a format that is interesting and intellectually stimulating. In a half-hour's time, an enormous amount of knowledge is conveyed because television can compact information through fast-moving images, graphics, and tightly packed commentary.

Of course, each video program highlights only a limited number of major points, introduces a few major contributors, touches on some historical background, and presents a brief view of current research or practical applications in a given area. But the hope is that by adding this unique visual component to the wealth of information in the textbook and the exercises and activities in this guide, psychology will come alive as never before.

UNIT 1

PAST, PRESENT, AND PROMISE

Science is the attempt to make the chaotic diversity of our sense-experience correspond to a logically uniform system of thought.

Albert Einstein

Unit 1 introduces psychology as the scientific study of behavior and mental processes. It looks at how psychologists work from a variety of theoretical models and traditions, record and analyze their observations, and attempt to unravel the mysteries of the mind.

Objectives

After viewing the television program and completing the assigned readings, you should be able to:

1. Define *psychology*

2. Understand the differences among the micro, molecular, and macro levels of analysis

3. Describe the five major goals of psychology

4. Describe what psychologists do and give some examples of the kinds of questions they may be interested in investigating

5. Summarize the history of the major theoretical approaches to psychology

6. Describe six current psychological perspectives

Reading Assignment

After viewing Program 1, read pages 1-26 in *Psychology and Life.*

Key People and Terms

As you watch the program and read the assignment, pay particular attention to these people and terms. People and terms defined in the text will be found on the given page numbers.
The following people and terms are used in Program 1 but are not defined in the text.

base rate (10)
behavior (4)
behaviorism (17)
behavioral data (5)
behavioristic approach (17)
biological approach (16)
cognitive approach (18)
determinism (13)
dispositional variable (9)
evolutionary approach (19)
functionalism (14)
humanistic approach (17)
intervening variables (8)
model (15)

organismic variables (9)
psychodynamic approach (16)
scientific method (4)
situational or environmental variables (9)
structuralism (14)

John Dewey (14)
Sigmund Freud (16)
William James (13)
Edward Titchener (13)
John Watson (17)
WilhelmWundt(13)

ERP (Event-Related Potentials)—variations in brain waves as recorded by the electro-encephalograph (EEG) which are triggered by specific internal or external events

Heisenberg indeterminacy principle—principle stating that our impressions of other people are distorted by how we observe and assess them

Emanuel Donchin-discovered that brains measure surprise before we are aware of it

Christine Hall- studies the disguised behavior of members of minority groups

G.Stanley Hall-founded the first American Psychology lab in 1883

Robert Rosenthal-showed that body language can reflect what we are thinking and feeling

Program Summary

Psychology is a field that asks questions about the relationships among the mind, brain, and behavior. Why do people laugh and cry? What is intelligence? Are we molded more by heredity or experience? What makes us fall in love? And how can we cure mental illness?

Psychologists are people who ask questions about the puzzles of human nature. Like most of us, they are people watchers who make assumptions about their observations. But as scientists, they test their ideas under special, controlled conditions.

During the next 26 programs we will see psychology in action and discover that it has a lot in common with many other fields of study. From understanding the smallest chemical reaction in the brain to recognizing the special needs of astronauts in space, psychology constantly seeks to answer this fundamental question: What is the nature of human nature?

Professor Philip Zimbardo, the host for the series, will introduce psychologists who work in many different settings: laboratories, classrooms, clinics, hospitals, and prisons. They study animals and people asleep and awake, healthy and ill, alone and in groups. But no matter what their field of expertise, all psychologists are dedicated to gaining a better understanding of behavior. We'll see how they observe behavior and attempt to describe it objectively, using their knowledge to predict behavior, and sometimes to control it.

Psychologists assume that our behaviors—our brain waves, gestures, eye movements, and word choices-are external signs of an inner reality. Even our slightest reaction can raise a host of questions about our underlying perceptions, expectations, feelings, and ideas.

Whatever type of behavior psychologists choose to study, they try to make sense of it by relating the behavior to certain aspects of the individual and to elements of the situation. They ask what it is about the person—gender, cultural background, past experiences—that could account for a particular reaction. By looking at the situation and the environment, they try to identify the elements that could have influenced the response.

But not all psychologists work in the same way. In 1975, a psychologist named Emanuel Donchin discovered that our brains register surprise even before we are aware of it. By recording the brain's electrical activity, he discovered that events trigger specific brain wave patterns. When psychologists focus on a small unit of behavior such as a brain wave, they are working at the micro level of analysis.

Most psychologists operate on the molecular level. They study larger units of behavior such as body language. Psychologist Robert Rosenthal has shown that our body language can reflect much of what we're thinking and feeling. Rosenthal describes how we can predict behavior in certain situations but emphasizes that the same gestures can have very different meanings in different situations.

At the molar level of analysis, researchers investigate the whole person in complex situations, focusing even more on cultural background and social experiences. Psychologists working at the molar level might study sexual attraction, worker morale, or the nature of prejudice. Because psychologists are scientists, they must always be aware of the limits to their powers of observation and assessment and to their ability to be truly objective.

Like all disciplines, psychology can be better understood in its own historical context. Modern psychology began in 1879 when Wilhelm Wundt founded the first experimental psychology laboratory in Germany. There he designed studies to collect data on such behaviors as reaction times to sensory stimuli, attention, judgment, and word associations.

The history of psychology took another step forward when G. Stanley Hall founded the first American psychology lab in 1883. Hall became the first president of the American Psychological Association, and he introduced Sigmund Freud to the United States through his translation of Freud's *General Introduction to Psychoanalysis.*

Then in 1890 Harvard professor William James published *Principles of Psychology,* considered by many to be the most important psychology text of all time. And James found a place in psychology for human consciousness, emotions, the self, personal values, and religion.

But James's methods—observation, introspection, and reasoning—were rejected by the Wundtian psychologists as too soft for science. They insisted on patterning psychology on the physical sciences, focusing on such areas as sensation and perception, and later adding studies on learning, memorization, and conditioning.

Since its inception, the field of psychology has included people with very different ideas about what to study and how to study it. Although the field has changed and expanded dramatically, the very ideas that originated over a century ago form the basis of psychological inquiry today.

Review Questions

Program Questions

1. What is the best definition of *psychology?*

    a. The scientific study of how people interact in social groups
    b. The philosophy explaining the relation between brain and mind
    c. The scientific study of the behavior of individuals and of their mental processes
    d. The knowledge used to predict how virtually any organism will behave under specified conditions

2. The program shows a woman who is suffering from multiple personality disorder. Which statement about these different personalities is true?

    a. Each is unaware of the others.
    b. Each has its own biology.
    c. Each is rather similar to the others.
    d. All began functioning at the same time.

3. What is the main focus of Donchin's research involving the P-300 wave?

    a. The relation between brain and mind
    b. The role of heredity in shaping personality
    c. The development of mental illness
    d. The role of situational factors in perception

4. What is the main goal of psychological research?

    a. To cure mental illness
    b. To find the biological bases of the behavior of organisms
    c. To predict and in some cases control behavior
    d. To find out how people think

5. The reactions of the boys and the girls to the teacher in the "Candid Camera" episode were essentially similar. Professor Zimbardo attributes this reaction to

    a. how easily adolescents become embarrassed.
    b. how an attractive teacher violates expectations.
    c. the way sexual titillation makes people act.
    d. the need people have to hide their real reactions.

6. What do EEGs measure?

    a. Heart rate
    b. Changes in hormone levels in the body
    c. Energy expended in overcoming gravity
    d. Brain activity

7. According to Robert Rosenthal's research, you are most likely to detect a liar by

    a. observing eye movements.
    b. listening to tone of voice.
    c. considering cultural factors.
    d. looking at body language.

8. Which cluster of topics did William James consider the main concerns of psychology?

    a. Reaction times, sensory stimuli, word associations
    b. Consciousness, self, emotions
    c. Conditioned responses, psychophysics
    d. Experimental design, computer models

9. What do we learn from our misreading of the "Paris in the spring" sign?

    a. We are accustomed to an artist's use of perspective.
    b. Experience disposes us to respond in a particular way.
    c. Unexpected events trigger P-300 waves in the brain.
    d. We laugh at those things that violate our expectations.

10. Christine Hall is conducting research on group behavior. She is particularly interested in how behavior varies based on

    a. the relative status of those present.
    b. the type of task the group is working on.
    c. how recently the group was formed.
    d. how many people there are in the group.

11. In her research, Christine Hall factors in the individual's cultural background and social experiences. Such research is being conducted at the

    a. micro level.
    b. molecular level.
    c. organic level.
    d. molar level.

12. Who founded the first psychology laboratory in the United States?

    a. Wilhelm Wundt
    b. William James
    c. G. Stanley Hall
    d. Sigmund Freud

13. How did Wundtian psychologists such as Hall react to William James's concept of psychology?

    a. They accepted it with minor reservations.
    b. They expanded it to include consciousness and the self.
    c. They rejected it as unscientific.
    d. They revised it to include the thinking of Sigmund Freud.

Textbook Questions

14. The most complete definition of psychology is

    a. the scientific study of human and animal behavior.
    b. the scientific study of behavior and mental disturbance.
    c. the scientific study of behavior and mental processes.
    d. the scientific study of human behavior and animal instincts.

15. Data are best described as

    a. collections of numbers.
    b. reports of observations.
    c. groups of hypotheses.
    d. evaluations of behaviors.

16. All of the following are goals of scientific psychology EXCEPT to

    a. predict.
    b. control.
    c. explain.
    d. classify.

17. The majority of psychologists have specialized in

    a. clinical and counseling psychology.
    b. social and experimental psychology.
    c. industrial and organizational psychology.
    d. counseling and community psychology.

18. Which of the following pairs is made up of "experimental psychologists"?

   a. Wilhelm Wundt and B.F. Skinner
   b. Sigmund Freud and Carl Jung
   c. William James and Abraham Maslow
   d. Rollo May and Carl Rogers

19. An important assumption of Wundt and the other early psychologists was that

   a. methods from the natural sciences could be used to study psychological processes.
   b. the mind was not subject to natural laws and principles.
   c. God determined how human beings behaved and responded.
   d. the decisions human beings make are predetermined.

20. Structuralists attempted to study _____ through the use of _____.

   a. the evolution of the mind; consciousness
   b. the contents of the mind; introspection
   c. the functioning of the mind; the behavioristic approach
   d. human emotions and motivations; experimentation

21. Both structuralists and functionalists agreed that the proper subject matter for psychology was

   a. consciousness.
   b. behavior.
   c. mental disorder.
   d. the brain.

22. Function is to functionalist as

   a. nature is to behaviorists.
   b. introspection is to evolutionists.
   c. contents are to structuralists.
   d. habits are to determinists.

23. All of the following may interfere with an accurate description of behavior EXCEPT

   a. expectations.
   b. inferences.
   c. objectivity.
   d. biases.

24. Who founded the first formal psychology laboratory?

    a. Johns Hopkins
    b. Wilhelm Wundt
    c. Herman von Helmholtz
    d. Edward Titchener

25. Titchener is to James as

    a. determinism is to evolutionism.
    b. creationism is to structuralism.
    c. functionalism is to humanism.
    d. structuralism is to functionalism.

26. Structuralism was criticized for being mentalistic. This means structuralists were interested only in

    a. animal behavior that could be measured.
    b. learned habits that aided in adaptation.
    c. those awarenesses that could be described verbally.
    d. overt observable behavior.

27. The two central processes in Charles Darwin's theory of evolution are

    a. evolution and determinism.
    b. natural selection and creationism.
    c. mutation and behavior genetics.
    d. natural selection and mutation.

28. The modern evolutionary approach emphasizes the biological significance of behavior. The perspective resembles that of

    a. behaviorism.
    b. humanism.
    c. structuralism.
    d. functionalism.

29. Psychodynamic approach is to biological approach as

    a. Freud is to Sperry.
    b. Sperry is to Watson.
    c. Watson is to Jung.
    d. Jung is to Maslow.

30. All of the following are humanistic psychologists EXCEPT

    a. Rollo May.
    b. Albert Bandura.
    c. Carl Rogers.
    d. Abraham Maslow.

Questions to Consider

1. Although psychologists are involved in many different kinds of research and professional activities, there are certain fundamental issues that form the basic foundation of psychology. What are they?

2. Why do some people believe that psychology is only concerned with abnormal behavior?

3. Why are critical thinking skills important?

4. How do your culture, age, gender, education level, and past experience bias your observations about events, your own actions, and the behavior of others?

5. Is thinking a behavior? How can it be studied?

Optional Activity

Start a personal journal or a log. Make a daily practice of recording events, thoughts, feelings, observations, and questions that catch your attention each day. Include the ordinary and the unusual. Then analyze what you observed, first listing as many questions as you can about the event. Speculate on the possible forces causing your behavior. As you progress through the course, review your notes and see how your observations and questions reflect what you have learned.

Additional Resources

Books and Articles

Adler, A.L. & Rubin, R. W. (Eds). (1994). *Aspects of the History of Psychology in America 1892-1992.* New York, New York: Academy of Sciences: Washington, D.C.: American   Psychological Association.

Hilgard, E. (1987). *Psychology in America.* New York: Harcourt Brace Jovanovich.

Stanovich, K. E. (1992). *How to Think Straight About Psychology*, 3rd ed. New York: HarperCollins.
    This "consumer's guide" to psychology sketches out what the behavioral science is—and is not.

12

UNIT 2

UNDERSTANDING RESEARCH

Whatever knowledge is attainable must be attainable by scientific method; and what science can not discover, mankind can not know.

Bertrand Russell

Unit 2 demonstrates the hows and whys of psychological research. By showing how psychologists rely on systematic observation, data collection, and analysis to find out the answers to their questions, this unit reveals why the scientific method is used in all areas of empirical investigation.

Objectives

After viewing the television program and completing the assigned readings, you should be able to:

1. Explain the concept of observer bias and cite some techniques experimenters use to eliminate personal bias

2. Define *placebo effect* and explain how it might be avoided

3. Define reliability and validity and explain the difference between them

4. Describe various psychological measurement techniques such as self report, behavioral and physiological measures

5. Define *correlational* methods and explain why it does not establish a cause and effect relationship

6. Summarize the American Psychological Association's ethical guidelines for the treatment of humans and animals in psychological experiments, and explain why they are necessary

7. Discuss some ways to be a wiser consumer of research

Reading Assignment

After viewing Program 2, read pages 27-54 in *Psychology and Life*.

Key People and Terms

As you watch the program and read the assignment, pay particular attention to these people and terms. People and terms defined in the text will be found on the given page numbers.

A-B-A design (36)
alternative explanations (33)
behavioral measures (44)
between-subjects designs (35)
confounding variable (35)
context of discovery (28)
control condition (35)
control procedures (35)
controlled experiment (42)
correlation coefficient (36)
correlational methods (36)
cross cultural research (39)
debriefing (49)
dependent variable (33)
descriptive statistics (45)
determinism (29)
double-blind control (35)
expectancy effects (33)
experimental method (36)
experimental condition (35)
hypothesis (29)
independent variable (33)
inferential statistics (45)
observer bias (31)
operational definition (32)

paradigm (29)
placebo control (35)
placebo effect (34)
psychological test (546)
randomization (43)
reliability (42)
self-report measures (43)
scientific method (31)
standardization (32)
validity (43)
variable (32)
within-subjects design (36)

Jane Goodall (46)
Anthony Greenwald (41)
Hugo Musterberg (31)
Robert Rosenthal (33)

The following terms and people are used in Program 2 but are not defined in the text.

field study—research carried on outside the laboratory where naturally occurring, ongoing behavior can be observed

random sample—an unbiased population selected at random

subjective reality—the perceptions and beliefs that we accept without question

Daryl Bem-psychologist who illustrated the importance of critical thinking in scientific experiments

Norman Cousins- used laughter to cure himself of osteoarthritis in his back after regular doctors had failed him

Jerome Frank-psychiatrist who studies the common features of miracle cures and healings, political and religious conversions and psychotherapy

Leonard Saxe- studies the use and misuse of polygraphs to detect lying

Program Summary

Tune in to any television or radio talk show, and you are likely to find someone peddling psychic powers, astrology, ESP, or mind reading. Because psychology is so often sensationalized and misrepresented, it is difficult for the average person to distinguish science from pseudoscience, fact from fiction.

Program 2 demonstrates how psychologists separate superstition and irrational beliefs from fact and reason. Understanding how ideas are tested enables us to become skeptical consumers of media information and to develop critical thinking skills to protect us against deception and fraud.

Psychologists are guided by a set of procedures for gathering and interpreting evidence using carefully controlled observations and measurements. This is called the scientific method and requires that research be conducted in an orderly, standardized way. Then the results are published so that others can review and perhaps repeat the process.

Scientists employ a variety of study methods. They conduct experiments in laboratories, administer surveys, and take measurements in the field where they observe people and animals in natural settings. Seeing how scientists try to eliminate error and bias from their work helps us avoid some of the faulty reasoning in our own lives.

One factor that scientists consider is the placebo effect. In medicine, a placebo is a substance that is chemically inert, such as a sugar pill. It may nevertheless have a therapeutic effect. The placebo effect complicates the job of a researcher because the mere suggestion of a believable treatment will make many people feel better. Some researchers have found that despite different settings or tactics, the power of any change agent relies on the person's absolute belief in the change agent's power.

Any medical or psychological treatment can only be considered successful if it demonstrates a level of effectiveness beyond the placebo effect. To do this, researchers use the double-blind procedure in which neither the participant nor the experimenter knows who is getting the real drug and who is taking the placebo. That information is held by another researcher who has no contact with the experimenter or subjects.

In order to analyze a miracle cure or a magic truck, we must evaluate all kinds of beliefs and theories. It is important to test hypotheses, define success, account for chance, and establish controls. Consider the case of Norman Cousins, the respected editor of the *Saturday Review* who had a form of spinal arthritis that is usually incurable. Dissatisfied with traditional medicine, he designed his own treatment based on a regimen of laughter. He claimed that 10 minutes of laughter gave him at least two hours of pain-free sleep. Cousins later recovered from spinal arthritis.

But was laughter the sole cause of his cure? The scientific method requires that we separate its effects from all the other possible sources of influence on Cousins' state of mind and health. When several factors (in this case, Cousins' optimism and high doses of vitamin C) might be responsible for the outcome, we must try to determine which one deserves the credit. It may be that Cousins' cure was influenced by the combination of these factors.

We must resist the temptation to conclude that things that merely occur together necessarily have a cause and effect relationship. There may be a third factor that causes the other two. Consider a report that suggests that when the time spent watching TV goes up, grades go down. Should we conclude that watching TV causes poor grades? In fact, students who watch a lot of TV might spend less time on their homework. But students who get bad grades might watch more television because they don't like homework. They would get bad grades whether they watched TV or not.

When interpreting data, we have to make sure that the subjects in an experiment are a representative sampling of the population they are meant to represent. Shere Hite's controversial report on women's attitudes about sex and marriage highlights a sampling problem. Her conclusions were based on only 4 percent of all the people who had received her questionnaire. She had taken no steps to ensure that her sample would be representative of the age, education level, and race distribution in the general population. Hite's sample method was too flawed to be useful (see figure below).

Shere Hite Study	ABC News and *Washington Post* Study
4% of sample responding	random sampling
98% dissatisfied with some aspect of their relationship	*93% satisfied* with their relationship
75% involved in extramarital affairs	7% involved in extramarital affairs

Figure 1: Comparison of Sex and Marriage Studies
Shere Hite's study of women's attitudes toward sex and marriage did not include a representative sampling since only 4 percent of the women she contacted responded. A similar study conducted by ABC News and the *Washington Post*, which included a random sampling of women, found very different results.

Professionals as well as the general public can be taken in by pseudoscientific technology. The polygraph, or lie detector, for example, measures changes in physical arousal such as heart rate or the galvanic skin response. But these machines are fallible. Research has shown that innocent people who believe they might be mistakenly identified may show anxiety. And guilty people may fool the machine by taking drugs or purposely tensing and relaxing their muscles. This so-called lie detector can play a crucial role in people's lives; sometimes it is used to help make decisions about hiring and firing employees.

Getting at the truth about psychological phenomena is difficult, but there are guidelines that help us avoid common pitfalls: Don't assume that two things that occur together are cause and effect. Seeing isn't always believing. Question data that aren't collected using rigorous procedures. Keep in mind the power of placebos. Restrain enthusiasm for scientific breakthroughs. Beware of people claiming absolute truth and of attempts to persuade rather than educate. And remember that conclusions are always open to revision.

Review Questions

Program Questions

1. In the science section of a newspaper, there is an article about recent psychological research on differences between men and women. According to Professor Zimbardo, how should you approach such articles?

    a. With a skeptical attitude
    b. With complete disbelief
    c. With a willingness to accept them completely
    d. Such accounts are not worth reading at all.

2. The scientific method is defined as a set of

    a. theories.
    b. truths.
    c. procedures.
    d. statistical methods.

3. What is the main reason that the results of research studies are published?

    a. So researchers can prove they earned their money
    b. So other researchers can try to replicate the work
    c. So the general public can understand the importance of spending money on research
    d. So attempts at fraud and trickery are detected

4. Why does the placebo effect work?

    a. Because researchers believe it does
    b. Because subjects believe they are receiving a treatment
    c. Because human beings prefer feeling they are in control
    d. Because it is part of the scientific method

5. What is the purpose of a double-blind procedure?

    a. To test more than one variable at a time
    b. To repeat the results of previously published work
    c. To define a hypothesis clearly before it is tested
    d. To eliminate experimenter bias

6. If you had been one of the subjects in the lie detector study, what information would have helped you earn some money?

    a. The results depend on the skill of the person administering the lie detector test.
    b. Lie detectors only measure arousal level, not lying.
    c. The polygraph is used to make millions of decisions each year.
    d. The placebo effect works with lie detectors.

7. What suggestion does Jerome Frank make that would help explain why Norman Cousins' method worked so well?

    a. People need a sense of mastery.
    b. Laughter makes us feel good.
    c. Psychotherapy has much in common with faith healing.
    d. A healing saying is an important feature of a cure.

8. A report on children's television watching found that children who watch more TV had lower grades. What cause-effect conclusion are we justified in making on the basis of this study?

    a. TV watching causes low grades.
    b. Poor school performance causes children to watch more TV.
    c. Cause-effect conclusions can never be based on one study.
    d. Cause-effect conclusions cannot be based on correlation.

9. What was the major weakness of the Hite report on women's attitudes toward sex and marriage?

    a. The sample was not representative.
    b. Hypotheses were not clearly stated beforehand.
    c. Experimenter bias arose because the double-blind procedure was not used.
    d. No control group was used.

10. A prediction of how two or more variables are likely to be related is called a

    a. theory.
    b. conclusion.
    c. hypothesis.
    d. correlation.

11. Imagine a friend tells you that she has been doing better in school since she started taking vitamin pills. She urges you to take vitamins too. On the basis of the program, what objection might you make?

    a. You remember reading somewhere that healthy people don't need vitamins.
    b. You realize that if a person believes something will help, there's a good chance it will.
    c. You will believe her only if she takes a polygraph test.
    d. You think that she would be doing well in school in any case.

12. Why can't psychologists do a controlled experiment on the effect a mother's use of cocaine has on her baby?

    a. The placebo effect would be too strong.
    b. Causation could not be established.
    c. It would be unethical.
    d. People who use drugs make unreliable subjects.

Textbook Questions

13. Critical thinking involves all of the following EXCEPT

    a. evaluating information.
    b. understanding causation and correlation.
    c. relying on authorities and the media.
    d. asking the right questions.

14. The term placebo effect refers to

    a. a change in condition or behavior due to observer bias.
    b. the side effects of new and untested medications.
    c. a change in response due to a belief that a particular factor would affect it.
    d. improvement in a behavior or condition due to the passage of time.

15. Freud's model of unconscious motivation and Skinner's model of response-consequence relationships are examples of

    a. hypotheses.
    b. paradigms.
    c. new technologies.
    d. deterministic ideas.

16. A psychologist would strive for all of the following EXCEPT

    a. open-mindedness.
    b. public verifiability.
    c. secrecy.
    d. a critical and skeptical attitude.

17. Why are operational definitions important in psychological research?

    a. To maintain an open-minded attitude among researchers and students
    b. To ensure ethical treatment of subjects
    c. To avoid ambiguity and ensure verifiability of stimuli and responses
    d. To standardize data reports and records

18. Researchers try to anticipate and control confounding variables in order to

    a. increase the reliability of the independent variable.
    b. increase the validity of the independent variable.
    c. eliminate alternative explanations.
    d. get results that are significant.

19. Carol took the Know-It-All Intelligence Test three times last year. She scored 100, 49 and then 156. This test lacks

    a. validity.
    b. reliability.
    c. objectivity.
    d. control procedures.

20. Which of the following statements about A-B-A design is true?

    a. The control group is measured twice.
    b. There are several dependent variables.
    c. The dependent variable is not measured.
    d. The same subjects are used in all conditions.

21. Central tendency is to variability as

    a. mode is to median.
    b. standard deviation is to range.
    c. mean is to standard deviation.
    d. range is to median.

22. When a difference between two sets of scores is considered "statistically significant", this means

    a. the mean of one group is higher than the other.
    b. the standard deviation is larger than the mean.
    c. the results are unlikely to be due to chance.
    d. the results are unlikely to be found again.

23. A subject comes to the Psychology Lab and is asked to sign a form describing what procedures will take place, any potential risks, and some benefits which might be expected. When she signs this form, she is

    a. surrendering her rights as a subject.
    b. indicating informed consent.
    c. stating her willingness to be deceived.
    d. stating her awareness of risk/gain assessment

24. Observer bias influences our

    a. perception.
    b. preferences.
    c. judgement.
    d. creativity.

25. If you were to offer a tentative and testable statement about the relationship between two or more variables, you would be offering a

    a. theory.
    b. paradigm.
    c. hypothesis.
    d. model.

26. The term "scientific method" refers to

    a. the use of new technology to study phenomena.
    b. the creation of theory based on observation.
    c. a set of theories combined into a new paradigm.
    d. a set of procedures for gathering and interpreting data.

27. All of the following characterize scientific attitudes or practices, EXCEPT

    a. secrecy.
    b. objectivity.
    c. skepticism.
    d. open-mindedness.

28. Using a double-blind procedure eliminates

    a. observer bias.
    b. expectancy bias.
    c. confounding variables.
    d. placebo effects.

29. Procedural control is to confounding variables as

    a. objectivity is to personal bias.
    b. reliability is to validity.
    c. independent variable is to dependent variable.
    d. placebo is to double-blind control.

30. Questionnaire is to interview as

    a. standardized is to interactive.
    b. open-ended is to representative.
    c. survey is to self-report.
    d. correlation is to experiment.

Questions to Consider

1. If some people really get healed by faith healers, why condemn the practice of faith healing?

2. Would you like to be graded on a curve? Why or why not?

3. What are some of the objections to studying mental processes?

4. Why is there so much uncertainty in psychology?

5. If the placebo effect can make a person feel better, do you think a person's disbelief can undermine the effects of drugs known to be effective?

6. Are animals adequately protected by the APA's guidelines? Why or why not?

7. Why is a study that uses only volunteers likely to be biased?

Optional Activities

1. Write operational definitions of the following:

success	aggression	wealth
love	anger	learning
affection	intelligence	hunger
attractiveness	power	

2. Design a study that would test the validity of one of the following proverbs:

   Birds of a feather flock together.
   Spare the rod and spoil the child.
   You can't teach an old dog new tricks.
   Actions speak louder than words.
   A stitch in time saves nine.
   If it ain't broke, don't fix it.

Additional Resources

Books and Articles

Agnew, N. M., and S. W. Pyke.(1978). *The Science Game: An Introduction to Research in the Behavioral Sciences.* 2d ed. Englewood Cliffs, N.J.: Prentice-Hall. Explores the basic methods, procedures, and tools of behavioral scientists.

Cousins, N.(1983). *The Healing Heart.* New York: Norton. Determined to take charge of his recovery from heart failure, Norman Cousins developed his own health plan, which included not only proper diet and exercise but also hobbies and humor.

Edward, A.L. (1985). *Experimental Design in Psychological Research.* New York: Harper & Row.

Page, J.(1988, November). "Dilutions of Grandeur." *American Health,* 78-82. The placebo effect can make even quack treatments look good. Jake Page takes a critical look at flawed research and scientific fraud.

Randi, J. (1980). *Flim Flam: The Truth About Unicorns, Parapsychology and Other Delusions.* New York: Lippincott & Crowell. Randi exposes individuals who claim paranormal, occult, and supernatural powers. He shows how scientific procedures can reveal the truth behind illusions.

Thompson, R. (1975). *Introduction to Physiological Psychology.* New York: Harper & Row.

UNIT 3

THE BEHAVING BRAIN

There is no scientific study more vital to man than the study of his own brain. Our entire view of the universe depends on it.

Francis Crick

Psychologists who study the structure and composition of the brain believe that all our thoughts, feelings, and actions have a biological and chemical basis. Unit 3 explains the nervous system and the methods scientists use to explore the link between physiological processes in the brain and psychological experience and behavior.

Objectives

After viewing the television program and completing the assigned reading, you should be able to:

1. Explain the major concepts of evolutionary theory such as natural selection, and variation.

2. Identify several methods used to study the brain and give a significant finding associated with each

3. Identify the major structures and specialized functions of the brain

4. Cite examples of how the endocrine system affects mood and emotion

5. List and describe the major divisions and subdivisions of the nervous system and the functions of each.

6. Describe the structure of a neuron

7. Explain the mechanism of neural transmission

8. Describe the process of synaptic transmission and list the six important neurotransmitters.

9. Describe hemispheric separation and individual difference within that

Reading Assignment

After viewing Program 3, read pages 55-100 in *Psychology and Life*. This textbook reading covers Units 3 and 4.

Key People and Terms

As you watch the program and read the assignment, pay particular attention to these people and terms. People and terms defined in the text will be found on the given page numbers.

action potential (83)

all-or-none principle (84)

amygdala (73)

association cortex (74)

auditory cortex (74)

autonomic nervous system (ANS) (69)

axon (80)

bipedalism (58)

brain stem (71)

Broca's area (65)

central nervous system (CNS) (68)

cerebellum (72)

cerebral cortex (73)

cerebral hemispheres (73)

cerebrum (73)

cerebral dominance (91)

corpus callosum (74)

dendrites (80)

echo-planar MRI (68)

electrode (66)

electroencephalogram (EEG) (66)

encephalization (58)

endocrine system (77)

environment (57)

estrogen (79)

evolution (57)

excitatory (82)

genes (62)

genetics (62)

genotype (57)

positron emission tomography (PET scanner) (67)

refractory period (85)

resting potential (80)

glial cells (glia) (81)

graded potentials (82)

heredity (57)

hippocampus (71)

homeostasis (73)

hormones (77)

human behavior genetics (62)

hypothalamus (73)

ion channels (84)

inhibitory (82)

interneurons (80)

lesions (65)

limbic system (72)

magnetic resonance imaging (MRI) (67)

medulla (71)

motor cortex (75)

motor neurons (80)

natural selection (57)

nature (57)

neural networks (89)

neuromodulator (88)

neuroscience (64)

neuron (79)

neurotransmitters (86)

nurture (57)

parasympathetic division (69)

peripheral nervous system (PNS) (68)

phenotype (57)

pituitary gland (78)

pons (71)

reticular formation (71)
sensory neurons (80)
sex chromosomes (62)
soma (80)
somatic nervous system (69)
somatosensory cortex (75)
spatial summation (83)
sympathetic division (69)
synaptic transmission (86)
synapse (86)
temporal summation (82)
terminal buttons (80)
testosterone (79)
thalamus (71)
visual cortex (76)

Paul Broca (65)
Santiago Ramon y Cajal (64)
Charles Darwin (57)
Rene Descartes (64)
Michael Gazzaniga (92)
Peter Grant (57)
Donald Hebb (64)
Walter Hess (66)
Eric Kandel (90)
Doreen Kimura (95)
Wilder Penfield (66)
Sir Michael Sherrington (64)
Roger Sperry (92)

The following terms and people are used in Program 3 but are not defined in the text.

agonist—a chemical or drug that mimics the action of a neurotransmitter

amnesia-forgetting

antagonist—a chemical or drug that blocks the action of a neurotransmitter

physostigmine-enhances the effect of acetylcholine in the brain by inhibiting the enzyme which breaks it down

sopolamine-depletes the availability of acetylcholine in the brain by blocking the receptors for acetylcholine

Fred Gage-studies new strategies for overcoming brain damage

E. Roy John-studies neurometrics and uses precise electrophysiological measures to determine neural functioning

Joseph Martinez-studies how brain chemical effect learning and memory

Program Summary

All information that we receive, process, and transmit depends on the functions of the brain, the most complex structure in the known universe. Program 3 describes the brain's biological and chemical foundation for all our thoughts, feelings, and actions.

There are about 10 trillion nerve cells in the brain. These cells, called neurons and glia, use a combination of electrical and chemical messengers to perform their specialized functions. Dendrites, or receptor fibers, gather incoming messages and send them to the cell body, or soma. Then the messages are sent on as electrical discharges down the axon to the neuron's terminal button, which releases a chemical message to adjacent neurons.

Some chemicals generate a nerve impulse by exciting nearby receptors; others reduce or block nerve impulses and regulate the rate at which neurons fire. These nerve impulses are the basis for every change that takes place in the body, from moving our muscles to learning and remembering our multiplication tables.

Although the brain works in a holistic way, some of its parts specialize in particular jobs. The brain stem, which connects the brain to the spinal cord, controls breathing, heartbeat, waking, and sleeping. The cerebellum coordinates body movement and maintains equilibrium. The amygdala, part of the limbic system, seems to control sensory impulses, such as aggressive urges. For example, a mouse receiving electrical stimulation to the amygdala will attack a cat. And suppressing the amygdala will stop a bull in his tracks. The hypothalamus is the liaison between the body and the rest of the brain, releasing hormones to the pituitary gland. The thalamus acts as a relay station, sending signals from the body to the brain.

The cerebrum translates nerve impulses into higher-level cognitive processes, using images and symbols to form ideas and wishes. Its outer layer, the cerebral cortex, is the center of conscious thought and action. The cerebrum's two halves, or hemispheres, are connected by a bundle of millions of nerve fibers called the corpus callosum, which acts as a conduit of messages between the right and left sides of the brain.

Scientists use a variety of methods to understand better the structure and functions of the brain. In the past, autopsies revealed how impaired abilities might be the result of damaged brain tissue. Later, experimenters purposely destroyed specific parts of animal brain tissue so they could observe what sensory or motor losses occurred. Researchers also stimulated specific regions with electricity or chemicals. Today we can get actual pictures of the brain's inner workings using a technique called imaging. Scientists can also record nerve signals from a single neuron or electrical wave patterns from the entire brain. This brain wave pattern is known as an electroencephalogram, or EEG.

But how do scientists know what constitutes normal electrical activity in the brain? By analyzing and comparing brain wave patterns from people all over the world, they have concluded that all healthy members of the human species have similar brains. Variations in electrical patterns may reveal environmental influences such as poor nutrition or even living at unusually high elevations. This methodology helps scientists identify structural or chemical causes for thought, mood, and behavioral disorders, thus making it easier to evaluate different therapies.

Other neuroscientists study the brain's biochemical activity. They look at many groups of neurotransmitters and hormones which affect brain functions and behavior. Nerve cells manufacture opiatelike molecules known as endorphins, part of the complex system of neurotransmitters. Endorphins can affect our moods, emotions, and perception of pain. Some long-distance runners report a feeling of euphoria, or "runner's high," after a strenuous workout. This may be the result of exercise's increasing the body's endorphin activity.

Endorphins are only one of many chemical influences on the brain. Some scientists investigate the influence of brain chemicals on learning and memory. By comparing the performance of experimental rats given drugs that block or mimic specific neurotransmitters with that of untreated animals, scientists hope to discover which changes in the brain produce specific actions. So, by learning how the brain works or fails to work, they can begin to prescribe new drug therapies to prevent, minimize, even cure diseases, such as learning deficits or memory losses, and Alzheimer's disease.

In addition to better understanding the brain, scientists are also improving how it works. Some researchers are actually designing new ways to overcome brain damage. In one lab, a scientist grafts healthy brain tissue into dead or damaged brain areas and finds that the tissue can survive and grow. Rats have gained learning and memory abilities following tissue transplants from aborted fetuses. These results may eventually help people with Parkinson's disease, a degenerative disorder caused by a loss of dopamine-producing brain cells, which affects more than a million people in the United States alone. Though fetal brain tissue transplants in human patients raise many ethical questions, scientists seek to understand whether successful transplants result from a strong placebo effect, some actual release of dopamine caused by the surgery, or the adjustment of medication before or after the surgery.

Although research involving human tissue transplants is highly controversial, even in the scientific community, scientists are continuing to uncover the biochemical mechanisms that underlie the complexities of behavior in an effort to prevent, control, and cure disease, and to improve the quality of life.

Review Questions

Note: Review Questions for Units 3 and 4 are provided in Unit 4.

Questions to Consider

1. What is the advantage of knowing that mental illness is caused by neurochemical problems if we don't know how to correct them?

2. There are millions of people who will try just about anything to control their weight. They buy diet pills and nutritional supplements that claim to alter the chemistry of their appetite. Some are so desperate that they have their mouths wired shut. Why don't doctors treat people with eating disorders by placing electrodes in their brains?

3. Why should you be suspicious of studies claiming that high doses of vitamins or nutritional supplements are necessary for preventing physical or mental disorders, maintaining health, or curing diseases?

4. Different technologies for measuring brain activity help psychologists view structures and functioning of the brain. What advantages do these advanced techniques offer?

Optional Activity

Can you feel the effects of your hormones? Try this: Imagine yourself falling down the stairs, stubbing your toe, or suddenly losing control of your car on a busy highway. Did your heart skip a beat? Did you catch your breath or feel a tingle up your back? Did the hair on your neck stiffen? Your imagination has caused a biochemical reaction in your brain, and you are feeling the effect of the hormones it produces. Can you name the hormones involved?

Additional Resources

Books and Articles

Boddy, J. (1989). The benefits of physiological psychology. *British Journal of Psychology*, 80, 4, pp. 479-498.

Diamond, M., A. Schneibel, & L. Elson.(1985) *The Human Brain Coloring Book.* New York: Harper & Row. An entertaining, illustrated guide to the human brain.

Gazzaniga, M. S. (1985). "The Social Brain." *Psychology Today,* 28-38. Are our brains divided into independent units that often work apart from our conscious and verbal selves? This article, like Gazzaniga's book of the same name, discusses a new theory of brain organization.

Holmes, C. (1992). Psychology as an evolving science. *Psychological Science*, Sept. 3, 5, 320-321.

Restak, R. (1984). *The Brain.* New York: Bantam Books. Chapter 1, "The Enlightened Machine," is a good, clearly written introduction to brain structures and functions.

Scientific American, (1979), 241, 9. This issue, devoted to the study of the brain, offers a good review of topics in the unit. Articles focus on various aspects of brain organization, chemistry, and functions.

Sinclair, J. D. (1983). "The Hardware of the Brain." *Psychology Today* December, 8-12. Will computers ever think the way humans do? Sinclair looks at how computers and human beings store and process information.

Valenstein, E. (1988). "Science Fiction, Fantasy, and the Brain." *Psychology Today* July, 28-39. Examines how the psychological experiments of science fiction compare with actual research.

UNIT 4

THE RESPONSIVE BRAIN

The Human Brain is a most unusual instrument of elegant and as yet unknown capacity.

Stuart Lyman Seaton

Unit 4 takes a closer look at the dynamic relationship between the brain and behavior. We'll see how the brain controls behavior and, conversely, how behavior and environment can cause changes in the structure and the functioning of the brain.

Objectives

After viewing the television program and reviewing the assigned reading, you should be able to:

1. Cite examples of the brain's capacity to adapt to environmental change

2. Describe the mechanism by which touch deprivation is related to stunted growth

3. Explain how early experience can affect brain mechanisms that influence stress tolerance in later life

4. Cite research studies that contribute to an understanding of the role enriched environments play in brain development

5. Describe the concept of critical periods of development and cite the evidence that supports or contradicts it

6. Explain how individual maturation is controlled by social needs and group behavior

7. Explain the value of observation studies of animals in their natural habitats and how these studies complement laboratory research

Reading Assignment

After viewing Program 4, review pages 55-100 in *Psychology and Life.*

Key People and Terms

People and terms defined in the text for this unit are provided in Unit 3.

The following terms and people are used in Program 4 but are not defined in the text.

enzymes—protein molecules that act as catalysts in body chemistry by facilitating chemical reactions

glucocorticoid—substances produced by the adrenal cortex that act on the hippocampus to alter the stress response

maternal deprivation—the lack of adequate affection and stimulation from the mother or mother substitute

Tiffany Field--studies the effect of infant massage on the cognitive and motor development of infants

Russell Fernald--neuroethologist who studies how brain, behavior and the environment interact in animals in their natural habitat

Michael Meaney--developmental psychologist who studies how early experiences can change the brains and behavior of animals, especially under stress

Saul Schanberg--works with infant rats to demonstrate how touch is a brain based requirement for normal growth and development. Argues that a mother's touch has real biological value to offspring which is required to maintain normal growth and development

Robert Sapolsky--neurobiologist who studies the social structure of baboon communities. Argues that dominance affects physiological functioning, with higher ranks being associated with greater control, predictability and better physiological functioning

Program Summary

The brain is the place where an endless stream of electrical nerve impulses, chemical transmitters, and hormone messengers get transformed into experience, knowledge, feelings, beliefs, and consciousness. Learning how it functions helps us better understand human and animal behavior.

The reciprocal relationship between the brain and behavior is the subject of Program 4. The brain controls behavior, and behavior feeds back information to influence the brain. The brain can even alter its own functioning and structure. This capacity for internal modification makes it one of the most dynamic systems on earth.

Several studies demonstrate the responsiveness of the brain's neurochemical system. In one, we learn that humans and animals thrive when they get adequate contact and suffer when they do not. For some infants, especially those born prematurely, touch can mean the difference between illness and health, even life and death.

Psychologist Tiffany Field explains her study in which some premature infants received gentle massages and others received routine care. Those in the massaged group gained more weight, were able to leave the hospital earlier, and showed long-term developmental advantages over the babies who received routine care. This research clearly demonstrates the therapeutic value of touching and suggests a way to save millions of dollars in hospital costs.

Psychologist Saul Schanberg, who conducted research with touch-deprived rats, demonstrated that maternal deprivation can stunt growth. But he also demonstrated that retarded growth can be reversed. Placing the stunted baby rats with their mothers or stroking them with a wet paintbrush restored normal growth.

Lack of touching also seems to affect the production of human growth hormones. When researchers removed touch-deprived, growth-stunted children from their unloving homes and placed them in more affectionate families, they grew dramatically.

Another study demonstrates that early experiences can cause permanent alterations in the structure of the brain. Rats raised in stimulating, visually enriched environments had a thicker cortex and were superior learners compared with rats raised in ordinary or deprived environments. The stimulated rats had more neurotransmitters, more enzymes in the glial cells, and more and larger spines on the dendrites.

Other research studies on early experience and the brain also show long-term effects of touching. Newborn rats who had regular handling were better able to cope with stress throughout their lives. They also showed signs of slower aging and of reduced learning and memory losses.

Developmental psychologist Michael Meany investigates how early experiences can change the brain and behavior. He explains that when an individual faces a threat, the adrenal glands release hormones called glucocorticoid, which prepare the body to handle stressful situations. But repeated exposure to stress hormones inhibits the glucocorticoid neurons in the hippocampus, a part of the brain that regulates stress and plays a key role in learning and memory. Handling the baby rats in the first three weeks of life seems to reduce the loss of glucocorticoid cells and improves the hippocampus's ability to turn off the stress response.

Field research is just as important as controlled experiments performed in the laboratory. Russell Fernald of the Institute of Neuroscience in Oregon studied the African Chiclid fish as an example of how the brain is altered when behavior changes. He observed that dominant male Chiclids have brightly colored patterns and dark eye bars. When these fish acquired territory, changes in the Chiclids brain caused the fish to grow rapidly and colorfully. When they lost territory, they lost their coloration and sexual maturity.

Another study, conducted by Stanford biologist Robert Sapolsky, demonstrated that in baboon colonies, social rank is the most important principle of social organization. When baboons attained high social rank, they also became healthier and more physically resistant to wear and tear. With reverses in status, they showed a corresponding loss of health and tolerance for stress.

All these studies contribute to a better understanding of the interplay of environment, behavior, and biology. In the controlled setting of the laboratory, researchers can look more closely at how the brain changes. In the field, they can observe how animals naturally respond to demands from the environment.

Review Questions

Program Questions

1. What section of a nerve cell receives incoming information?

   a. The axon
   b. The terminal button
   c. The synapse
   d. The dendrite

2. In general, neuroscientists are interested in the

   a. brain mechanisms underlying normal and abnormal behavior.
   b. biological consequences of chemicals produced by the body.
   c. comparison of neurons with other types of cells.
   d. computer simulation of intelligence.

3. Which section of the brain coordinates body movement and maintains equilibrium?

    a. The brain stem
    b. The cerebellum
    c. The hippocampus
    d. The cerebrum

4. Where in the brain are emotions centered?

    a. In the cortex
    b. In the brain stem
    c. In the limbic system
    d. In the cerebellum

5. Which method of probing the brain produces actual pictures of the brain's inner working?

    a. Autopsies
    b. Lesioning
    c. Brain imaging
    d. Electroencephalograms

6. E. Roy John cites the example of the staff member responding to a personal question to show how imaging can detect

    a. abnormal structure in the brain.
    b. abnormal biochemical activity in the brain.
    c. abnormal but transient states.
    d. pathological states such as alcoholism.

7. If a scientist was studying the effects of endorphins on the body, the scientist would be likely to look at a subject's

    a. memory.
    b. mood.
    c. ability to learn new material.
    d. motivation to compete in sports.

8. Joseph Martinez taught rats a maze task and then gave them scopolamine. What effect did the drug have on brain functioning?

    a. It enhanced the rats' memory.
    b. It made the rats forget what they had learned.
    c. It enabled the rats to learn a similar task more quickly.
    d. It had no effect.

9. Research related to acetylcholine may someday help people who

    a. have Alzheimer's disease.
    b. have Parkinson's disease.
    c. suffer spinal cord trauma.
    d. suffer from depression.

10. In research conducted by Fred Gage, what effect did neuronal transplantation have on the performance of aged rats in the hidden platform task?

    a. The rats could no longer perform the task.
    b. The rats performed better than young rats did.
    c. The rats could then perform the task.
    d. The rats performed at the same level as before.

11. When we say the relationship between the brain and behavior is reciprocal, we mean that

    a. the brain controls behavior, but behavior can modify the brain.
    b. behavior determines what the brain will think about.
    c. the brain and behavior operate as separate systems with no interconnection.
    d. the brain alters behavior as it learns more about the world.

12. Before an operation, men and women were gently touched by a nurse. What effect did this touch have on the patients' anxiety levels?

    a. It decreased anxiety in both men and women.
    b. It increased anxiety in both men and women.
    c. It decreased anxiety in men, but increased it in women.
    d. It increased anxiety in men, but decreased it in women.

13. A group of people comfortable with touching others is compared with a group uncomfortable with touching others. Those comfortable with touch were generally higher in

    a. self-esteem.
    b. social withdrawal.
    c. conformity.
    d. suspicion of others.

14. What long-term effect did Tiffany Field find massage had on premature infants?

    a. Massaged infants had better social relationships.
    b. Massaged infants were physically and cognitively more developed.
    c. Massaged infants slept and ate better.
    d. There were no long-term effects noted.

15. What is the relationship between the results of Saul Schanberg's research and that of Tiffany Field?

    a. Their results are contradictory.
    b. The results of Schanberg's research led to Field's research.
    c. Their results show similar phenomena in different species.
    d. Their results are essentially unrelated.

16. What area of the brain seems to be affected in psychosocial dwarfism?

    a. The hippocampus
    b. The cerebellum
    c. The brain stem
    d. The hypothalamus

17. What physical change did Mark Rosenzweig's team note when they studied rats raised in an enriched environment?

    a. A thicker cortex
    b. More neurons
    c. Fewer neurotransmitters
    d. No physical changes were noted, only functional changes.

18. In Michael Meany's research on aged rats' performance in a swimming maze, the rats that performed best were those that

    a. had received doses of glucocorticoid.
    b. had been subjected to less stress in their lives.
    c. had been handled early in life.
    d. could use spatial clues for orientation.

19. In his study of Chiclid fish, Russell Fernald found that there was growth in a specific area of the brain following

    a. improved diet.
    b. social success.
    c. gentle handling.
    d. loss of territory.

20. In Robert Sapolsky's study of stress physiology among baboons, what is the relationship between high status and "good" physiology?

    a. Animals attain high status because they have good physiology.
    b. Attaining high status leads to good physiology.
    c. Lowering one's status leads to improved physiology.
    d. Animals with poor physiology acquire low status.

Textbook Questions

21. Genotype is to inheritance as phenotype is to

    a. habitat conditions.
    b. recognizable features.
    c. natural selection.
    d. selective breeding.

22. Traits such as eye color, sex, hair color, and so on are determined at

    a. birth.
    b. conception.
    c. first cell division.
    d. ovulation.

23. Jane and Jim are twins. They are

    a. monozygotic.
    b. dizygotic.
    c. identical.
    d. concordant.

24. Which of the following people believed that human beings and animals are very different?

    a. Charles Darwin
    b. Rene Descartes
    c. Paul Broca
    d. Tiffany Field

25. Neuroscientists use all of the following techniques to study brain function EXCEPT

    a. marking DNA in brain neurons.
    b. recording brain activity.
    c. observing brain-damaged patients.
    d. lesioning specific brain sites.

26. A new diagnostic technique involving the comparison of someone's EEG with those of individuals with specific disorders is called

    a. CT scanning.
    b. neurometrics.
    c. magnetic resource imaging.
    d. microelectrode therapy.

27. The limbic system is to motivation as

    a. cerebellum is to thinking.
    b. cerebral cortex is to breathing.
    c. central core is to memory.
    d. central core is to internal regulation.

28. Structures of the limbic system include the

    a. hippocampus, amygdala, and hypothalamus.
    b. thalamus, hypothalamus, and medulla.
    c. amygdala, pons, and reticular formation.
    d. cerebellum, medulla, and hippocampus.

29. What do the nervous system and the endocrine system have in common?

    a. Both are controlled by the limbic system
    b. Both are concerned with communication
    c. Both are involved with reflexes
    d. Both systems process auditory data

30. Which of the following best describes the characteristics of the action potential? It is most like

    a. slowly opening a valve to increase the flow of water.
    b. pulling the trigger on a gun.
    c. bursts of energy of unpredictable intensity.
    d. a spotlight sweeping across an area.

31. Your textbook author describes the brain as "responsive" because it

    a. controls many complex functions.
    b. monitors internal and external environments.
    c. adapts the environment to the individual.
    d. is charged by the behavior it generates.

32. All of the following represent important human adaptations EXCEPT

    a. competition.
    b. encephalization.
    c. bipedalism.
    d. language.

33. The mechanism that nature uses to select individuals on the basis of phenotypes is

    a. competition.
    b. variation.
    c. concordance.
    d. flexibility.

34. Genes are

    a. tiny units of DNA.
    b. collections of chromosomes.
    c. important in observing phenotypes.
    d. affected by learning.

35. Down syndrome is caused by

    a. a mother's alcoholism.
    b. lack of intellectual stimulation.
    c. teenagers' life-styles.
    d. an extra chromosome.

36. One of the ultimate goals of genetic mapping is to

    a. genetically code for destiny as well as potential.
    b. improve a phenotype's selective advantage.
    c. prevent further encephalization.
    d. intervene in and treat genetically based disorders.

37. Rene Descartes is most associated with the term

    a. genetic mapping.
    b. animal spirits.
    c. natural selection.
    d. concordance.

38. Paul Broca showed a direct connection between a particular part of the brain and a particular function when he discovered

    a. the mechanics of the reflex arc.
    b. sensory and motor nerves have distinctive functions.
    c. specific stimuli activate specific parts of the brain.
    d. left brain damage impairs language ability.

39. All of the following are techniques for producing lesions on the brain EXCEPT

    a. surgically removing brain tissue.
    b. connecting an EEG.
    c. cutting neural connections.
    d. employing laser technology.

40. From an evolutionary perspective, the "oldest part" of the human brain is the

    a. central core.
    b. cerebral cortex.
    c. limbic system.
    d. corpus callosum.

41. Which of the following is the correct order for evolutionary development?

    a. Limbic system, central core, cerebral cortex
    b. Central core, limbic system, cerebral cortex
    c. Limbic system, cerebral cortex, central core
    d. Central core, cerebral cortex, limbic system

42. Endocrine system is to nervous system as

    a. CNS is to PNS.
    b. pituitary is to adrenal.
    c. parietal is to adrenal.
    d. hormone is to neurotransmitter.

43. The purpose of the myelin sheath is to

    a. increase the frequency of firing.
    b. increase the speed of neural conduction.
    c. increase the number of neurotransmitters.
    d. increase the ration of action potentials.

44. Dyslexia and other reading disabilities are most likely to occur in people who are _____ and whose _____ cerebral hemisphere is dominant for language functions.

    a. right-handed; right
    b. right-handed; left
    c. left-handed; right
    d. left-handed; left

45. The two cerebral hemispheres are connected by the

     a. hippocampus.
     b. interneurons.
     c. pons.
     d. corpus callosum.

Questions to Consider

1. Many different factors influence your performance on a test: your study habits, recollection of the material, familiarity with the test format, and confidence. Given the choice, would you take a drug that might improve your performance? Would you take a beta-blocker that interferes with the effects of adrenaline (used by some actors and musicians to reduce stage fright) or a drug that enhances retention and recall of information? Would taking a drug give you an unfair advantage over other test takers? Is there any danger in taking drugs for this purpose?

2. What are the biological benefits of touching? Program 4 suggests that children raised with significantly different patterns of physical contact and touching will develop different behavioral, social, and personality characteristics. What differences would you expect to observe between children from undemonstrative families and those from families whose members touch each other frequently?

3. Consider the roles that biologically determined factors, such as your health and looks, play in your life. How might social or environmental conditions influence your health and looks? How might your health and looks influence social and environmental conditions?

4. Considering what is known about the damaging effects of poor nutrition, drugs, cigarettes, and alcohol on the fetus, what can be done to protect a baby from the effects of its mother's activities? Should any legal action be taken?

Optional Activity

Interview a few parents from different generations about the infancy of their children. Did they read books on child development or follow an expert's advice? Did they sleep with their babies? How did they comfort them? Which early experiences do they believe were most influential in their children's future development?

Additional Resources

Books and Articles

Alper, J. (1989). "The Chaotic Brain: New Models of Behavior." *Psychology Today,* May. Seemingly chaotic patterns of electrical activity of the brain are being better understood, thanks to the new "science of chaos." Chaotic models help link such patterns to changes in behavioral states.

Beaumont, J.G. (1983). *Introduction to Neuropsychology.* New York: Guilford Press.

Gazzaniga, M (1985). *The Social Brain: Discovering the Networks of the Mind.* New York: Basic   Books.

Kolb, B. (1990). *Fundamentals of Human Neuropsychology.* New York: Freeman.

Wartman, R. J. (1982). "Nutrients That Modify Brain Functions." *Scientific American,* April, 50-59. Nutrients in our food can act like drugs. Certain nutrients give rise to significant changes in the brain's chemical makeup, changes that affect how we think and feel.

UNIT 5

THE DEVELOPING CHILD

When we hear the baby laugh, it is the loveliest thing that can happen to us.

Sigmund Freud

Unit 5 looks at how advances in technology and methodology have revealed the abilities of newborn infants, giving researchers a better understanding of the role infants play in shaping their environment. In contrast to the nature versus nurture debates of the past, today's researchers concentrate on how heredity and environment interact to contribute to the developmental process.

Objectives

After viewing the television program and completing the assigned readings, you should be able to:

1. State the primary interest of developmental psychologists

2. Describe the various ways that development is documented, including longitudinal, cross-sectional and sequential

3. Identify Piaget's stages of cognitive development

4. Describe some contemporary perspectives on early cognitive development

5. Describe physical development across the lifespan

6. Describe cognitive development across the lifespan

Reading Assignment

After viewing Program 5, read pages 137-169 in *Psychology and Life*.

Key People and Terms

As you watch the program and read the assignment, pay particular attention to these people and terms. People and terms defined in the text will be found on the given page numbers.

accommodation (158)
Alzheimer's disease (169)
assimilation (158)
body image (154)
centration (159)
chronological age (139)
cognitive development (156)
conservation (159)
constitutional factors (146)
critical period (145)
cross-sectional design (141)
developmental age (139)
developmental stages (144)
egocentrism (159)
foundational theories (163)
genes (146)
longitudinal design (140)
maturation (153)
menarche (154)
nature-nurture controversy (143)
normative investigations (139)
object permanence (158)

physical development (148)
postformal thought (165)
puberty (154)
schemes (157)
selective optimization with compensation
sequential designs (142)
wisdom (167)
Renée Baillergeon (161)
Margaret Baltes (168)
Paul Baltes (168)
Elliott Blass (151)
Robert Fantz (151)
Jean Marc Itard (143)
John Locke (143)
Jean Piaget (157)
Jean-Jacques Rousseau (143)

The following terms and people are used in Program 5 but is not defined in the text.

stage theory—a theory that describes development as a fixed sequence of distinct periods of life

Judy DeLoache-studies cognitive development in older children and how they come to understand symbols

Jerome Kagan-studies inherited behavioral differences between bold and timid children

Steve Suomi-studies the behavior of genetically shy monkeys. Argues that at least some shyness is an inheritable tendency

Program Summary

Historically, the debate about the true essence of human nature was defined as "nature versus nurture." Empiricists, like John Locke, gave all credit for human development to experience and believed that we arrived in this world as blank tablets devoid of knowledge or skills. Nativists sided with Jean-Jacques Rousseau, arguing that what we bring into the world at birth most affects our development. This debate was sharpened by the discovery of "The Wild Boy of Aveyron" in 1800 and the attempts by Dr.

Itard to educate him. Today, developmental psychologists focus on how heredity and experience interact from the beginning of life throughout the life span.

In the field of child development, the subject of Program 5, there have been many important changes in attitudes about the capacities of newborns. Advances in technology and methodology have rapidly expanded our ability to read the silent language of infants. The growing ability to test for and map their psychological states has led scientists to conclude that infants are born ready to perform many feats and are able to participate in shaping their environment.

Psychologist William James depicted the infant as totally helpless in confronting the world. But today researchers have powerful evidence that a newborn's behavior is meaningful. Newborns come ready to eat, turn away from bad odors, make friends, and mimic our expressions. We know that newborns can follow a moving face and express a preference for sights, sounds, tastes, and textures.

Researchers infer what newborns are thinking, seeing, and feeling by using techniques that measure how long they look at something or how intensely they suck when presented with stimuli. Researchers can also record and measure electrical responses in the brain, the degree of pupil dilation, and changes in heart rate. Using such indicators, it is possible to determine a baby's preferences and abilities, such as whether a baby is more interested in stripes or spots and whether it recognizes its mother.

One of the first researchers to use a baby's ability to express distinct preferences was Robert Fantz. He was able to show that babies preferred complexity and whole faces over jumbled parts of faces, thus demonstrating their cognitive capacities.

But it is the Swiss psychologist Jean Piaget who has contributed most to understanding the cognitive development of children. Piaget posed a variety of problems for children to solve, and after comparing their responses he demonstrated that understanding of the world varies with age. Piaget theorized that each child passes through four distinct levels of understanding in a fixed sequence, or stages—some children more slowly than others.

Despite his major contribution to psychology, Piaget vastly underestimated what children could do and overestimated the ages at which abilities emerged. Today, researchers are careful to design tasks that distinguish a child's ability to perform a task from the ability to explain or understand a concept. The results convince us that infants and children know more than we think they know—and they know it much earlier.

Researcher Renée Baillergeon of the University of Illinois has demonstrated that even sixmonth-old infants understand the concept of object permanence. Her colleague Judy DeLoache has shown that changes in children's ability to use symbols occur between ages two and a half and three. Another well-known experiment that uses the visual cliff has clearly shown that infants develop a fear of heights at about eight and a half months old, around the time they learn to crawl.

Researchers have identified activity level and shyness as the personality traits that show the most genetic influence. Harvard psychologist Jerome Kagan, who specializes in the study of inherited behavioral differences between timid and bold children, has found that being born shy does not necessarily mean a lifetime of shyness. Even inherited tendencies can be modified by learning, training, and experience. Researcher Steven Suomi explains how shyness decreased when he placed shy baby monkeys with extremely nurturant foster mothers, demonstrating that both nature and nurture play a significant role in many complex behaviors.

Review Questions

Program Questions

1. Imagine that someone familiar with the last 20 years of research on babies was able to converse with William James. What would this time traveler probably say to James?

   a. "You were ahead of your time in understanding babies."
   b. "Babies are more competent than you thought."
   c. "Babies' senses are less sophisticated than you said."
   d. "Babies' perceptions actually depend on their cultures."

2. Which smell do newborns like?

   a. The smell of a banana
   b. The smell of shrimp
   c. Newborns can't smell anything.
   d. Newborns can smell, but we have no way of knowing what smells they prefer.

3. What task of infancy is aided by a baby's ability to recognize its mother's voice?

   a. Avoiding danger
   b. Seeking sustenance
   c. Forming social relationships
   d. Learning to speak

4. A toy company wants to use Robert Fantz's research to design a new mobile for babies to look at in their cribs. The research suggests that the mobile should

   a. be as simple as possible.
   b. use soft colors such as pink.
   c. be made of a shiny material.
   d. have a complex design.

5. Which of a baby's senses is least developed at birth?

   a. Hearing
   b. Taste
   c. Sight
   d. Touch

6. Jean Piaget has studied how children think. According to Piaget, at what age does a child typically master the idea that the amount of a liquid remains the same when it is poured from one container to another container with a different shape?

   a. Two years old
   b. Four years old
   c. Six years old
   d. Eight years old

7. A baby is shown an orange ball a dozen times in a row. How would you predict the baby would respond?

   a. The baby will make the same interested response each time.
   b. The baby will respond with less and less interest each time.
   c. The baby will respond with more and more interest each time.
   d. The baby will not be interested at any time.

8. Dr. Baillergeon and other researchers have investigated object permanence in babies. How do their results compare with Piaget's views?

   a. They show Piaget's age estimates were too high.
   b. They contradict Piaget's concept of object permanence.
   c. They support Piaget's timetable.
   d. They indicate that babies show more variation than Piaget found.

9. When Dr. DeLoache hid the small and large toy dogs, what was she investigating?

   a. Stranger anxiety
   b. Activity level
   c. Conservation of volume
   d. Symbolic representation

10. In a discussion of the nature–nurture controversy, who would be most likely to cite Steven Suomi's research on shyness in monkeys to support his or her point of view?

    a. Someone arguing that nature is primary
    b. Someone arguing that nurture is primary
    c. Someone arguing that nature can be modified by nurture
    d. The research does not support any of these viewpoints.

11. At what stage in their development do babies refuse to cross the visual cliff?

    a. As soon as their eyes can focus on it
    b. When they develop conditioned fears
    c. Just before they are ready to walk
    d. About a month after they learn to crawl

12. What conclusion has Jerome Kagan come to about shyness in young children?

    a. It is inherent but can be modified by experience.
    b. It is created by parents who misunderstand their child's temperament.
    c. It is an inherited trait that cannot be changed.
    d. It is normal for all children to be shy at certain stages.

13. How does Steven Suomi modify shyness reactions in young monkeys?

    a. By putting them in an enriched environment
    b. By providing highly supportive foster mothers
    c. By placing a shy monkey with other shy monkeys
    d. By administering drugs that reduce the level of social anxiety

Textbook Questions

14. Germ cell is to body cell as

    a. XX is to XY.
    b. adenine is to nucleotide base pairs.
    c. single helix is to double helix.
    d. 23 is to 46.

15. Which of the following organisms is likely to show the most stereotyped behavior?

    a. Donald, the dog
    b. Sylvia, the seagull
    c. Sam, the salmon
    d. Kanzi, the chimp

16. All of the following are common in drug-dependent babies EXCEPT

    a. mental retardation.
    b. impaired motor skills.
    c. hyperactivity.
    d. PKU.

17. Habituation and dishabituation in infants demonstrates that infants can

    a. coordinate their movements.
    b. imitate other people.
    c. assimilate.
    d. perceive differences.

18. A new developmental theory states that in the course of a lifetime, there are nine distinct stages of emotional relating. The originator of this theory has a

    a. continuous perspective.
    b. discontinuous perspective.
    c. quantitative orientation.
    d. critical period orientation.

19. Research indicates that severe malnutrition just before and shortly after birth can do permanent damage to certain cognitive abilities. Malnutrition at other times does not have this effect. This demonstrates the concept of

    a. nature versus nurture.
    b. discontinuity.
    c. plasticity.
    d. critical period.

20. You are babysitting with a newborn baby. To calm the baby you should

    a. let it suck on a bottle containing sugar and water.
    b. make clicking and clucking noises.
    c. imitate its crying sounds.
    d. play music.

21. An infant is frequently seen to grasp objects and shake them. In Piagetian terms, this is

    a. a reflex.
    b. a scheme.
    c. object permanence.
    d. centration.

22. New research has shown that

    a. assimilation and accommodation do not explain formal operational thought.
    b. children as young as age 3 show conservation of quantity.
    c. infants as young as 3.5 months have object permanence.
    d. egocentric thinking sometimes extends into adolescence.

23. Harlow's research suggests that _____ is the basis for the attachment of infants to their mothers.

    a. eye contact
    b. food and water
    c. contact comfort
    d. good nutrition

24. An organism begins to experience the effects of environment

    a. prenatally.
    b. at birth.
    c. after birth.
    d. during the first year of life.

25. If you were a developmental psychologist with a strong nativist perspective, you would enthusiastically applaud a speech by

    a. Jean-Jacques Rousseau.
    b. John Locke.
    c. Jean Itard.
    d. Steven Suomi.

26. The developmental theories of Freud, Piaget, and Erikson emphasize

    a. quantitative differences.
    b. plasticity.
    c. discontinuity.
    d. continuity.

27. The schemes of an infant are

    a. symbolic.
    b. representational.
    c. cephalocaudal.
    d. sensorimotor.

28. A major criticism of Piagetian theory has been that

    a. his concepts of assimilation and accommodation have not proven useful or valid.
    b. adolescent thinking is not typically abstract.
    c. his stage theory has not been well utilized by other researchers.
    d. limitations in memory better explain preoperational and concrete operational differences.

29. Socialization begins with

    a. good friends.
    b. emotional attachment.
    c. adequate imprinting.
    d. scheme formation.

30. Ambivalent child is to disorganized child as

    a. inability to be comforted is to contradictory behavior.
    b. distress is to anger and resistance.
    c. desire for contact is to aloofness.
    d. contradictory behavior is to desire for contact upon reunion.

Questions to Consider

1. What are the advantages and disadvantages of being bold? Does boldness imply the same thing when used to describe both boys and girls? How might training and experience lead boys and girls to express boldness in different ways?

2. Consider different theories of infant abilities, and contrast the influence of both Gesell and Watson on developmental psychology and childrearing practices.

3. How might the knowledge of developmental norms affect a parent's response to a child? Speculate on what would happen if parents raised their children following inaccurate or out-of-date theories of child development.

4. Is reading the body language of an adult different from reading the body language of a child? How can some of the measures used to detect an infant's interest or learning be used to measure adult cognitive functioning?

5. Do you think it is possible to "spoil" an infant by holding it too much?

Optional Activities

1. Recall your earliest memory. Speculate as to why you recall it and what effects the event has had on your development.

2. Compare yourself to your siblings. What traits, abilities, and interests do you share? Speculate on the roles of genetics and environment in the development of your similarities and differences.

3. Get permission from a day care center to observe two different age groups of children. Observe their play and social interactions. At approximately what age does it appear that children engage in cooperative play? Can cooperative play be taught?

Additional Resources

Books and Articles

Asher, J. (1987). "Born to Be Shy." *Psychology Today* April, 56–64. Some recent studies indicate there may be a genetic basis for shyness, but research also suggests that children "born to be shy" can learn to overcome their shyness.

Bettelheim, B. (1976). *The Uses of Enchantment: The Meaning and Importance of Fairy Tales.* New York: Vintage Books. Stories help children make sense of the world and themselves, as well as reflect struggles children face growing up. A renowned child psychologist looks at Cinderella, Snow White, and other classic fairy tales.

Flavell, J. (1993). *Cognitive Development.* Englewood Cliffs, NJ: Prentice-Hall.

Gardner, H. (1982). *Developmental Psychology: An Introduction.* Boston: Little, Brown & Co.

Gibson, E. J., & Walk, R. (1960). "The Visual Cliff." *Scientific American*, 202, 64–71. Classic study of the development of depth perception and the emotion of fear in children.

Itard, J. (1962). *The Wild Boy of Aveyron. Translated by G. Humphrey and M. Humphrey.* New York: Appleton-Century-Crofts. Itard's early nineteenth-century memoir tells of his attempts to educate and socialize a child reared in the wild.

Slamphill (Ed.) (1976). *An introduction to Jean Piaget through his own words.* New York: Wiley.

Shaffer, D. (1993). *Developmental Psychology: Childhood and Adolescence.* Pacific Grove, CA: Brooks/Cole Pub. Co.

Films

Child's Play: Prodigies and Possibilities. NOVA #1209, Time-Life Video. 1985. This film introduces us to prodigies who excel in several fields and to current research hoping to uncover more about the nature of giftedness.

The Wild Child. Directed by François Truffaut. 1969. Dr. Jean Itard, a nineteenth-century scientist, adopted and attempted to socialize a 12-year-old boy found in the wild. This film, based on Itard's memoirs, explores how children learn language and bond with others. It also shows how the values and expectations of scientists direct their research and may bias their conclusions.

The following popular films capture various aspects of children's perceptions of themselves, adults, and the world around them.

Big. Directed by Penny Marshall. 1988.

E.T. the Extra-Terrestrial. Directed by Steven Spielberg. 1982.

Fanny and Alexander. Directed by Ingmar Bergman. 1983.

My Life as a Dog. Directed by Lasse Hallström. 1985.

Small Change. Directed by François Truffaut. 1976.

UNIT 6

LANGUAGE DEVELOPMENT

*The birth of language is the dawn of humanity. The
line between man and beast—between the highest ape
and the lowest savage—is the language line.*
Suzanne K. Langer

Unit 6 examines how children acquire language and demonstrates the methods psychologists use to study the role of biology and social interaction in language acquisition. It also looks at the contribution of language to children's cognitive and social development.

Objectives

After viewing the television program and completing the assigned reading, you should be able to:

1. Describe the structure of language, including syntax, grammar and semantics

2. Define a child's "language making capacity"

3. Explain Chomsky's hypothesis that humans are born with an innate biological capacity for language acquisition

4. Explain how "motherese" (or "parentese") helps babies learn to communicate

Reading Assignment

After viewing Program 6, read pages 169-179 in *Psychology and Life.*

Key People and Terms

As you watch the program and read the assignment, pay particular attention to these people and terms. People and terms defined in the text will be found on the given page numbers.

child directed speech (171)   Noam Chomsky (175)
habituation (172)   Anne Fernald (171)
language making capacity (176)   Dan Slobin (176)
motherese/parentese (171)   Janet Werker (172)
overregularization (177)
phoneme (171)

The following terms and people are used in Program 6 but are not defined in the text.

> *psycholinguists*—researchers who study how the structure of language is related to speaking and listening

> *Jean Berko Gleason*-developmental psychologist who studies the central impact of social interaction on language acquisition

Program Summary

Learning language, the subject of Program 6, is one of the most amazing of all human accomplishments. How a baby learns to talk so quickly with so little help stimulates intense scientific interest and debate. Until the late 1950s, linguists assumed that children learned to speak by imitating their parents. But observations of young children reveal that early language patterns are unique, and parents rarely try to teach their children to talk.

In 1957, Noam Chomsky revolutionized the study of language when he suggested that babies were born with a built-in language acquisition device. He claimed that babies have the innate capacity for extracting meaning from the words and sentences they hear.

Ideas about the biological capacity for language gave rise to a new field: developmental psycholinguistics. Some psycholinguists, like Jean Berko Gleason, concentrate on the role of social interaction in language development. Gleason explains that environmental and hereditary factors contribute to the process of language acquisition. Communication depends on the ability of both speakers to decode and express their intentions, and includes the use of words and formats with shared meanings.

Research has shown that biology does play a role in language acquisition. Children all over the world follow the same steps as they learn the sounds, words, and rules of their own language. All babies have a built-in preference for voices and can pick out their mother's speech within the first few days of life.

The fact that every child goes through the same sequences suggests that learning depends on some form of biological maturation. Scientists believe that a developmental timetable regulates both the maturation of the brain and the muscles in the mouth and tongue that are needed for communication.

Although true language develops later, communication begins at birth. All normal babies cry and coo and can imitate facial expressions. After a couple of months, they begin babbling and make many varied sounds. By the end of their first year, they tend to specialize in those sounds that have meaning in their own language.

Using words as symbols represents an advance in thinking skills and a new kind of relationship with objects and people. Children increasingly use words as tools for achieving their goals as they move from one- to two-word utterances and simple sentences. Later, they use language for abstract purposes, such as discussing past events.

Age	Language Skills
first few days of life	cry, coo, recognize mother's voice
2 months	babbling, varied sounds
1 year	specialized sounds in own language
18 months	babbles, knows some words
2 years	two-word phrases, knows more than 50 words
3 years	knows more than 1,000 words
by age 6	understands grammar and syntax

Note: The ages in this chart are approximations. Not all children acquire language at the same rate.

Language development occurs in a regular pattern, leading some researchers to think that language is biologically innate.

Just as the first steps in language development are universal, so is the tendency for parents everywhere to use simplified, high-pitched, melodic baby talk. Anne Fernald explains that people everywhere speak to babies in this adapted style that linguists call motherese, parentese, or child-directed speech (CDS).

Parentese is typically slow, with longer pauses and shorter utterances than the speech used with older children and other adults. It seems to help babies understand units of speech and conveys an emotional content. Researchers observe that caregivers typically adapt to the child's level of language as language skills grow more complex.

The biggest task before age 6 is discovering the underlying regularities of language—the rules of grammar and syntax. Berkeley psychologist Dan Slobin explains that regularities in children's words and word combinations show that they use a system of grammatical rules that is not based on imitation.

For example, children say "foots" and "mouses," although adults do not use those words or reinforce them. The children are using the right rules but in the wrong places.

The complicated social and linguistic strategies of children are part of the language development process. Children need to learn multiple uses of language, how to ask a question, and how to begin and end a conversation. Parents and caregivers teach children the rules of dialogue by asking questions, then teaching them the proper response, like "Thank you" and "Yes, please." These lessons not only help children learn how to use language but also prepare them for more advanced social interactions.

Review Questions

Program Questions

1. Lori's parents are thrilled that their daughter has just said her first word. Based on this information, how old would you estimate Lori is?

   a. 3 months
   b. 6 months
   c. 12 months
   d. 18 months

2. Before Chomsky's work, what assumption was generally made about language acquisition?

   a. Babies have an innate capacity for extracting meaning.
   b. There is a built-in language acquisition device.
   c. Language development varies widely, depending on culture.
   d. Language is a skill learned by imitating parents.

3. What sounds do very young babies prefer?

   a. Ocean sounds
   b. Human voices
   c. Other babies
   d. Soft music

4. How does an infant react when its mother's voice is paired with the face of a stranger?

   a. By becoming upset
   b. By laughing
   c. By paying closer attention
   d. An infant is not capable of noting any discrepancy.

5. What kind of sentences does a mother use in talking to her baby?

   a. One-word commands
   b. Short, simple sentences
   c. Telegraphic sentences that lack function words
   d. Sentences that violate standard English word order

6. How does the development of language competence compare from culture to culture?

   a. It varies greatly.
   b. It is remarkably similar.
   c. Certain cultures are similar, while others are very different.
   d. This topic is just beginning to be explored by researchers.

7. Jean Berko Gleason has studied mothers and their babies. Her major focus is on the role of

   a. neurological maturation in language development.
   b. melodic patterns used by mothers in different cultures.
   c. social interaction in language development.
   d. parental patterning of conversational conventions.

8. One difference between cooing and babbling is that babbling allows a baby to

   a. say real words.
   b. express discomfort.
   c. develop its vocal cords.
   d. vary intonations.

9. A 7-month-old American child with American parents is babbling. The sounds that the child produces include

   a. sounds from many different languages.
   b. only sounds used in English.
   c. only sounds found in Western languages.
   d. sounds unlike those of any language.

10. When Anne Fernald says "the melody is the message," she means that

   a. babies take meaning from pitch contours.
   b. mothers need to sing to their babies.
   c. babies need to learn the intonation patterns of their native language.
   d. mothers speak slowly and clearly to their babies.

11. If you heard a mother using a rise–fall pattern with a high pitch and a sharp peak, what would you guess the mother would be saying?

    a. "Don't do that."
    b. "That's a good baby."
    c. "See the dog."
    d. "Are you hungry?"

12. What mental ability must a child have developed in order to use words as symbols?

    a. Storing and retrieving memory codes
    b. Recognizing the letters of the alphabet
    c. Composing questions
    d. Recognizing the spatial relationships between objects

13. If you hear a child saying "Go store," what is a good estimate of the child's age?

    a. 1 year old
    b. 1½ years old
    c. 2 years old
    d. 3 years old

14. What is the typical word order in English?

    a. Object, action, actor
    b. Actor, object, action
    c. Object, actor, action
    d. Actor, action, object

15. What does a sentence such as "I bringed the toy" show about how children acquire language?

    a. They imitate their parents, including the parents' errors.
    b. They have no interest in grammar and need training.
    c. They acquire grammatical rules on their own.
    d. They make errors based on watching television and listening to their peers.

16. What has Dan Slobin's research shown about children's language acquisition?

    a. Children are persistent in building regularity.
    b. Correct word order is difficult for children to grasp.
    c. Children learn conversation conventions at an early age.
    d. Some languages are easier than others to learn.

17. Which of the following is NOT one of the essential features of dialogue?

    a. Signaling the willingness to converse
    b. Understanding rules for taking turns
    c. Using proper forms of address
    d. Closing conversations by mutual agreement

Textbook Questions

18. Noam Chomsky is to Harry Harlow as

    a. motherese is to scaffolding.
    b. babbling is to crying.
    c. phoneme is to morpheme.
    d. LAD is to contact comfort.

19. DeCasper and Spence's pre-natal listening hypothesis was supported when they found that

    a. parents corrected their children's speech to make it more truthful rather than grammatically accurate.
    b. babies modified their sucking to hear a familiar story.
    c. caretakers use motherese universally.
    d. all infants began babbling at the same age.

20. Motherese helps infants acquire language by

    a. making use of and refining intonations developed in babbling.
    b. accelerating movement from one-word utterances to telegraphic speech.
    c. coordinating verbal and nonverbal expression.
    d. helping infants attend and remain interested in adult's interactions with them.

21. Which phrase is an example of telegraphic speech

    a. Do it now.
    b. Randy no like beets.
    c. She eated all her beets.
    d. I wanna eat it.

22. All of the following factors are important in children's ability to learn language EXCEPT
    a. LAD.
    b. high social interest.
    c. prenatal language audition.
    d. developmental plasticity.

23. When a father tells a child she should give someone else a turn to talk and not interrupt, he is teaching the child

    a. morphology.
    b. pragmatics.
    c. semantics.
    d. phonemes.

24. A mother is most likely to use short staccato bursts when she says

    a. "It's nighty-nite time."
    b. "Eat one more bite for mommy."
    c. "Smile for your grandpa."
    d. "Don't pull Kitty's tail."

25. Parents gradually increase their demands on children's attempts to communicate. This is called

    a. motherese.
    b. over extension.
    c. scaffolding.
    d. telegraphic speech.

26. Which term is out of place here?

    a. Overregularization
    b. Two-word stage
    c. Protodialogue
    d. Telegraphic

Questions to Consider

1. Is human language unique? Is language unique to humans? Although chimps and gorillas lack the vocal apparatus for spoken language, they can use symbols and signs for communication. Consider your textbook's definition of language. Why is there so much resistance to the idea that animals use language?

2. How closely tied are language and thought? Is language ability necessary for thought?

3. What role does nonverbal communication play in language development? How is it learned?

4. Why do people talk to animals? Why do people often use baby talk when they talk to their pets?

5. If a parent does not use "parentese," what implications might that have for an infant?

6. If most children acquire language before age 6, why is grammar instruction such an important part of the school curriculum?

Optional Activities

1. Watch television with the sound turned off. How much speech and sound is necessary to understand what is happening? Compare a familiar show with one you have never watched. Does familiarity make it easier to interpret the action? Compare a news program with a situation comedy or commercial. How much information depends on language? Visual cues? Listen to a show without watching the picture. How much content is verbal? Do you think young children and adults respond to program and advertising content in the same way?

2. Arrange to observe in a home or day care center. Observe a 1-year-old and a 2-year-old conversing, one at a time, with an adult, preferably their own mother. For at least 15 minutes, write down everything each child and the adult say to each other. After you have observed both adult-child pairs, analyze your transcripts. Describe and compare each child's word choices and language skills. Describe the adult's word choices, intonations, and voice and speech patterns. How well did they fit the child's level of language?

Additional Resources

Books and Articles

Chapman, R. (Ed.) (1992). *Process in Language Acquisition and Disorders*. St. Louis: Mosby Year Book.

Erneling, C. (1993). *Understanding Language Acquisition: The Framework of Learning*. Albany: SUNY Press.

Goodluck, H. (1991). *Language Acquisition*. Oxford, England: Blackwell.

MacWhinney, B. (1987). *Mechanisms of Language Acquisition*. Hillsdale, NJ: L. Erlbaum & Assoc.

Miller, G. A. (1981). *Language and Speech*. San Francisco: Freeman. This basic text examines language and its development in the individual and in the human species.

Moskowitz, B. A. (1978). "The Acquisition of Language." *Scientific American.*   November, 92-108.   Children learn to speak in a highly methodical way.   This article looks at the methods and rules children use to acquire language.

Motley, M. T. (1987). "What I Meant to Say." *Psychology Today.* February, 24-28.   Freud believed slips of the tongue exposed actual thoughts and desires.   Some psychologists and linguists disagree.

Pines, M. (1981). "The Civilizing of Genie." *Psychology Today,* September, 28-34.   In 1970, the discovery of a "wild child" in California stirred up many old and new questions about language development.

UNIT 7

SENSATION AND PERCEPTION

We are told about the world before we see it. We imagine most things before we experience them. And those preconceptions, unless education has made us acutely aware, govern deeply the whole process of perception.

Walter Lippmann

Unit 7 explores how we make contact with the world outside our brain and body. We'll see how biological, cognitive, social, and environmental influences shape our personal sense of reality, and we'll gain an understanding of how psychologists use our perceptual errors to study how the constructive process of perception works.

Objectives

After viewing the television program and completing the assigned reading, you should be able to:

1. Define and compare *sensation* and *perception*

2. Describe how visual stimulus gets translated into "sight" in the brain.

3. Describe the study of psychophysics

4. Be able to distinguish notions of distal and proximal stimuli

5. Explain why illusions provide clues to perceptual rules

6. Describe Gestalt psychology

7. Describe the phenomenon of perceptual constancy

8. Know the difference between figure and ground

9. Know the psychological dimensions of sound and be able to describe the physiology of hearing

10. Describe the difference between top-down and bottom-up processing

11. Discuss the senses of smell, taste and touch

12. Be able to outline attentional processes

13. Describe identification and recognition processes

Reading Assignment

After viewing Program 7, read pages 215-302 in *Psychology and Life*.

Key People and Terms

As you watch the program and read the assignment, pay particular attention to these people and terms. People and terms defined in the text will be found on the given page numbers.

absolute threshold (219)
accommodation (226)
amacrine cells (228)
ambiguity (263)
apparent motion (285)
attention (270)
auditory cortex (243)
auditory nerve (243)
basilar membrane (243)
bipolar cells (228)
bottom-up processing (294)
brightness (232)
closure (280)
cochlea (243)
complementary colors (232)
cones (227)
cutaneous senses (249)
decibels (241)
dichotic listening (272)
difference threshold (222)
distal stimulus (261)
erogenous zones (249)
figural goodness (280)

figure (279)
fovea (227)
frequency theory (245)
ganglion cell (228)
gate control theory (253)
gestalt psychology (268)
goal directed selection (270)
ground (279)
guided search (275)
hertz (240)
horizontal cell (228)
hue (231)
identification and recognition (260)
illusion (264)
illusory conjunction (276)
induced motion (284)
just noticeable difference (222)
kinesthetic sense (251)
lateral geniculate nucleus (229)
lateral inhibition (238)
law of common fate (282)
law of pragnanz (283)
law of proximity (282)

law of similarity (282)
loudness (241)
magnitude estimation (224)
neuropathic pain (252)
nociceptive pain (252)
olfactory bulb (247)
opponent-process theory (234)
optic nerve (228)
orientation constancy (293)
pain (251)
perceptual constancy (290)
perceptual grouping (281)
perceptual organization (259) (278)
phantom limb phenomenon (253)
pheromones (248)
phi phenomenon (285)
phonemic restoration (295)
photoreceptors (227)
pitch (241)
place theory (245)
preattentive processing (274)
proximal stimulus (261)
psychometric function (219)
psychophysics (219)
receptive field (236)
reference frames (280)

relative motion parallax (287)
response bias (220)
retina (227)
rods (227)
saturation (232)
sensation (259)
sensory adaptation (218)
sensory physiology (217)
shape constancy (292)
signal detection theory (221)
size constancy (291)
spatial-frequency model (238)
stimulus-driven capture (270)
subjective contours (280)
superior colliculus (229)
taste buds (248)
theory of ecological optics (268)
timbre (242)
top-down processing (294)
transduction (217)
trichromatic theory (234)
unconscious inference (268)
visual cortex (228)
vestibular sense (250)
volley principle (245)
Weber's law (223)

Linda Bartoshuk (254)
Georg von Bekesy (245)
Irving Brederman (296)
Donald Broadbent (272)
Gustav Fechner (219)
James Gibson (268)
Hermann von Helmholtz (234) (268)
Ewald Hering (234)
David Hubel (238)
Leo Hurvich (235)
Dorothea Jameson (235)
Wolfgang Kohler (268)

Kurt Koffka (268)
Ronald Melzack (253)
Johannes Muller (217)
Sir Isaac Newton (231)
SS Stevens (224)
Anne Treisman (278)
Ernst Weber (222)
Max Wertheimer (268)
Torsten Weisel (238)
Sir Thomas Young (234)

The following term and person are used in Program 7 but is not defined in the text.

receptor—a specialized nerve cell sensitive to particular kinds of stimulus energy

Misha Pavel-studies the successive stages of information processing that take place as we continually perceive the world

Program Summary

Can we believe our eyes? For centuries, magicians and artists have entertained, deceived, and delighted us because we tend to believe what we see. Most of the time our perceptions are remarkably error-free. They have to be; survival in our ever-changing, complex environment depends on accurate perception.

Although psychologists study all sensory processes, including hearing, smell, touch, and taste, Program 7 focuses on visual perception and the processes we rely on to create meaning out of the world's myriad objects and events.

To sense, perceive, and understand the world, we use two different processes. When our eyes, ears, and other sensory apparatus detect stimulation and send the data to the brain, it is called "bottom-up" processing. Then "top-down" processing occurs, adding in what we already know and remember.

First, the raw sensory data is relayed to the thalamus, which analyzes and directs it to specialized areas in the cortex, the outermost covering of the brain. The cortex processes this information and, scientists believe, combines it with old data stored in the memory.

Visual perception takes place in three different areas: the retina, the pathways through the brain, and the visual cortex. It is in the visual cortex that flashes of light are broken down and decoded, enabling us to distinguish one object from another.

In addition to identifying objects, the brain has to compute size, distance, and boundaries. It must make these decisions almost instantaneously so we can go about our daily routines safely and smoothly.

Memories, expectations, culture, and language also influence how we derive meaning from sensory information. Unlike a camera, which merely copies an image, our perceptual process is actively processing the world by selecting, classifying, and judging. Consider that a simple curve and a line in the right place on a sheet of paper may took like a nose and a mouth. But when we put these same lines in another context, they may look like random, meaningless marks, or even like some different object.

The brain also must work to eliminate confusing signals and fill in the blanks. We know that a railroad track doesn't converge and disappear in the distance when we look toward the horizon. And if a shadow falls on our newspaper, we know that the paper isn't really turning black. Perception goes beyond sensory information to impose stability on a constantly changing flow of information.

Psychologists have learned a great deal about how perception works from studying illusions—the perceptual traps we fall into because we use perceptual principles as shortcuts to deal with a flood of sensory input. Fortunately, these shortcuts work most of the time. For example, even when a stop sign is partially obscured by leaves, we still "see" the sign. Although we understand only about 70 percent of the words we hear, we can make sense out of a spoken message because our minds fill in the rest from context.

Have you ever failed to recognize people you knew when you encountered them in a place where you didn't expect to see them? The reason is that our expectations and personal biases have a powerful effect on perception. We may fail to see something because we don't expect or want to see it, which is one reason why people are often unreliable eyewitnesses to an accident or crime.

All of our senses put us in touch with the world around us. But it is our brain that organizes our perceptions, letting us know what's out there and how we should react. Because the perceptual process is the basis for everything we learn, think, and do, scientists and laypersons alike are interested in finding out more about how this extremely sophisticated system works.

Review Questions

Program Questions

1. Imagine that a teaspoon of sugar is dissolved in two gallons of water. Rita can detect this level of sweetness at least half the time. This level is called the

   a. distal stimulus.
   b. perceptual constant.
   c. response bias.
   d. absolute threshold.

2. What is the job of a receptor?

   a. To transmit a neural impulse
   b. To connect new information with old information
   c. To detect a type of physical energy
   d. To receive an impulse from the brain

3. In what area of the brain is the visual cortex located?

   a. In the front
   b. In the middle
   c. In the back
   d. Under the brain stem

4. What is the function of the thalamus in visual processing?

   a. It relays information to the cortex.
   b. It rotates the retinal image.
   c. It converts light energy to a neural impulse.
   d. It makes sense of the proximal stimulus.

5. David Hubel discusses the visual pathway and the response to a line. The program shows films from an experiment where the response to a moving line changes dramatically with changes in the line's

   a. thickness.
   b. color.
   c. speed.
   d. orientation.

6. Misha Pavel is using computer graphics to study how

    a. we process visual information.
    b. rods differ from cones in function.
    c. we combine information from different senses.
    d. physical energy is transduced in the visual system.

7. Imagine that a psychologist equips a male baseball player with special glasses that shift the player's visual field up 10 degrees. When he wears these glasses, the player sees everything higher than it actually is. After some practice, the player can hit with the glasses on. What will happen when the player first tries to hit with the glasses off?

    a. He will think the ball is higher than it is.
    b. He will think the ball is lower than it is.
    c. He will accurately perceive the ball's position.
    d. It is impossible to predict an individual's reaction in this situation.

8. Imagine that a dog is walking toward you. As the dog gets closer, the image it casts on your retina

    a. gets larger.
    b. gets darker.
    c. gets smaller.
    d. stays exactly the same size.

9. You want to paint your room yellow, so you get some samples at the paint store. When you hold the sample against your white wall, it looks different from the way it looks against the green curtain. A psychologist would attribute this to

    a. perceptual constancy.
    b. visual paradoxes.
    c. contrast effects.
    d. threshold differences.

10. Because perception must work quickly, it relies especially on information about an object's

    a. color.
    b. relative size.
    c. edges.
    d. central point.

11. The program shows a drawing that can be seen as a rat or as a man. Subjects were more likely to identify the drawing as a man if they

    a. were men.
    b. had just seen pictures of people.
    c. were afraid of rats.
    d. looked at the picture holistically rather than analytically.

12. When we see a visual paradox such as the Escher picture, why do we have difficulty interpreting it?

    a. There is too much difference between the proximal stimulus and the distal stimulus.
    b. The difference threshold is the same as the absolute threshold.
    c. What we know contradicts what we see.
    d. There is too much unfamiliar information to take in.

Textbook Questions

13. Which best defines sensation?

    a. Enjoying the physical responses of the body
    b. Giving meaning to incoming stimuli
    c. Connecting incoming stimuli to memories and previous knowledge
    d. Stimulation of a receptor that results in awareness of a condition

14. How do the neurons of your auditory system let your brain know the difference between a whisper and a shout?

    a. By firing more frequently when there is shouting
    b. By firing more intensely when there is shouting
    c. By the greater number of neurons firing when there is shouting
    d. By firing more irregularly when there is shouting

15. In strictly physical terms, the differences between blue and yellow lie in their

    a. wavelength.
    b. saturation.
    c. brightness.
    d. photon strength.

16. When a receptor cell on the retina is stimulated, its rate of firing increases and the rate of firing of neighboring cells decreases. This is called

    a. the Hubel–Wiesel effect.
    b. the DeValois effect.
    c. facilitative interaction.
    d. lateral inhibition.

17. Where does transduction take place in the auditory system?

    a. At the hairs of the basilar membrane
    b. At the tympanic membrane of the outer ear
    c. At the hammer, anvil, and stirrup of the middle ear
    d. At the cochlea of the inner ear

18. Sensory processes serve to

    a. integrate and interpret incoming stimuli.
    b. put the brain in contact with sources of stimuli.
    c. reduce the flow of incoming stimulation.
    d. regulate internal states.

19. Sensory physiology is to psychophysics as

    a. transduction is to experiences of stimulation.
    b. sensuality is to information gathering apparatuses.
    c. neural processes are to transduction.
    d. initial receiving center is to secondary receiving/integrating center.

20. Which stimulus involves sensation via a mechanoreceptor?

    a. Moonlight
    b. Bread baking
    c. A cup of hot tea
    d. A telephone ringing

21. The theory of Signal Detection predicts that a person's likelihood of correctly detecting the presence of a stimulus partially depends on

    a. the intensity of the stimulus.
    b. anticipated gains and losses involved in the decision.
    c. the absolute threshold of the subject.
    d. the just noticeable difference equation.

22. Camera is to film as

    a. eye is to cornea.
    b. lens is to pupil.
    c. shutter is to fovea.
    d. eye is to retina.

23. The specialized neurons that send visual data to relay stations in the brain are called

    a. rods.
    b. cones.
    c. bipolar cells.
    d. ganglion cells.

24. Timbre is to sound as

    a. color is to vision.
    b. brightness is to color.
    c. hue is to color.
    d. saturation is to color.

25. Improper cleaning of the ear could result in hearing loss due to damage of the

    a. cochlea.
    b. tympanic membrane.
    c. basilar membrane.
    d. inner ear.

26. Rods and cones in the visual system are comparable to _____ in the auditory system.

    a. hair cells
    b. ossicles
    c. the basilar membrane
    d. anvils

27. Which statement best reflects the relationship between place theory and frequency theory?

    a. Pitch is determined first by the spot vibrating on the basilar membrane and then by how often neurons fire.
    b. The addition of the volley principle demonstrates frequency theory to be more correct.
    c. Frequency of firing determines the pitch of low frequency sounds while place theory explains high frequency audition.
    d. Place theory determines the amplitude of low sounds while frequency of firing explains how we hear loud sounds.

28. Audition is to the vestibular sense as

    a. deafness is to motion sickness.
    b. occipital lobe is to temporal lobe.
    c. cochlea is to semicircular canals.
    d. saccule is to basilar membrane.

29. All of the following describe the nature of perception EXCEPT

    a. comparison of different stimuli.
    b. organization and interpretation of stimuli.
    c. reaction to the physical properties of a stimulus.
    d. discovery of invariant features of the environment.

30. A good definition of "illusion" is

    a. a strongly held false belief.
    b. a breakdown in transmission of the proximal stimulus.
    c. a distortion of information threatening to self-esteem.
    d. a breakdown in accurate perception of a distal stimulus.

31. All ambiguous figures are characterized by

    a. instability.
    b. lateral inhibition.
    c. delusions.
    d. bottom-up processing.

32. In attempting to explain perceptual processes, Helmholtz emphasized _____ and Gibson emphasized _____.

    a. neural mechanisms; perceptual hypotheses
    b. perceptual hypotheses; neural mechanisms
    c. experience; environmental cues
    d. environmental cues; experience

33. A string section melody is to a symphony as

    a. nativist is to empiricist.
    b. element is to Gestalt.
    c. environment is to ecology.
    d. proximal is to distal.

34. Treisman's attenuation theory differs from Broadbent's filter theory in proposing that

    a. unattended messages get some higher-level processing.
    b. there is conscious awareness of unattended stimuli.
    c. sensory systems enhance the intensity of unattended stimuli.
    d. each sensory system has its own information processing channel.

35. According to the Gestalt psychologists, we organize our perceptual world as simply and efficiently as we can. This statement is the essence of the law of

    a. pragnanz.
    b. attenuated processes.
    c. perceptual organization.
    d. figural goodness.

36. The rod and frame test is used to evaluate

    a. field dependence.
    b. depth perception.
    c. attentional processes.
    d. object identification.

37. Transduction occurs in the _____ stage of perceptual processing; synthesis occurs in the _____ stage.

    a. perception; identification
    b. perception; recognition
    c. sensation; perception
    d. sensation; identification

38. How do hallucinations differ from illusions?

    a. They are not shared by others.
    b. They occur in the absence of distal stimuli.
    c. They are more likely to occur in altered states of consciousness.
    d. they differ in all of the above ways

39. If your professor stated she believed that we would understand more about perception by examining the environment in which we perceive rather than the physiological process of perception, she would be a follower of

    a. Gibson's ecological theory.
    b. Helmholtz's classical theory.
    c. Richard's gestalt theory.
    d. Oppel's geometrical theory.

40. If you were a perception researcher in the area of artificial intelligence, you would be most concerned with

    a. neurophysiology of perception.
    b. the regular, predictable operational principles of perception.
    c. the physical properties of perceived stimuli.
    d. formation of whole configurations from separate elements.

41. Which of the following is NOT a good metaphor for attention?

    a. Spotlight
    b. Bridge
    c. T.V. channel
    d. Open door

42. Your brain uses information that comes from color and texture changes for the process of:
    a. dichotic visualization.
    b. region segregation.
    c. focusing attention.
    d. grouping.

Questions to Consider

1. As the population ages, adapting the environment for people with a range of sensory abilities and deficits will become increasingly important. Architects will need to improve access to and safety of buildings, taking into account that older people need about three times as much light as young people in order to distinguish objects. They also need higher visual contrasts to detect potential hazards such as curbs or steps. Evaluate your home environment, and identify some changes you could make to create a safer, more comfortable environment for a disabled, or visually or hearing impaired person.

2. Investigations of people who claim to have extrasensory perception reveal that the better controlled the study, the less likely it is to support claims of ESP. Does it do any harm to believe in ESP? Why do most psychologists suggest that we should be skeptical of people who claim to have extrasensory perception?

3. Gestalt rules of organization are evident in any good page layout. Related items are often placed together or have some design similarities. Magazine advertisers know that it is not only the design but the positioning of the ad that is crucial for grabbing and holding the reader's attention. Analyze several page layouts in a popular magazine. How are color, size, copy, and pictures used? Are Gestalt principles used to convey ideas? If so, how?

4. Describe how film and television directors use sight and sound techniques to create meaning and feeling. As you watch a television commercial, program, or film, notice the way the camera frames the image and how angle and motion create a mood or point of view. Notice the use of sound. Consider how these elements shape viewers' needs, expectations, and feelings.

Optional Activities

1. Closure and continuity of line are organizing principles that we use to make sense out of stimuli. Make line drawings of familiar objects by tracing pictures from the comics, children's coloring books, or magazines. Leave out sections of the drawing, and ask family members or friends to identify the objects. See how incomplete the line drawing can be and still be identified.

2. Blindfold yourself. (Have someone standing by to prevent injury or damage.) Contrast the experience of moving about in a familiar room such as your bedroom or kitchen with the experience of moving about a room in which you spend little time. Note the expectations and significant sensory cues you depend on to avoid tripping and bumping into things. How relaxed or tense were you in each room?

Additional Resources

Books and Articles

Ackerman, Diane (1990). *A Natural History of the Senses*. New York: Random House.

Cobb, Vicki. (1981). *How to Really Fool Yourself: Illusions for All Your Senses.* New York: Lippincott. Offers do-it-yourself demonstrations to trick your own senses and explains how each illusion works.

Coren, Stanley. (1984). *Sensation and Perception*. 2nd Ed. Orlando, FL: Academic Press.

Goldstein, Bruce.(1989). *Sensation and Perception*. 3rd. Ed.   Belmont, CA: Wordsworth Publishing Co.

Keller, Helen.(1954). *The Story of My Life*. Garden City, N.Y.: Doubleday. World-famous autobiographical account of a deaf and blind woman's struggle to learn to communicate with others and to live with severe handicaps.

Koffka, K. (1959). *The Growth of the Mind*. Paterson, NJ: Littlefield.

Kohler, W. (1947). *Gestalt Psychology*. New York: Leveright Publishing Corp.

Monmaney, T. (1987, September). "Are We Led by the Nose?". *Discover, 56,* 48-54. Odors trigger memories, help rats find mates, and save us from eating toxic foods. Monmaney explores these and other fascinating functions of smell.

Mosin, Sergio (Ed.). (1993). *Foundations of Perception Theory.* New York: North-Hobard.

Norwich, K. (1993). *Information, Sensation and Perception.* San Diego, CA: Academic Press.

Sacks, Oliver.(1985). *The Man Who Mistook His Wife for a Hat and Other Clinical Tales.* New York: Summit Books. Perception of the outside world and of oneself can be distorted in bizarre ways by neurological disorders. Fascinating accounts of actual case histories.

Films

Houdini. Directed by George Marshall. 1953. A fictional screen biography of the master magician and escape artist Harry Houdini. Includes faithful recreations of dozens of Houdini's tricks and illusions and his efforts to expose mediums and spiritualists as frauds.

Roshomon. (In the Woods.) Directed by Akira Kurosawa. 1950. A murder is recounted by four people, including the victim. Each point of view and each story is different, illustrating how people can experience and interpret the same event in different ways. The audience must determine what is real.

The Thin Blue Line. Directed by Errol Morris. 1988. A remarkable and true detective story showing the limits and distortions of perception. Errol Morris calls it "a movie about how truth is difficult to know—not a movie about how truth is impossible to know."

UNIT 8

LEARNING

*Effective learning means a living at new power, and
the consciousness of new power is one of the most
stimulating things in life.*

Janet Erskine Stuart

Learning is the process that enables humans and other animals to profit from experience, anticipate events, and adapt to changing conditions. Unit 8 explains the basic learning principles and the methods psychologists use to study and modify behavior. It also demonstrates how cognitive processes such as insight and observation influence learning.

Objectives

After viewing the television program and completing the assigned reading, you should be able to:

1. Define *learning*

2. Describe the process of classical conditioning and show how it demonstrates learning by association

3. Cite examples of extinction, spontaneous recovery, generalization, and discrimination

4. Describe the process of operant conditioning

5. Define positive and negative reinforcement

6. Know the distinction between positive and negative punishment

7. Describe how observational learning occurs

8. Discuss how biofeedback can teach a person to modify autonomic responses

9. Discuss the varieties of reinforcement schedules, including fixed ratio, variable ratio, fixed interval and variable interval

10. Describe cognitive influences on learning

11. Define instinctual drift

Reading Assignment

After viewing Program 8, read pages 303-342 in *Psychology and Life*.

Key People and Terms

As you watch the program and read the assignment, pay particular attention to these people and terms. People and terms defined in the text will be found on the given page numbers.

acquisition (313)
animal cognition (334)
behavior analysis (307)
biological constraints of learning (331)
blocking (313)
classical conditioning (307)
cognition (334)
cognitive map (334)
conditioned reinforcers (326)
conditional response (309)
conditional stimulus (308)
connectionism (339)
discriminative stimuli (323)
experimental analysis of behavior (321)
extinction (314)
instinctual drift (332)
law of effect (317)
learning (305)
learning performance distinction (305)
negative punishment (323)
negative reinforcer (322)
observational learning (337)
operant (321)
operant conditioning (321)
operant extinction (322)
partial reinforcement effect (328)
performance (305)
positive punishment (323)
positive reinforcer (322)
Premack principle (327)
primary reinforcers (326)
psychoneuroimmunology (318)
punisher (323)
reflex (308)

reinforcement contingency (322)
savings (314)
schedules of reinforcement (328)
shaping by successive approximations (329)
spontaneous recovery (314)
stimulus discrimination (315)
stimulus generalization (315)
taste aversion learning (332)
three term contingency (323)
unconditional stimulus (308)
unconditional response (308)
Robert Ader (318)
Albert Bandura (337)
Keller & Marion Breland (331)
Nathan Cohen (318)
John Garcia (332)
Donald Hebb (340)
David Hume (331)
Leon Kamin (312)
Ivan Pavlov (307)
David Premack (327)
Robert Rescorla (309)
Shepard Siegal (319)
B.F. Skinner (306)
Edward Thorndike (320)
Edward Tolman (334)
Edward Wasserman (336)
John B. Watson (306)

Program Summary

Learning is the process by which people and all other animals profit from experience. During the process of learning, behavior is modified. Individuals acquire new skills that ultimately help them survive because they find new ways to anticipate the future and fine-tune their ability to control their environment. In Program 8, we will learn the basic principles of learning along with two methods, developed more than 50 years ago, that psychologists still use today to study behavior, help people to overcome old patterns of behavior, and learn new ones.

One method is called classical conditioning or signal learning. It takes advantage of our ability to anticipate what will happen. The second method is called instrumental conditioning, which takes into account the influence of consequences on future behavior.

Research on learning dominated American psychology for most of the twentieth century. It began around the turn of the century when the Russian scientist Ivan Pavlov noticed that the dogs in his digestion experiments began salivating before they even touched their food. In fact, anything they associated with food caused them to drool—the sight of the food dish, even the sound of Pavlov's footsteps. Pavlov decided to find out why and thereby discovered the basic principles of classical conditioning. He demonstrated that by presenting any stimulus, such as a light or a bell, before the food, the dogs would drool when the stimulus was presented without the food.

Pavlov and others also studied the extinction of such conditioned responses. They found that it was possible for a subject to learn over time that the stimulus no longer elicited the desired event (food, in the dogs' case), so the light or bell no longer elicited drooling. These simple experiments led to an important conclusion: any stimulus an animal can perceive can elicit any response the animal is capable of making.

While the Russians were working on classical conditioning, the American psychologist Edward Thorndike was studying how humans and animals learned new habits and skills. He observed and measured trial and error behavior and discovered that actions that brought a reward became learned—that, in fact, learning is controlled by its consequences. This became known as instrumental conditioning.

John B. Watson, another American psychologist influenced by Pavlov, studied observable behavior. He believed that he could use conditioning and environmental control to train any infant to become anything, regardless of talents or preferences.

Watson's famous test case involved 8-month-old Little Albert. In an experiment that today's ethical guidelines would prohibit, Watson conditioned the boy to fear a white rat by pairing the rat with the sound of a loud gong. Albert learned to fear not only the rat but anything that resembled it-even a fur coat. Years later, Watson's associate, Mary Cover Jones, developed a way to remove conditioned fears.

Then, by focusing only on observable events that precede and follow behavior, Harvard psychologist B. F. Skinner refined instrumental conditioning. His basic experimental device, the Skinner box, has become the symbol of radical behaviorism. In Skinner's simplest experiments, a pigeon learned to control the rate at which it received a reward (food) by pecking a disk. Because the rate of response varied directly with the reinforcing consequences, the behavior could be changed by changing the consequences. Skinner's version of instrumental conditioning is called operant conditioning.

Although Skinner's view that any behavior can be stripped down to its antecedents and consequences is controversial, it also has many practical applications. Dogs and monkeys have been trained to help disabled people lead more independent lives. Behavioral principles are also the basis for token systems used to reward healthy behaviors in disturbed patients and criminal offenders. Behavior therapy is also used to help people lose weight, quit smoking, and overcome phobias.

Behavioral principles are very powerful—so powerful that they can actually affect our body's immune system. Current research studies that have grown out of these basic learning theories may even shed light on how to enhance our ability to fight off disease.

Review Questions

Program Questions

1. Which of the following is an example of a fixed-action pattern?

   a. A fish leaping at bait that looks like a fly
   b. A flock of birds migrating in winter
   c. A person blinking when something gets in the eye
   d. A chimpanzee solving a problem using insight

2. What is the basic purpose of learning?

   a. To improve one's genes
   b. To understand the world one lives in
   c. To find food more successfully
   d. To adapt to changing circumstances

3. How have psychologists traditionally studied learning?

   a. In classrooms with children as subjects
   b. In classrooms with college students as subjects
   c. In laboratories with humans as subjects
   d. In laboratories with animals as subjects

4. In his work, Pavlov found that a metronome could produce salivation in dogs. Why?

   a. It signaled that food would arrive.
   b. It was the dogs' normal reaction to a metronome.
   c. It was on while the dogs ate.
   d. It extinguished the dogs' original response.

5. What is learned in classical conditioning?

    a. A relationship between an action and its consequence
    b. A relationship between two stimulus events
    c. A relationship between two response events
    d. Classical conditioning does not involve learning.

6. What point is Professor Zimbardo making when he says "Relax" while finding a pistol?

    a. There are fixed reactions to verbal stimuli.
    b. The acquisition process is reversed during extinction.
    c. Any stimulus can come to elicit any reaction.
    d. Unconditioned stimuli are frequently negative.

7. What point does Ader and Cohen's research on taste aversion in rats make about classical conditioning?

    a. It can be extinguished easily.
    b. It takes many conditioning trials to be effective.
    c. It is powerful enough to suppress the immune system.
    d. It tends to be more effective than instrumental conditioning.

8. What is Thorndike's law of effect?

    a. Learning is controlled by its consequences.
    b. Every action has an equal and opposite reaction.
    c. Effects are more easily determined than causes.
    d. A conditioned stimulus comes to have the same effect as an unconditioned stimulus.

9. According to John B. Watson, any behavior, even strong emotion, could be explained by the power of

    a. instinct.
    b. inherited traits.
    c. innate ideas.
    d. conditioning.

10. In Watson's work with Little Albert, why was Albert afraid of the Santa Claus mask?

    a. He had been classically conditioned to fear the mask.
    b. The mask was an unconditioned stimulus creating fear.
    c. He generalized his learned fear of the rat.
    d. Instrumental conditioning created a fear of strangers.

11. What was the point of the Skinner box?

    a. It kept animals safe.
    b. It provided a simple, highly controlled environment.
    c. It set up a classical conditioning situation.
    d. It allowed psychologists to use computers for research.

12. Skinner found that the rate at which a pigeon pecked at a target varied directly with

    a. the conditioned stimulus.
    b. the conditioned response.
    c. the operant antecedents.
    d. the reinforcing consequences.

13. Imagine a behavior therapist is treating a person who fears going out into public places. What would the therapist be likely to focus on?

    a. The conditioning experience that created the fear
    b. The deeper problems that the fear is a symptom of
    c. Providing positive consequences for going out
    d. Reinforcing the patient's desire to overcome the fear

Textbook Questions

14. Which of the following organisms would show greater plasticity in behavior?

    a. Chameleon
    b. Pigeon
    c. Wolf
    d. Rat

15. John B. Watson changed the course of psychology by rejecting _____ as a research method and establishing _____ as appropriate subject matter for psychology.

    a. observation; child behavior
    b. experimentation; behavior
    c. introspection; learning
    d. introspection; mental events

16. When Little Albert began to show fear at the sight of any furry objects, _____ had occurred.

    a. discrimination
    b. generalization
    c. spontaneous recovery
    d. a conditioned social behavior

17. Skinner would disapprove of which one of the following statements?

    a. Bar pressing doubled when it became contingent for rat chow.
    b. Bell ringing was extinguished in the chimp.
    c. The pigeon pecked the key because it was thirsty.
    d. Contingent shock reduced key pecking.

18. The cumulative recorders that are used in conjunction with operant chambers record the ___ of responding.

    a. latency
    b. duration
    c. rate
    d. strength

19. Increased response rate is to decreased response rate as

    a. positive reinforcement is to negative reinforcement.
    b. punishment is to extinction.
    c. negative reinforcement is to punishment.
    d. conditioned reinforcement is to negative reinforcement.

20. In Skinner's model of behavior the signal that communicates that a particular behavior will be followed by a particular consequence is called a

    a. token economy.
    b. discriminative stimulus.
    c. conditioned reinforcer.
    d. differential reinforcer.

21. Classical is to operant as

    a. reward is to consequence.
    b. learned is to cognitive.
    c. reflex is to observation.
    d. association is to consequence.

22. The best definition for learning is

    a. mastery of a new ability, such as walking.
    b. relatively permanent modification in behavior.
    c. permanently changed thinking pattern.
    d. repeated improved performance.

23. Which of the following psychologists would probably give you an F for a term paper entitled: "Dreams and Daily Mood States?"

    a. John B. Watson
    b. Sigmund Freud
    c. Wolfgang Köhler
    d. Edward C. Tolman

24. All of the following are associated with behaviorism EXCEPT

    a. John B. Watson
    b. B. F. Skinner
    c. Ivan Pavlov
    d. Wolfgang Köhler

25. In classical conditioning, it is important to consider the attention-getting characteristics of the

    a. UCS.
    b. UCR.
    c. CS.
    d. CR.

26. After many exposures to a bell alone, Pavlov's dogs stopped salivating. The next day, he presented the tone again and the dogs salivated. This is an example of

    a. stimulus generalization.
    b. extinction.
    c. the partial reinforcement effect.
    d. spontaneous recovery.

27. Generalization gradients tell us that

    a. a wide range of stimuli can be used as the conditioned stimulus.
    b. the more similar a stimulus is to the original CS, the stronger the response will be.
    c. the most important attribute of a conditioned stimulus is its attention-getting ability.
    d. animals have high sensitivity to tone intensity.

28. If you want to punish a child's behavior effectively, you should

    a. punish after the child has thought about the troublesome behavior.
    b. be sure that only one parent consistently punishes
    c. be sure that physical pain is part of the punishment.
    d. make the punishment brief and immediate.

29. Albert Bandura's research has made us all conscious of the influence of

    a. noncontingent shock in producing feelings of helplessness.
    b. physical punishment on a developing personality.
    c. observed models on subsequent behavior.
    d. behavior chains on mastering complex.

30. Which of the following brought Gestalt principles to our understanding of how learning occurs?

    a. Donald O. Hebb
    b. Albert Bandura
    c. Edward C. Tolman
    d. Wolfgang Köhler

Questions to Consider

1. Approximately 2 percent of Americans are hooked on gambling, which experts claim can be just as addictive as drugs or alcohol. Is compulsive gambling a disease or a learned behavior? Consider the kind of reinforcement gamblers get. What techniques do you predict would work best to help compulsive gamblers change their behavior? Which would be a better goal, controlled gambling or no gambling at all?

2. You are the city manager of a medium-size city. In an effort to reduce traffic congestion and improve air quality, you encourage workers to form car pools or choose alternative ways of traveling to work. What kinds of incentives might be effective for getting people to change their habits?

3. What role does intention play in classical and operant conditioning?

Optional Activities

1. Design your own behavior change program based on the learning principles described in Unit 8. First identify a specific behavior. Instead of setting a broad goal, such as losing weight, design a strategy to reinforce a desired behavior—limiting second helpings, cutting out midnight snacks, or choosing low-calorie foods. Analyze the specific behavior you would like to change in terms of antecedents-behavior-consequences. Then get a baseline measurement of the target behavior, try out your plan for a predetermined amount of time, and evaluate the results.

2. Have someone teach you something new, such as how to juggle, iron a shirt, roller skate, or serve a tennis ball. Analyze the teacher's method. How does it apply principles of theories of learning?

Additional Resources

Books and Articles

Adam, Jack. (1980). *Learning and Men: An Introduction*. Homewood, IL: Dorsey Press.

Burgess, Anthony. (1963). *A Clockwork Orange*. New York: Norton. In a nightmarish world of the future, authority figures attempt to reform, through conditioning, a violent young thug.

Gilbreath, Frank B & Carey, E.(1949). *Cheaper by the Dozen*. New York: Crowell. A light-hearted novel about a time-management expert's use of behavioral techniques to organize and educate his large family.

Harris, B. (1979). "Whatever Happened to Little Albert?". *American Psychologist* 34, 151-60. Examines Watson's famous case in which fear was conditioned in a young child.

Hitz, Randy & Driscoll, A. (1988, July). "Praise or Encouragement? New Insights into Praise: Implications for Early Childhood Teachers." *Young Children,* 6-13. Taking a position contrary to the popular one promoting praise in classrooms everywhere, the authors show how praise can work as a negative reinforcer because many students experience it as intrusive and controlling.

Sahakian, William. (1984). *Introduction to the Psychology of Learning.* 2nd Ed. Itasca, IL: FE Peacock Pub.

Skinner, B. F.(1971). *Beyond Freedom and Dignity.* New York: Knopf. A reflection on the philosophical implications of behaviorism. Skinner discusses, in particular, the issue of determinism versus free will.

Skinner, B. F. (1972). *Walden Two.* New York: MacMillan. Skinner's famous vision of Utopia built from the principles of operant learning.

Films

A Clockwork Orange. Directed by Stanley Kubrick. 1971. In the film based on the novel, Malcolm McDowell plays a young thug conditioned to become sick when he thinks of sex or violence.

The List of Adrian Messenger. Directed by John Huston. 1963. Based on Philip MacDonald's novel, this detective film includes some fancy murder methods that illustrate themes of the unit.

The Manchurian Candidate. Directed by John Frankenheimer. 1962. The power of hypnosis plays a central role in the plot of this sophisticated political satire and thriller.

UNIT 9

REMEMBERING AND FORGETTING

Memory is not just the imprint of the past upon us; it is the keeper of what is meaningful for our deepest hopes and fears.

Rollo May

Unit 9 explores memory, the complex mental process that allows us to store and recall our previous experiences. It looks at both the ways cognitive psychologists investigate memory as an information-processing task and at the ways neurobiologists study how the structure and functioning of the brain affect how we remember and why we forget.

Objectives

After viewing the television program and completing the assigned reading, you should be able to:

1. Define *memory*

2. Compare implicit and explicit memory

3. Compare declarative and procedural memory

4. Describe the processes of encoding, storage, and retrieval

5. Describe the characteristics of short-term, long-term, and sensory memory

6. Define *schema*

7. Describe the accuracy of memory as a reconstructive process

8. Define amnesia

9. Describe processes of encoding and retrieval in Long Term Memory (LTM)

10. Describe short term memory (STM), note its limitation capacity, and discuss two ways to enhance STM

11. Compare semantic and episodic memory

12. Discuss interference

Reading Assignment

After viewing Program 9, read pages 343-384 in *Psychology and Life*.

Key People and Terms

As you watch the program and read the assignment, pay particular attention to these people and terms. People and terms defined in the text will be found on the given page numbers.

amnesia (382)
chunk (354)
chunking (354)
context distinctiveness (362)
declarative memory (347)
echoic memory (352)
encoding (348)
encoding specificity principle (360)
engram (379)
episodic memory (359)
explicit memory (346)
iconic memory (350)
implicit memory (346)
interference (360)
levels of processing theory (364)
long-term memory (357)
maintenance rehearsal (354)
memory (344)
metamemory (368)
mnemonics (367)

priming (365)
procedural memory (347)
prototype (370)
recall (358)
recognition (358)
repressed memories (378)
retrieval (348)
retrieval cues (358)
savings method (345)
schemas (373)
semantic memory (359)
sensory memory (350)
sensory register (350)
serial position effect (362)
short-term memory (353)
storage (348)
working memory (356)
Sir Frederick Bartlett (375)
Hermann Ebbinghaus (345)
Karl Lashley (379)
Elizabeth Loftus (377)
George Miller (353)
George Sperling (351)
Saul Sternberg (356)
Richard Thompson (380)
Endel Tulving (359)

The following person is used in Program 9 but is not mentioned in the text.

Gordon Bower-demonstrates mnemonic training techniques which enhance memory.

Program Summary

When we misplace our keys, forget a name, or go blank in the middle of an exam, we become acutely aware of the complexities of memory. Forgetting can be mildly irritating, or it can be a major frustration. Chronic forgetfulness can even be a symptom of disease. Program 9 explores memory, the basis for all learning, and a process that enables us to survive, by linking the past to the present and the present to the future. To psychologists and neuroscientists, memory is an essential tool for studying the functions of the mind and the structures of the brain.

The early experimental study of memory began 100 years ago when German psychologist Hermann Ebbinghaus attempted to memorize random, three-letter combinations in meaningless series. But his memory faded quickly; he had no frame of reference or familiar context for the nonsense syllables. Because they had no meaning, order, or organization, he forgot them.

With the advent of the computer in the 1960s, psychologists were able to create a working model of the memory. Their approach depicted the mind as an information processor that could be divided into its component processes: selecting, encoding, storing, retaining, and retrieving knowledge.

Today we know that there are two kinds of memory: long-term and short-term. Long-term memory contains everything we know about the world and ourselves. It has infinite capacity and stores concepts, smells, words, movements, and all our personal experiences in a complex network of associations. It functions as a passive storehouse, not as an active dispatcher.

The short-term memory holds information currently in use but only for a very brief time. When we talk with friends, read, or take in the sights and sounds of our environment, we are using our short-term, or working, memory. But without active attention and rehearsal, all items in short-term memory are quickly forgotten and lost forever—unless we transfer them into long-term memory where they become permanent.

Sigmund Freud was the first to recognize that what we remember and forget can help us maintain our personal integrity and sense of self-worth. He labeled this process repression. But even when we push these unacceptable ideas into the unconscious, some of them escape and show up in our dreams, slips of the tongue, or mental preoccupations.

Memory is not an exact record of our experience. What we select, retain, and retrieve is influenced by many factors. Our attitudes, expectations, interests, and fears affect what we remember and how we remember it. A student assigned to read a book that seems boring will not retain as much as another student who finds the book fascinating. A witness may provide a distorted report of an accident because of personal expectations or preconceptions. Our schemas—that is, our own set of beliefs about people, objects, and situations—often cause us to ignore some details and add or alter others.

Scientists are learning more about how the memory actually works. When something is remembered the brain changes physically. In fact, every bit of information we remember is encoded in our brains. These traces, or engrams, form the biological foundation for everything we know and do.

Clearly, memory is essential to individuality and personal identity. But sometimes people do lose their memories. The best known type of memory loss is functional amnesia. It is temporary and is often restored through hypnosis or psychotherapy. Organic amnesia, on the other hand, may well be the result of injury to the brain, disease, or alcohol addiction. As the memory fades, so does the personality, and eventually life itself. Sadly, life without memory is life without a past or a future.

Review Questions

Program Questions

1. What pattern of remembering emerged in Hermann Ebbinghaus's research?

    a.   Loss occurred at a steady rate.
    b.   A small initial loss was followed by no further loss.
    c.   There was no initial loss, but then there was a gradual decline.
    d.   A sharp initial loss was followed by a gradual decline.

2. The way psychologists thought about and studied memory was changed by the invention of

    a.   television.
    b.   electroconvulsive shock therapy.
    c.   the computer.
    d.   the electron microscope.

3. What do we mean when we say that memories must be encoded?

    a.   They must be taken from storage to be used.
    b.   They must be put in a form the brain can register.
    c.   They must be transferred from one network to another.
    d.   They must be put in a passive storehouse.

4. About how many items can be held in short-term memory?

    a.   3
    b.   7
    c.   11
    d.   An unlimited number

5. Imagine you had a string of 20 one-digit numbers to remember. The best way to accomplish the task is through the technique of

   a. selective attention.
   b. peg words.
   c. rehearsing.
   d. chunking.

6. According to Gordon Bower, what is an important feature of good mnemonic systems?

   a. There is a dovetailing between storage and retrieval.
   b. The acoustic element is more important than the visual.
   c. The learner is strongly motivated to remember.
   d. Short-term memory is bypassed in favor of long-term memory.

7. According to Freud, what is the purpose of repression?

   a. To protect the memory from encoding too much material
   b. To preserve the individual's self-esteem
   c. To activate networks of associations
   d. To fit new information into existing schemas

8. In an experiment, subjects spent a few minutes in an office. They were then asked to recall what they had seen. The subjects were most likely to recall those objects that

   a. fit into their existing schema of an office.
   b. carried little emotional content.
   c. were unusual within that particular context.
   d. related to objects the subjects owned themselves.

9. The paintings Franco Magnani made of an Italian town were distorted mainly by

   a. repression causing some features to be left out.
   b. a child's perspective altering relationships.
   c. sensory gating changing colors.
   d. false memories of items that were not really there.

10. What was Karl Lashley's goal in teaching rats mazes and then removing part of their cortexes?

   a. Finding out how much tissue was necessary for learning to occur
   b. Determining whether memory was localized in one area of the brain
   c. Discovering how much tissue loss led to memory loss
   d. Finding out whether conditioned responses could be eradicated

11. What has Richard Thompson found in his work with rabbits conditioned to a tone before an air puff?

    a.   Rabbits learn the response more slowly after lesioning.
    b.   Eyelid conditioning involves several brain areas.
    c.   The memory of the response can be removed by lesioning.
    d.   Once the response is learned, the memory is permanent despite lesioning.

12. What is the chief cause of functional amnesia?

    a.   Alzheimer's disease
    b.   Substance abuse
    c.   Traumatic injury to the brain
    d.   Severe anxiety or hysteria

Textbook Questions

13. The three memory systems differ in

    a.   capacity.
    b.   duration of storage.
    c.   method of encoding.
    d.   all of the above.

14. Which technique for measuring the capacity of sensory memory gave a more accurate account of its capacity?

    a.   Selective attention procedure
    b.   Masking procedure
    c.   Whole report procedure
    d.   Partial report procedure

15. All of the following statements about STM are true EXCEPT

    a.   Material is retained for about a second.
    b.   It is part of our conscious awareness.
    c.   Capacity is limited to about 7 chunks.
    d.   It is called the working memory.

16. In his study, Sternberg found that we retrieve data from STM via

    a.   parallel-processing search.
    b.   serial exhaustive scanning.
    c.   elaborative rehearsal.
    d.   semantic encoding.

17. Encoding in STM is _____, whereas in LTM it is _____.
    a.   iconic; echoic
    b.   by icon; by category
    c.   by chunking; by meaning
    d.   acoustic; by meaning

18. Levels of processing theory is to duplex theory of memory as

    a.   depth of processing is to separate memory systems.
    b.   STM is to LTM.
    c.   memory data flow is to depth of processing.
    d.   serial position effect is to free recall.

19. The high-frequency stimulation of the hippocampus that increases memory strength for new learning is called

    a.   long-term potentiation.
    b.   accelerated consolidation.
    c.   synaptic alteration.
    d.   glutamate supplementation.

20. All of the following processes are aspects of memory EXCEPT

    a.   encoding data.
    b.   retrieving data.
    c.   modifying data.
    d.   creation of data.

21. Which of the following is the best metaphor for your memory of your life?

    a.   Continuous videotaping
    b.   A photo album
    c.   Selected excerpts
    d.   A documentary film

22. All of the following concepts are associated with H. Ebbinghaus EXCEPT

    a. serial learning.
    b. criterion performance.
    c. savings method.
    d. proactive interference.

23. In what way is human memory similar to computer memory?

    a. Both engage in parallel processing.
    b. Memories are equally stable in both.
    c. Both select data to encode.
    d. Both experience loss of data.

24. George Sperling used the _____ procedure to study _____ memory.

    a. partial report; iconic
    b. partial report; echoic
    c. full-report; iconic
    d. full-report; echoic

25. All data encoded in STM is generally held there

    a. in the form of icons and echoes.
    b. until it can be retrieved.
    c. in an acoustic form.
    d. for 5-15 seconds.

26. Material in LTM is stored in small abstract units of knowledge called

    a. icons.
    b. schemas.
    c. propositions.
    d. mnemonics.

27. The technical term for "photographic memory" is

    a. iconic memory.
    b. echoic memory.
    c. semantic memory.
    d. eidetic memory.

28. If you believe that a person's memory is strongly influenced by his or her history, values, and expectations then you would agree with

    a. the concept of a duplex memory.
    b. a level of processing memory model.
    c. the idea of memory as a constructive process.
    d. the concept of encoding specificity.

29. Elizabeth Loftus's memory research demonstrated

    a. the use of schemas in memory construction.
    b. how the memories of eyewitnesses can be distorted.
    c. how the serial position effect can influence our memory for complex events.
    d. the technique of using cues to improve retrieval from LTM.

30. There is convincing evidence that decay occurs in

    a. sensory memory and long-term memory.
    b. sensory memory and short-term memory.
    c. short-term memory and long-term memory.
    d. sensory memory, short-term memory, and long-term memory.

Questions to Consider

1. What memory strategies can you apply to help you better retain the information in this course?

2. What is your earliest memory? Can you recall an experience that happened before you could talk? If not, why not? How does language influence what we remember? How do photographs and other mementos aid memory?

3. Learning the ABCs by singing them is almost universal. Why does singing the ABCs make it easier to remember them?

4. Many quiz shows and board games like Trivial Pursuit are based on recalling items of general knowledge that we do not use every day. Why is it so much fun to recall such trivia?

5. As a member of a jury, you are aware of the tendency to reconstruct memories. How much weight do you give to eyewitness testimony? Is it possible ever to get "the whole truth and nothing but the truth" from an eyewitness?

Optional Activities

1. Do you have an official family historian? In individual interviews, ask family members to recall and describe their memories of a shared past event, such as a wedding or holiday celebration. Perhaps a photograph or memento will trigger a story. Compare how different people construct the event and what kind of details are recalled. What are different people revealing about their personal interests, needs, and values when they describe the experience?

2. Without looking, try to sketch all the features on the front or back face of a quarter or a dollar bill. Make the sketch as detailed as possible. Evaluate your sketch for accuracy. Did you include and locate the features correctly?

Additional Resources

Books and Articles

Ellis, H. (1989). *Fundamentals of Human Memory and Cognition.* Dubuque, IO: WB Brown.

Haliston, John. (1986). *Fundamentals of Learning and Memory.* New York: Harcourt Brace Jovanovich.

Loftus, E. & Ketcham, K. (1994). *The myth of repressed memory: False memories and allegations of sexual abuse.* New York: St. Marten's Press.

Neisser, U. (1982). *Memory Observed: Remembering in Natural Contexts.* San Francisco: Freeman. A collection of papers on practical aspects of memory, such as flashbulb memories, eyewitness testimony, memory for poetry and prose, and memory aids.

Ofshe, R. (1995). *Making Monsters: False memories, psychotherapy and sexual hysteria.* New York: Scribners.

Schacter, D. & Tulving, E. (Eds.) (1994). *Memory Systems.* Cambridge, MA: MIT Press.

Singer, J. & Salovey, P. (1993). *The Remembered Self: Emotion and Memory in Personality.* New York, Free Press.

Welty, Eudora. *One Writer's Beginnings.* Cambridge: Harvard University Press, 1983. Memories of childhood through the voice of a gifted writer.

UNIT 10

COGNITIVE PROCESSES

I think, therefore I am.
René Descartes

The study of mental processes and structures—perceiving, reasoning, imagining, anticipating, and problem-solving—is known as cognition. Unit 10 explores these higher mental processes, offering insight into how the field has evolved and why more psychologists than ever are investigating the way we absorb, transform, and manipulate knowledge.

Objectives

After viewing the television program and completing the assigned reading, you should be able to:
1. Compare inductive and deductive reasoning

2. Define the concept "problem" in information processing terms and describe some ways to improve problems solving abilities

3. Discuss the "historical roots of methods for revealing mental processes"

4. Describe the study of language production

5. Explain language understanding and the ambiguity of meaning

6. Explain the role of visual imagery in cognition

Reading Assignment

After viewing Program 10, read pages 385-416 in *Psychology and Life*.

Key People and Terms

As you watch the program and read the assignment, pay particular attention to these people and terms. People and terms defined in the text will be found on the given page numbers.

audience design (395)
attention (392)
automatic processes (392)
belief bias effect (413)
cognitive neuroscience (393)
cognitive science (388)
controlled processes (392)
deductive reasoning (412)
functional fixedness (412)
inductive reasoning (414)
inferences (403)
language production (395)
mental models (414)
mental set (416)
parallel processes (391)
problem solving (408)
problem space (409)
reasoning (408)
reaction time (390)
serial processes (390)
think aloud protocols (410)

Bernard Baars (398)
Kathryn Bock (399)
Noam Chomsky (388)
Herbert Clark (396)
F.C. Donders (389)
H. Paul Grice (395)
Allen Newell (388)
Allan Paivio (404)
Jean Piaget (388)
Herbert Simon (388)
John Von Neumann (388)

The following people are used in Program 10 but are not defined in the text.

Howard Gardner-leading cognitive psychologist who studies various kinds of intelligences

Robert Glaser-studies learning

Michael Posner-uses brain imaging techniques like PET to explore what parts of the brain are used in accomplishing specific cognitive tasks

Program Summary

Cognition is the term we use for all forms of knowing-remembering, reasoning, imagining, anticipating, planning, problem solving, and communicating. In Program 10, we'll find out how psychologists study these mental processes and what they have learned about how people think.

In 1958, British psychologist Donald Broadbent used a flow chart to demonstrate how people receive, process, and store information as words, pictures, and patterns in the memory. His model interpreted the workings of the mind as if it were a computer. Using the information-processing model, many cognitive psychologists today, including Nobel Prize–winner Herbert Simon, are beginning to answer questions about how our experiences are transformed into knowledge that guides our actions.

One of the basic functions the mind performs is categorizing. We sort, label, and store all stimuli based on common features, similar functions, or other resemblances. The categories we form in our minds are called concepts. Although some concepts are simple and some complex, our minds link virtually all elements into coherent relationships.

Scientists have speculated that we store concepts in our minds by including a representation of the most typical member of a category: a prototype. For example, most people in our culture have in mind a prototype of a bird that looks like a robin, rather than a turkey or flamingo. Using this prototype allows us mentally to organize objects in an efficient way.

Complex concepts are known as schemas. They require us to organize a body of knowledge around prior experience, related events, and expectations. When we hear the word *picnic,* for example, we can immediately imagine what items go into a picnic basket, what to wear to a picnic, and in what environment the picnic is likely to take place. The more something fits into an established schema, the more it will make sense to us. If something doesn't fit our expectations or doesn't belong to our mental picture of the world, we may not even notice it.

Our concepts are formed not only as words or labels but also as mental pictures. Evidence of visual thinking comes from laboratory experiments in which subjects' delayed responses indicate that they are mentally rotating or scanning images. Psychologists can also measure changes in brain wave activity or blood flow to areas of the brain to show how the brain reacts to surprises.

Visual thought builds on our experience of spatial or geographical relationships. We use mental maps to give directions, decide on an alternate route to work, and get around the house without turning the lights on. But cognitive maps also reflect our experience and values and may distort information. For example, our mental map of the rest of the world might enlarge nearby or familiar places and foreshorten faraway places.

While some researchers try to understand how the mind functions, others examine the brain's chemistry and architecture in an effort to find out how we reason, learn, and remember. Psychologist Michael Posner uses sophisticated brain scanning equipment to look at the chemical and electrical processes that occur when a person is reading or solving a problem. Then there are scientists like Robert Glazer who try to use cognitive knowledge to understand better how we learn. His research may help to improve formal education and everyday learning in the years to come.

Review Questions

Note: Review Questions for Units 10 and 11 are provided in Unit 11.

Questions to Consider

1. Where does the poem "Jabberwocky," by Lewis Carroll, get its meaning? Read the excerpt below and consider the concepts and rules of language and underlying structure that help you make sense of it. Can you paraphrase it?

> 'Twas brillig, and the slithy toves
> Did gyre and gimble in the wabe;
> All mimsy were the borogoves,
> And the mome raths outgrabe.

> Beware the Jabberwock, my son!
> The jaws that bite, the claws that catch!
> Beware the Jubjub bird, and shun
> The frumious Bandersnatch!

2. What does the expression "Act your age" mean? Do you have a script that applies to someone in your age group? Do you have different scripts for someone ten years older? Twenty years older? How does your script influence your behavior?

3. What is the symbolic power of political cartoons? How do people understand them?

4. What is common sense? Can a computer have it?

5. Can language and knowledge be separated? How do children acquire knowledge before they are able to use verbal labels?

Optional Activities

1. There are many variations on the game "Ghost." This version challenges players to manipulate concepts by using words in different contexts. Players may find it easier to think up new word pairs as time goes on. What might explain the change? How would you measure it?

    To play: The first player starts off by offering a pair of words that are commonly used together. They may be compounded, hyphenated, or entirely separate. The next player must come up with another pair of words, using the last word of the previous pair as the first word of the new pair. (Example: Baseball, ball game, game show, show girl, girlfriend, friendship.) Players keep the chain going until someone cannot come up with a word pair. He or she gets the letter "g." The game resumes. A player is out of the game when he or she gets all the letters of the word "ghost."

2. All of us tend to categorize the world into convenient units and to use common labels for our categories. Often those labels become permanent, and we tend to view our world in a rigid or stereotypical way. When this stops us from producing new ideas it is called functional fixedness. Can you overcome it?

    Try this: How many uses can you think of for an empty milk carton, a brick, a sock with a hole in it, a paper clip, a bandanna, or another ordinary household object? After you feel you've exhausted all possibilities, list as many attributes of the object as possible. Draw a picture of the object from various points of view. Then see if you can generate any new uses.

Additional Resources

Books and Articles

Alloy, L. (Ed.) (1988). *Cognitive Processes in Depression.*. New York: Guilford Press.

Bourne, L. (1986). *Cognitive Processes.* 2nd Ed. Englewood Cliffs, NJ: Prentice Hall.

Craik, F. & Trehub, S. (1982). *Aging and Cognitive Process.* New York: Plenum Press.

Fiske, S. & Taylor, S. (1991). *Social Cognition.* New York: McGraw-Hill.

Kosslyn, S. M. (1983). *Ghosts in the Mind's Machine.* New York: Norton. Good introduction to the issues of cognitive psychology.

Kosslyn, S. M.(1985, May). "Stalking the Mental Image." *Psychology Today,* 22ff. How we see things, manipulate images, and solve problems by visualizing with our "mind's eye."

Simon, H. (1992). *Economics, Bounded Rationality, and the Cognitive Revolution.* Brookfield, VT: E Elgin Pub. Co.

Thatcher, R. (1977). *Foundations of Cognitive Processes.* Hillsdale, NJ: Lawrence Erlbaum Assoc.

UNIT 11

JUDGMENT AND DECISION MAKING

If you have to make a choice and don't make it, that in itself is a choice.

William James

Unit 11 explores the decision-making process and the psychology of risk-taking, revealing how people arrive at good and bad decisions. It also looks at the reasons people lapse into irrationality and how personal biases can affect judgment.

Objectives

After viewing the television program and completing the assigned readings, you should be able to:

1. Describe contrasting views of why human thinking is irrational and prone to error

2. Explain the notions of heuristic thinking and analytical thinking

3. Compare definitions of judgment and decision making

4. Describe the anchoring bias, availability heuristic, and representativeness heuristic.

5. Discuss why the way a problem is framed can influence a decision

6. Define decision aversion

Reading Assignment

After viewing Program 11, read pages 416-426 in *Psychology and* Life.

Key People and Terms

As you watch the program and read the assignment, pay particular attention to these people and terms. People and terms defined in the text will be found on the given page numbers.

anchoring bias (421)
availability heuristic (419)
decision aversion (425)
decision making (417)
frame (423)
heuristics (417)
human factors (418)
judgment (417)
representativeness heuristic (420)

Daniel Kahneman (417)
Amos Tversky (417)

To review textbook terms, refer to the Key People and Terms in Unit 10. The following terms and people are used in Program 11 but are not defined in the text.

dread factor—the fear of unfamiliar or potentially catastrophic events which makes us judge them to be riskier than familiar events

framing—the way information is presented which tends to bias how it is interpreted

invariance—the principle stating that preferences between options should be independent of different representations

similarity heuristic—an error based on the tendency to sec a connection between belonging to a certain category and having the characteristics considered typical of members of that category

Max Bazerman-discusses the five most common cognitive mistakes that negotiators make

Leon Festinger-father of cognitive dissonance theory

Irving Janis-studied the Cuban Missile Crisis and looked at distorted "groupthink" reasoning

Program Summary

No matter how uncertain life is, we all have to think and act decisively. Every day we assess situations, take risks, and make judgments and decisions. In Program 11 we'll get a chance to participate in experiments that illustrate the psychology of making decisions and taking risks. And we'll find out what psychologists are discovering about why people make bad decisions and irrational judgments.

There are several explanations for human error and irrationality. Social psychologists point to the influence of the crowd; Freudians claim that animal passions and emotions tend to overpower our better judgment.

Amos Tversky of Stanford University and Daniel Kahneman of the University of California at Berkeley study how and why people make illogical choices. They believe that irrationality is based on the same processes that enable us to form concepts and make inferences. But we often make irrational decisions because these same mental strategies are not appropriate in all cases. Confronted with uncertainty or ambiguity, we tend to think that the most easily recalled events are the most likely. For example, when news reports are full of vivid accounts of plane crashes and hijackings, we overestimate the likelihood of these events and may avoid traveling altogether.

We make some decisions based on other mental shortcuts, often using prototypes to represent classes of objects, events, and people. These assumptions can mislead us into making poor judgments, because we may mistakenly categorize something based on one feature. How information is "framed," or presented, can also influence our decision making in mathematics, geography, politics—virtually any subject area.

Recently, the science of risk assessment has also been attracting a lot of interest. Researchers are discovering that most people avoid risks when seeking gains. But they also choose risks to avoid sure losses. Prolonged wars are a good example of loss avoidance; it's extremely difficult for one side to accept a sure loss (and cut its losses) and admit that there's no chance of winning. So both sides end up fighting longer and losing even more.

How people perceive a risk may also depend on complex psychological factors such as the "dread" factor. For example, we may be terrified of a nuclear accident but never think twice about jaywalking. That's because jaywalking is familiar, while a nuclear accident is unfamiliar and therefore seems more potentially catastrophic. Yet the odds of a nuclear accident are a tiny fraction of the odds of getting hurt while jaywalking.

Psychologists also study group decision making and have found that rationality often turns out to have little to do with intelligence, because decision making changes in groups. Psychologist Irving Janis studied the records of John F. Kennedy's cabinet meetings at which the disastrous decision to invade the Bay of Pigs was made. He found many examples of distorted reasoning, which he has labeled *group think*. Janis has also outlined some procedures that decision makers can implement in order to prevent irrational group decision making.

Another new field is the psychology of negotiation. It attempts to avoid the negative effects of bad decisions among individuals, groups, and institutions. Many people, especially government and business professionals, are taking a great interest in this area in an effort to improve their own negotiating skills.

What happens after a decision is made? The act of making a decision can set other processes in motion. Psychologists have found that whenever we decide something that conflicts with our prior beliefs, a state of "cognitive dissonance" results. We often try to reduce the tension and discomfort of cognitive dissonance by changing our attitude toward the decision or changing how others think about it.

Although bright, reasonable people often make irrational decisions and take unacceptable risks, the field of psychology is helping to shed light on our behavior and even provide guidelines for helping us catch ourselves before we go astray—or redirect ourselves if we do.

Review Questions

Program Questions

1. *Cognition* is a general term that refers to all forms of

    a.   remembering.
    b.   perceiving.
    c.   interacting.
    d.   knowing.

2. The movement in psychology called cognitive psychology developed primarily

    a.   at the turn of the century.
    b.   in the 1920s.
    c.   after World War II.
    d.   during the social unrest of the 1960s.

3. What analytic tool did David Broadbent use to model the process by which information is perceived and stored in memory?

    a.   Statistical analysis on a computer
    b.   A flow chart
    c.   A set of categories
    d.   An analogy to a steam engine

4. When Herbert Simon discusses the computer, he compares neurons to

    a.   punched cards.
    b.   display monitors.
    c.   central processing units.
    d.   wires.

5. When we distinguish between groups of letters on the basis of the kinds of lines that form them, we are performing the mental process of

    a.   relating.
    b.   categorizing.
    c.   creating prototypes.
    d.   activating schemas.

6. Concepts are mental representations. Which is a concept of an attribute?

    a.   Bed
    b.   Jumping
    c.   Slow
    d.   Courage

7. What is our prototype of a tree most likely to be?

    a.   A maple tree
    b.   A palm tree
    c.   A Christmas tree
    d.   A dead tree

8. According to the program, why do we assume that Montreal is farther north than Seattle?

    a.   Because we have learned it
    b.   Because we are less familiar with Montreal than with Seattle
    c.   Because Canada is north of the United States in our mental maps
    d.   Because we are not good at making such judgments

9. When Steve Kosslyn asked subjects about the picture of a motorboat he was primarily interested in

    a.   how subjects scanned a mental image.
    b.   how much detail subjects noted.
    c.   how subjects compared a new picture with a prototype.
    d.   how sure subjects felt about what they had seen.

10. What is one way in which human problem solving appears to be quite different from the way computers solve problems?

    a.   Humans can solve problems that don't involve numbers.
    b.   Humans are more logical in their approach to problems.
    c.   Humans have trouble when content is unfamiliar.
    d.   Humans are less likely to be misled by bias.

11. What did Michael Posner find when he conducted PET scans of people reading a word and associating it with a function?

    a.   Localized activity occurred, but the location varied widely.
    b.   Similar localized activity was seen in all the subjects.
    c.   Brain activity was general rather than localized.
    d.   No general pattern of activity was observed.

12. According to Robert Glaser, what is the general purpose of the research at the University of Pittsburgh's Learning and Research Development Center?

    a. To create new types of computers
    b. To model the organic functions of the brain
    c. To classify errors and mistakes
    d. To improve the way people use their intelligence

13. What is a cognitive illusion?

    a. A mental map that we can scan for information
    b. A biased mental strategy
    c. A concept formed on the basis of a perceptual illusion
    d. A decision motivated by emotion

14. How did Freud explain the fact that human beings sometimes make irrational decisions?

    a. They are driven by primitive needs.
    b. They are influenced by the emotions of the crowd.
    c. They are basing their decisions on availability.
    d. They are using standard human mental processes.

15. Why did the people questioned assume that there were more words beginning with k than with k as the third letter?

    a. There is a general tendency to favor the initial position.
    b. The anchoring effect biased their answers.
    c. It's easier to find examples of words beginning with k.
    d. It seems less risky as an answer.

16. A heuristic is a kind of

    a. mistake.
    b. tendency.
    c. mathematical model.
    d. shortcut.

17. A researcher asks two groups of students to estimate the average price of a new car. One group is asked if the price is more or less than $9,000. The other group is asked if the price is more or less than $18,000. Each group is asked to estimate the actual average price. How will the two averages compare?
    a. They will be essentially the same.
    b. The first group will have a slightly higher average.
    c. The second group mill have a slightly higher average.
    d. The second group will have a much higher average.

18. When people were confronted with a choice of a sure loss of $85 or an 85 percent chance of losing $100, how did most people react?

    a.   They chose the loss.
    b.   They chose the chance.
    c.   They pointed out the statistical equivalence of the alternatives.
    d.   They revised to make the choice.

19. Why would smokers be likely to underestimate the chance of developing lung cancer?

    a.   They do not dread the disease.
    b.   It is an unfamiliar risk.
    c.   It is not representative.
    d.   It represents a delayed consequence.

20. Irving Janis studied how the decision to invade Cuba was made during the Kennedy administration. What advice does Janis offer to promote better decision making?

    a.   Encourage group think by team-building exercises.
    b.   Appoint one group member to play devil's advocate.
    c.   Restrict the size of the group.
    d.   Assume that silence means consent on the part of all group members.

21. Imagine that you are a business leader who has been to a negotiating workshop led by Max Bazerman and Lawrence Susskind. Which statement shows something you should have learned from the experience?

    a.   "I will escalate conflict."
    b.   "I know this is a zero-sum game."
    c.   "I will enlarge my frame of reference."
    d.   "I am confident that I am right and will prevail."

22. How does cognitive dissonance make us feel?

    a.   We are so uncomfortable that we try to reduce the dissonance.
    b.   We enjoy it so much that we actively seek dissonance.
    c.   Our reaction to dissonance depends largely on personality.
    d.   It creates boredom, which we try to overcome.

23. In Festinger's experiment, which students felt dissonance?

    a.   Both the students who got $20 and those who got $1
    b.   The students who got $20 but not those who got $1
    c.   The students who got $1 but not those who got $20
    d.   Neither the students who got $1 nor those who got $20

Textbook Questions

24. A cognitive psychologist would be interested in which one of the following issues?

    a. How olfactory data is processed
    b. Maturation of the efferent system
    c. How to distinguish mania from schizophrenia
    d. How you decide which is the correct answer to this question

25. Which statement is accurate according to the information-processing model?

    a. Thinking can be seen as the response of a complex organism to an internal or external stimulus.
    b. There is a hierarchy of processing systems in the mind.
    c. Associations between and among stimuli are learned and thereby strengthened.
    d. The mind processes one datum at a time along a singular pathway.

26. Artificial Intelligence is best defined as a field that focuses on

    a. how thinking occurs.
    b. becoming smarter through computer interaction.
    c. chemicals that affect thinking processes.
    d. computer programs.

27. A technique for studying cognition that improved Wundt's methodology is called

    a. evoked potentials.
    b. think-aloud protocols.
    c. choice reaction time.
    d. introspection.

28. Which of the following is accurate concerning the "parallel distributed processing model" that is being worked on by David Rumelhart and his associates?

    a. It assumes that the same information can be stored in several locations.
    b. It incorporates both excitatory and inhibitory processes.
    c. It is a type of connectionist model.
    d. All of the above are accurate.

29. Our tendency to form concepts is evidence of the principle of
    a. perceptual organization.
    b. cognitive economy.
    c. categorical reasoning.
    d. inductive preference.

30. One of the first steps that occurs in the process that leads to thinking is

    a.   retrieval of schemas.
    b.   activation of concepts.
    c.   selection of scripts.
    d.   recognition of patterns.

31. The belief bias effect occurs when people

    a.   distort schemas to accommodate their own beliefs and preferences.
    b.   are influenced by content in deciding if a syllogism is valid.
    c.   define abstract concepts in terms of personal preferences.
    d.   make errors in inductive reasoning because they ignore or repress evidence.

32. The main difference between how a novice and an expert go about approaching a problem is

    a.   the amount of information and skill accumulated.
    b.   their metacognitive knowledge.
    c.   how rational their processes are.
    d.   whether they rely on algorithms or heuristics.

33. The contemporary perspective of evolutionary psychology views human cognition as the result of the functioning of

    a.   a single information processor that tackles all problems.
    b.   an irrational and unpredictable web of separate neural networks.
    c.   a collection of semi-independent processing modules.
    d.   a rational, logical, and single- channel processor.

34. We often make errors in judgement because we rely on

    a.   personal intuition.
    b.   statistical evidence.
    c.   algorithms.
    d.   deductive reasoning.

35. If you choose an option solely on the basis of the way it is presented to you, you are violating the

    a.   computational model.
    b.   availability principle.
    c.   invariance principle.
    d.   group think effect.

36. If you engage in unprotected sex with "good, well-educated" partners you might die from

    a.   your optimistic bias.
    b.   a faulty decision frame.
    c.   a case of group think.
    d.   functional fixedness.

37. Cognition involves all of the following EXCEPT

    a.   perception.
    b.   attention.
    c.   imagination.
    d.   decision making.

38. In terms of cognitive theory, children are to communication as

    a.   Von Neumann is to Piaget.
    b.   Chomsky is to Simon and Newell.
    c.   Piaget is to Chomsky.
    d.   Freud is to John.

39. Which of the following is the most accurate concerning the information-processing model of cognition?

    a.   It emphasizes parallel processing capabilities.
    b.   The components are related to structures in the nervous systems.
    c.   It analyzes products rather than processes.
    d.   The system is conceptualized as a series of subsystems.

40. All of the following statements describe PDP models EXCEPT

    a.   the mind consists of neural networks.
    b.   interactive systems process data.
    c.   various activities are carried out simultaneously.
    d.   data is processed in the sequential order it is received.

41. If a researcher wanted to find out if it takes longer to read long familiar words than it takes to read short unfamiliar words, the researcher would probably use _____ as the _____ variable.

    a.   reaction time; independent
    b.   reaction time; dependent
    c.   accuracy; independent
    d.   accuracy; dependent

42. A weakness in computational models of human thinking has been

    a. their failure to take irrationality into consideration.
    b. their lack of precision in duplicating logical reasoning.
    c. their inability to model metacognition.
    d. their dependence on heuristics rather than algorithms.

43. Seemingly unpredictable or irrational behavior that aids in survival or reproduction are called

    a. Protean algorithms.
    b. meaty systems.
    c. Darwinian algorithms.
    d. adaptive heuristics.

44. All of the following have been offered as sources of irrational behavior EXCEPT

    a. group influence.
    b. biological urges.
    c. misapplication of rational processes.
    d. metacognition.

45. You are asked to judge whether the percentage of eligible voters who are registered is above or below 80%. Your response is likely to be affected by

    a. self-fulfilling prophecies.
    b. an anchoring bias.
    c. selective exposure.
    d. overconfidence.

Questions to Consider

1. According to the *Journal of the American Medical Association*, strep throat is one of the most common reasons that children and young adults visit the doctor. It is difficult to diagnose by history or examination only. Ten doctors working in a university health center overestimated the incidence of strep throat by 81 percent. Of the 308 patients in the study, only 15—about 5 percent—actually had strep throat. What might explain the doctors' overestimation?

2. Knowing about problem-solving strategies and using them are two different things. Based on the information in the program and in your text, what are some of the pitfalls you need to avoid in both day-to-day problem solving and decision making about major life changes?

3. The profile of a creative person involves such qualities as nonconformity, curiosity, a high degree of verbal fluency, flexibility with numbers, concepts, a sense of humor, a high energy level, impatience with routine tasks, and a vivid imagination that may take the form of wild stories or fibs. What would be the implications for this type of child in the typical school classroom?

4. How does the scientific method try to guard against an experimenter's cognitive biases?

Optional Activity

Go to a busy intersection and observe pedestrian street-crossing behavior. Observe the kinds of risks people take crossing the street. What do you consider risky behavior? Who is most likely to engage in it? Why do you suppose certain people take more risks than others?

Additional Resources

Books and Articles

Arkes, H. & Hammond, K. (1986). *Judgment and Decision Making: An Interdisciplinary Reader.* New York: Cambridge University Press.

Bazerman, M. (1994). *Judgment in Managerial Decision Making.* 3rd Ed. New York: Wiley.

Hogarth, R. (1987). *Judgment and Chance.* Chicester, West Sussex: Wiley.

Janis, Irving. (1972). *Victim of Groupthink: A Psychological Study of Foreign-Policy Decisions and Fiascos.* 2d ed. Boston: Houghton Mifflin. Decision making in highly cohesive groups can be radical and even foolhardy. A sense of esprit de corps often appears connected with shared illusions and overconfidence.

Janis, I. & Mann, L. (1977). *Decision Making.* New York: Free Press.

Kahneman, D., Slovic, P. & Tversky, A. (Eds.) (1982). *Judgment Under Uncertainty: Heuristics and Biases.* Cambridge: Harvard University Press. How framing and other biases affect and often distort judgment.

Plous, S. (1993). *The Psychology of Judgment and Decision Making.* New York: McGraw-Hill, Inc.

Svenson, O. & Maule, A. J. (1993). *Time Pressure and Stress on Human Judgment and Decision Making.* New York: Plenum Press.

Turk, O. & Salovey, P. (Eds.) (1988). *Reasoning, Inference and Judgment in Clinical Psychology.* New York: Free Press.

UNIT 12

MOTIVATION AND EMOTION

*We may affirm absolutely that nothing great in the
world has been accomplished without passion.*
Georg Wilhelm Friedrich Hegel

What moves us to act? Why do we feel the way we do? Unit 12 shows how psychologists study the continuous interactions of mind and body, in an effort to explain the enormous variety and complexities of human behavior.

Objectives

After viewing the television program and completing the assigned reading, you should be able to:

1. Compare emotion and motivation

2. Describe three theories concerning the sources of motivation

3. Discuss some of the forces that drive the motivation to eat

4. Describe some of the factors behind the motivation for sex

5. Define the need for achievement

6. Outline the attributions for success and failure in terms of a locus of control orientation

7. Describe the research on the universality of the expression and decoding of emotion

8. Delineate Maslow's hierarchy of needs

9. Outline the major theories of emotion

10. Describe what an organizational psychologist does

11. Discuss the functions of emotions

Reading Assignment

After viewing Program 12, read pages 427-440 and 449-472 in *Psychology and Life*.

Key People and Terms

As you watch the program and read the assignment, pay particular attention to these people and terms. People and terms defined in the text will be found on the given page numbers.

amgydala (466)
anorexia nervosa (439)
attributions (452)
bulimia nervosa (439)
Cannon-Bard theory of emotion (468)
emotion (460)
emotion wheel (464)
equity theory (455)
expectancy theory (455)
fixed action patterns (431)
hierarchy of needs (456)
James-Lange theory of emotion (467)
Lazarus-Schacter theory of emotion (468)
locus of control orientation (451)
motivation (428)
need for achievement (450)
organizational psychologists (455)
thematic apperception test (TAT) (450)
Yerkes-Dodson law (471)

Gordon Bower (471)
Kelly Brownell (440)
Walter Cannon (435) (467)
Paul Ekman (462)
Sigmund Freud (432)
Fritz Heider (434)
Peter Herman (437)
Clark Hull (431)
William James (432) (466)
Richard Lazarus (468)
Joseph Le Doux (466)
Abraham Maslow (456)
David McClelland (449)
Henry Murray (449)
Robert Plutchik (464)
Janet Polivy (437)
Julian Rotter (434)
Stanley Schacter (468)
Martin Seligman (453)
Sylvan Tompkins (461)
Henry Triandis (456)
Robert Woodworth (430)
Robert Zajonc (469)

The following terms and person are used in Program 12 but are not defined in the text.

arousal—a heightened level of excitation or activation

optimism—the tendency to attribute failure to external, unstable, or changeable factors and to attribute success to stable factors

pessimism—the tendency to attribute failure to stable or internal factors and to attribute success to global variables

Norman Adler-studies the physiological and behavioral mechanisms of sexual behavior.

Program Summary

What moves people to act? What makes someone jump into freezing water, risking his or her own life, to save a stranger? Why do exhausted marathon runners stagger relentlessly toward the finish line, determined to complete a punishing race?

To explain the enormous variety and complexity of behavior, psychologists study the environment as well as the individual, the mind as well as the body, to find what moves people to take action. They have observed that we move toward some things and away from others.

When we can't help moving toward something, we have an addiction. When we have an unnatural aversion to something, we have a phobia. Between the two extremes of approach and avoidance, psychologists infer motives by noting what we choose, how intensely we involve ourselves, and how long we keep at it.

Seeking pleasure and avoiding pain explain many of our actions. But this same principle can also work against us. For example, alcohol and drugs may be pleasurable, but they are bad for us. And studying may be extremely difficult, but it can be good for us. As we grow older, we learn to do the things that will pay off in the future. But our true desires may never go away.

Freud theorized that behavior was based on our motivation to seek sexual satisfaction and to express aggressive urges against those who restrain our pursuit of pleasure. He explained that our basic sexual and aggressive desires are hidden from our conscious awareness but that they still influence our behavior and sometimes reveal themselves in dreams, fantasies, or slips of the tongue.

In contrast to Freud, Carl Rogers and Abraham Maslow, who studied normal, healthy people, saw a different side of human nature. They theorized that our lives are shaped by a basic tendency toward growth and mastery.

Sexual behavior is a good example of the complex interaction of psychological and biological forces. In contrast to the motivation of other animals, whose sexual mating behavior patterns promote the survival of the species, human sexual motivation is a readiness to experience intense pleasure and, often, romantic love. It combines physical arousal, strong emotion, and intense attraction to another person. Human sexual behavior is highly diverse and subject to a mixture of personal, social, situational, and cultural influences.

A related area of psychological interest is emotion, the complex pattern of changes involving feelings, thoughts, behavior, and physical arousal. Psychologist Robert Plutchik has proposed that there are eight basic emotions made up of four pairs of opposites, such as joy and sadness, and anger and fear, which we combine when we feel other emotions (see figure).

Psychologist Paul Ekman's cross-cultural studies reveal a remarkable universality in the way facial expressions communicate basic emotions. In fact, people all over the world decode emotions in much the same way. And they show similar changes in the brain, muscles, thoughts, and behavior.

Theorists such as Martin Seligman emphasize the role of cognitive appraisal in motivation and emotion. He suggests that what people do and how hard they try are influenced by basic optimism and pessimism. Our motivations and emotional states depend on how we view failure and success. An optimist failing a test would attribute the poor performance to external causes ("The test was too hard") or changeable factors ("I'll try harder and do better next time"). The pessimist would feel doomed by stable, unchangeable factors ("I guess I'm dumb and unlucky") and out of control ("Nothing I do will make a difference; I'll always be this way"). On the other hand, optimists take full credit for their successes, while pessimists see only luck or chance in anything good that happens to them. A person's explanatory style can influence performance in school and work and even his or her physical and mental well-being.

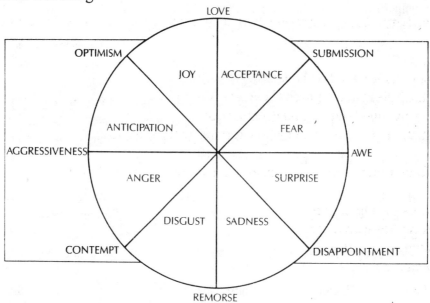

Wheel of Emotion
Psychologist Robert Plutchik created a wheel of emotion showing eight primary emotions and composites of adjacent emotions. According to this model, fear and surprise, when combined, become awe, and joy mixed with acceptance becomes love.

Review Questions

Program Questions

1. What is the general term for all the physical and psychological processes that start behavior, maintain it, and stop it?

    a. Explanatory style
    b. Repression
    c. Addiction
    d. Motivation

2. Phoebe has a phobia regarding cats. What is her motivation?

    a. Environmental arousal
    b. Overwhelming fear
    c. Repressed sexual satisfaction
    d. A need for attachment to others

3. What is the role of the pleasure-pain principle in motivation?

    a. We repress our pleasure in others' pain.
    b. We seek pleasure and avoid pain.
    c. We persist in doing things even when they are painful.
    d. We are more intensely motivated by pain than by pleasure.

4. Which activity most clearly involves a "reframing" of the tension between desire and restraint?

    a. Eating before you feel hungry
    b. Seeking pleasurable physical contact with others
    c. Working long hours for an eventual goal
    d. Getting angry at someone who interferes with your plans

5. Freud thought there were two primary motivations. One of these is

    a. expressing aggression.
    b. seeking transcendence.
    c. fulfilling creativity.
    d. feeling secure.

6. Compared with Freud's view of human motivation, that of Abraham Maslow could be characterized as being more

    a. negative.
    b. hormonally based.
    c. optimistic.
    d. pathologically based.

7. Behaviors such as male peacocks displaying their feathers or male rams fighting are related to which part of sexual reproduction?

    a. Providing a safe place for mating
    b. Focusing the male's attention on mating
    c. Selecting a partner with good genes
    d. Mating at the correct time of year

8. In Norman Adler's research on mating behavior in rats, what is the function of the ten or so mountings?

    a. To trigger hormone production
    b. To prepare the male for ejaculation
    c. To cause fertilization
    d. To impress the female

9. What kinds of emotions tend to be involved in romantic love?

    a. Mainly intense, positive emotions
    b. Mainly intense, negative emotions
    c. A mixture of intense and weak emotions that are mainly positive
    d. A mixture of positive and negative emotions that are intense

10. Darwin cited the similarity of certain expressions of emotions as evidence that

    a. all species learn emotions.
    b. emotions are innate.
    c. emotions promote survival of the fittest.
    d. genetic variability is advantageous.

11. Pictures of happy and sad American workers are shown to American college students and to Italian workers. Based on your knowledge of Paul Ekman's research, what would you predict about how well the groups would identify the emotions?

    a. Both groups will identify the emotions correctly.
    b. Only the Americans will identify the emotions correctly.
    c. Only the Italians will identify the emotions correctly.
    d. Neither group will identify the emotions correctly.

12. Theodore has an explanatory style that emphasizes the external, the unstable, and the specific. He makes a mistake at work about which his boss becomes very angry. Which statement is Theodore most likely to make to himself?

    a. "I always make such stupid mistakes."
    b. "I was just distracted by the noise outside."
    c. "All my life people have always gotten so mad at me."
    d. "If I were a better person, this wouldn't have happened."

13. Why does Martin Seligman believe that it might be appropriate to help children who develop a pessimistic explanatory style?

    a. These children are unpleasant to be around.
    b. These children lack contact with reality.
    c. These children are at risk for depression.
    d. These children seldom achieve much in life.

Textbook Questions

14. Theories such as that of Maslow's hierarchy of motives, McClelland's achievement motivation and even Freud's psychoanalytic theory are all

    a. instruct theories.
    b. deprivation driven.
    c. homeostatic theories.
    d. dynamic theories.

15. All of the following have been used as measures of motivation EXCEPT

    a. choices of tasks and rewards.
    b. consummatory behavior.
    c. response generalization.
    d. activity level.

16. Which one of the following psychologists would NOT applaud a speech entitled, "Instincts: The Best Explanation for Human Motivation?"

    a. William James
    b. Abraham Maslow
    c. Sigmund Freud
    d. William McDougall

17. The concept of "instinct" as an explanation for human motivation was flawed because

    a. human behavior is too complex.
    b. most human behavior is clearly learned.
    c. only animals can be shown to engage in fixed action patterns.
    d. psychoanalysts adopted this concept as one aspect of their theory.

18. Maslow would probably say that your decision to attend college and be successful is motivated by your need for

    a. attachment.
    b. esteem.
    c. creativity.
    d. self-actualization.

19. If you believe that what happens to you in life has a definite relationship to your efforts and behaviors, you would be

    a. motivated by a cognitive dissonance.
    b. motivated by the discrepancy between your current position and your goal.
    c. classified as having a need for power.
    d. classified as having an internal locus of control.

20. The current approach to understanding hunger and eating is referred to as the

    a. psychological factors approach.
    b. peripheral cues approach.
    c. brain center approach.
    d. multiple system approach.

21. All of the following processes are involved in motivation EXCEPT

    a. continuing activities.
    b. directing activities.
    c. enjoying activities.
    d. initiating activities.

22. Instinct theory was abandoned largely because

    a. many so-called "instincts" were shown to be learned behaviors.
    b. instincts were seen as too mechanistic.
    c. there were few examples of instinctive behaviors observed.
    d. introspection could not be used to study instincts.

23. Hullian drive theory was criticized because it

   a. failed to adequately explain biologically based motivation.
   b. hypothesized a nonspecific, nondirectional energy.
   c. could not adequately explain motivations such as exploration and manipulation.
   d. used instinct as a universal explanation for all observed behavior.

24. According to Rotter's social cognitive theory of motivation, we can estimate a person's motivation to reach a goal by

   a. measuring the discrepancy between the goal and the person's present position.
   b. taking the algebraic sum of the positive and negative aspects of the goal.
   c. subtracting the number of barriers that impede achievement from the value of the goal.
   d. multiplying the person's probability of achieving the goal by the value of the goal to the person.

25. Research suggests that compared to individualistic cultures, collectivist cultures emphasize

   a. self-discipline.
   b. immediate gratification.
   c. social relationships.
   d. economic goals.

26. Sympathetic system is to parasympathetic system as

   a. reticular activating system is to autonomic system.
   b. unpleasant stimulation is to pleasant stimulation.
   c. neuron is to hormone.
   d. intense is to mild.

27. James-Lange is to peripheralist as

   a. Lazarus-Schachter is to adaptive function.
   b. Darwin is to two-factor theory.
   c. Canon-Bard is to centralist.
   d. Tompkins is to mere exposure.

28. All of the following organs are involved in the expression of emotion EXCEPT

   a. the cortex.
   b. the adrenal glands.
   c. the limbic system.
   d. the cerebellum.

29. A model of emotion involving ten distinct emotions was proposed by

    a.   Caroll E. Izard.
    b.   Robert Plutchik.
    c.   Joseph LeDoux.
    d.   Charles Darwin.

30. Mood-dependent is to recall as

    a.   mood-congruent is to stress.
    b.   mood-ring is to facial expressiveness.
    c.   mood-congruent is to selective sensitization.
    d.   mood-altering is to adrenaline.

Questions to Consider

1. Human sexual motivation expresses itself in sexual scripts that include: attitudes, values, social norms, and expectations about patterns of behavior. Consider how males and females might develop different sexual scripts. How might lack of synchronization affect a couple? How might sexual scripts change as the bad news about sexually transmitted diseases and AIDS increases?

2. Do you consider yourself an optimist or a pessimist? Pick a recent success and a recent failure or disappointment and consider how an optimist and a pessimist would explain each experience. How did you handle each situation?

3. Does your body give away your true feelings? What is the role of emotion in nonverbal communication? When words and body language don't match, do you pay more attention to the words or to the behavior? Why?

4. Consider how eating disorders such as anorexia and bulimia contradict the pain-pleasure principle.

5. Why might both extremely sad and extremely happy events be stressful?

6. If you could choose between taking this course pass/fail (credit only) or getting a letter grade, which would you choose? How would your decision affect your study time, motivation, test-taking behavior?

Optional Activity

Are we sad because we cry, or do we cry because we are sad? Can making a sad face make us feel sad? Does going through the motions trigger the emotion?

Try this: Set aside 10 or 15 minutes for this experiment. Write down the words *happy, sad, angry,* and *fearful* on slips of paper. In front of a mirror, select one of the slips, and watch yourself as you create the facial expression for it. Hold the expression for at least a minute. Note the thoughts and physical reactions that seem to accompany your facial expression. Then relax your face and repeat the exercise with another slip of paper. Which theories does your experience support or challenge?

Additional Resources

Books and Articles

Beck. R. (1983). *Motivation.* 2nd Ed. Englewood Cliffs, NJ: Prentice Hall.

Ekman, P. (1994). *The Nature of Emotion.* New York: Oxford University Press.

Ekman, P. & Friesen, W. (1975). *Unmasking the Face: A Guide to Recognizing Emotions from Facial Cues.* Englewood Cliffs, N.J.: Prentice-Hall, 1975. A look at how emotions are communicated through facial expressions.

Evans, P. (1989). *Motivation and Emotion.* London: Routledge.

Freud, Sigmund.(1914). *The Psychopathology of Everyday Life.* New York: Macmillan. How slips of the tongue, dreams, fantasies, and other phenomena manifest forces of the unconscious that motivate behavior.

Fromm, Erich.(1946). *The Art of Loving.* New York: Harper & Row. Fromm suggests that, in order truly to experience love, we must have "courage, faith, and discipline." He looks at various types of love—motherly, brotherly, erotic, religious, and the love of oneself.

Maslow, Abraham.(1968). *Toward a Psychology of Being.* New York: Van Nostrand. This classic groundwork of humanistic psychology explores the human striving for self-actualization.

McClelland, D. (1976). *The Achieving Society.* New York: Irvington Pub.

Melzack, R. (1973). *Puzzle of Pain.* Harmoundsworth: Penguin.

Miller, Laurence. "The Emotional Brain." *Psychology Today* (February 1988): 34-42. Where do emotions originate? Recent studies trace different emotions to specific parts of the brain.

Nebraska Symposium on Motivation. (1994). *Integrative Views of Motivation, Cognition, and Emotion.* Lincoln, Nebraska: University of Nebraska Press.

Plutchik, Robert.(1980). *Emotion: A Psychoevolutionary Synthesis.* New York: Harper & Row. Discusses the evolution of eight basic emotions in human beings. Depicts these emotions as four pairs of opposites, such as joy and sadness.

Roberts, Marjory. (1987, March). "Baby Love." *Psychology Today,* 60. Two recent studies suggest that the nature of early attachments with parents affects how people view romance and love.

Zimbardo, Philip.(1990). *Shyness: What It Is, What to Do About It*, 2d ed. Reading, Mass.: Addison-Wesley. What causes shyness, and how can people overcome it. Philip Zimbardo looks at the often painful experience of shyness.

UNIT 13

THE MIND AWAKE AND ASLEEP

One of the most adventurous things left us is to go to bed. For no one can lay band on our dreams.

E. V. Lucas

Unit 13 describes how psychologists investigate the nature of sleeping, dreaming, and altered states of conscious awareness. It also explores the ways we use consciousness to interpret, analyze, even change our behavior.

Objectives

After viewing the program and completing the reading assignment, you should be able to:

1. Describe the functions of consciousness

2. Describe the different levels of consciousness and the kinds of processing that occur at each level

3. Define circadian rhythms

4. Describe the stages of sleep

5. Identify the major sleep disorders and the effects of sleep deprivation

6. Discuss the difference between night dreaming and day dreaming, and describe lucid dreaming

7. Explain Freud's theory of dreaming and contrast it with the Hobson-McCarley theory and the information-processing theory

8. Give examples of the difference between a dream's manifest content and latent content

Reading Assignment

After viewing Program 13, read pages 101-136 in *Psychology and Life*. This textbook reading covers Units 13 and 14.

Key People and Terms

As you watch the program and read the assignment, pay particular attention to these people and terms. People and terms defined in the text will be found on the given page numbers.

addiction (128)
circadian rhythm (114)
consciousness (102)
consensual validation (109)
daydreaming (113)
daytime sleepiness (121)
dream work (123)
dualism (106)
experience-sampling (105)
hallucinations (129)
hypnosis (125)
hypnotizability (126)
insomnia (120)
latent content (123)
lucid dreaming (124)

manifest content (123)
meditation (129)
monism (107)
narcolepsy (120)
nonconscious processes (104)
non-REM (NREM) sleep (115)
preconscious memories (104)
psychoactive drugs (131)
physiological dependence (131)
psychological dependence (132)
rapid eye movement (REM) sleep (115)
sleep apnea (120)
self-awareness (103)
think-aloud protocols (105)
tolerance (131)
withdrawal symptoms (131)

Rosalind Cartwright (118)
Sigmund Freud (105)
Ernest Hilgard (128)
J. Allen Hobson (120)
Stephen LaBerge (124)
James Maas (121)
Robert McCarley (120)
Jerome Singer (113)

The following term and person are used in Program 13 but is not defined in the text.

hypnagogic state—a period of reverie at the onset of the sleeping state

Ernest Hartmann-an expert on sleep who believes that it serves a restorative function

Program Summary

Throughout the day we experience changes in our biological processes and states of consciousness. Body temperature, blood pressure, pulse rate, blood sugar, and hormone levels fluctuate over the course of a day. As we will see in Program 13 these fluctuations affect our moods, motivations, energy level, and performance.

We are rarely aware of our body's automatic "housekeeping" functions. Nor are we aware of processing sensory input. But we are able to walk down the street without bumping into things because our brains automatically estimate distances and detect obstacles. Once we have mastered the routine tasks, we no longer need to direct and monitor our efforts.

Just as some cognitive psychologists use the metaphor of the computer to describe human cognition, William James used the stream, with its constantly changing flow, to explain the concept of consciousness. He also noted that the mind is selective and is able to reduce the continual bombardment of sensory input, freeing us to attend to what is most relevant to our survival.

Interest in the conscious mind has waxed and waned throughout the history of psychology. In nineteenth-century Germany, Wilhelm Wundt conducted studies of consciousness. He looked for an underlying structure of the mind by performing experiments in which his subjects reported their sensations. In the United States, Edward Titchener also explored the contents of consciousness—the "what" instead of the "how and why." This approach became known as structuralism. William James rejected the attempts of the structuralists to reduce consciousness to component parts, focusing instead on how the mind adapts to the environment. His approach was known as functionalism.

Then, in the 1920s, a leading behaviorist named John B. Watson declared the study of consciousness worthless and called for an objective science that studied behavior. He influenced the focus of American psychology for the first half of the twentieth century.

The study of consciousness was reintroduced in the late 1950s by a new breed of cognitive psychologists who took an interest in how and why we pay attention to some things and not to others. One of them, British psychologist Donald Broadbent, demonstrated that our attention has a limited capacity.

Further research showed the selective aspects of attention. For example, if someone mentions your name across a crowded, noisy room, it will probably catch your attention, whereas you probably wouldn't notice other names or words that were being spoken. This demonstrates mental activity at a preconscious level. Just outside of conscious awareness, ideas and feelings that are stored in memory and external stimuli are continuously processed or filtered.

Another state of consciousness is daydreaming. Although some people consider daydreaming a waste of time, psychologists believe daydreams are quite useful. They can be a source of creativity, a way of coping with problems and overcoming boredom, and a way of stimulating the brain.

In contrast, sleep helps reduce stimulation. But until the first half of this century we knew relatively little about it. In 1937, research revealed that brain waves change in form during the entire sleep cycle. In the early 1950s, studies led to the discovery of rapid eye movements, known as REM (see figure). When REM was limited to dreaming, researchers had a reasonably objective index of the dream.

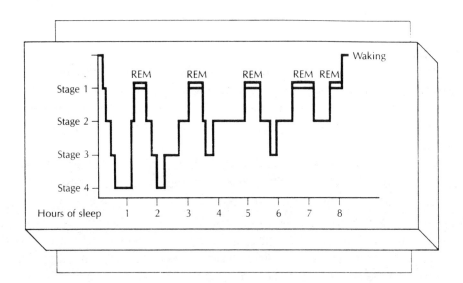

Sleep Cycles
For the typical sleeper, five periods of REM sleep alternate with non-REM sleep through an eight-hour night. Sleep is deeper earlier in the night, and REM sleep increases toward morning.

But what do dreams tell us about ourselves and our world? Freud claimed that they revealed the presence of deep secrets buried in the unconscious and that dreams protected the dreamer from disturbing wishes and thoughts. He believed that dreams were the key to understanding unconscious sexual and aggressive desires and fears.

Researchers Alan Hobson and Robert McCarley explain the controversial theory that dreams arise from spontaneous discharges of electrical impulses in the brain stem. They assert that REM sleep promotes brain development and does not have a psychological purpose. The electrical discharges activate the memories that appear in dreams as coherent images, but the psychological meaning is added afterward by the dreamer.

The middle view is that dreams are the result of the interplay of the physiological triggering of brain activity and the psychological function of its imaginative, interpretive parts. Electrical impulses activate concepts stored in memory, and the cerebral cortex helps to shape recall.

Steven LaBerge of Stanford University explores the power of the cerebral cortex to influence dreamers. He trains his study participants to report aloud their dreams without waking. They can also be given suggestions for directing their dreams. Some people claim this can enhance creativity and control of the unconscious; others object because such directed dreaming tampers with the unconscious. Psychologists find it fascinating because it represents a way of intentionally altering consciousness.

Review Questions

Note: Review Questions for Units 13 and 14 are provided in Unit 14.

Questions to Consider

1. Donald Broadbent conceived of attention as a selective filter which acts like a tuner on a radio, selecting one message from all the others. According to Broadbent, the unattended sensory information is sent to a buffer, where it either receives attention and gets processed or is ignored and lost. How is this buffer similar to the concept of the sensory memory? What role might it play in subliminal perception?

2. What are the benefits and drawbacks of mindlessness?

3. Consider the role of culture and language in structuring consciousness or focused perception. In what ways is awareness culturally determined?

Optional Activities

1. Keep a pad and pencil by your bed and start a dream journal. Just before you fall asleep, remind yourself to remember your dreams. Immediately upon awakening, record what you remember: images, actions, characters, emotions, events, and settings. Does your ability to recall your dreams improve over time? Does your recall become more vivid or more organized? Are there common elements, people, symbols, or themes? Can you shape your dreams by telling yourself at bedtime what you want to dream about?

2. Make a list of common examples of dissociation and divided consciousness. Do these examples support the concept of mini-minds or independent areas of the brain conducting their business? What other explanations might explain your ability to divide your consciousness?

Additional Resources

Books and Articles

Coleman, R. (1986). *Wide Awake at 3:00 A.M. By Choice or by Chance?* New York: Freeman. Excellent treatment of biological clocks and the role they play in work, jet lag, and insomnia.

Cartwright, R. (1978). *A Primer on Sleep and Dreaming.* Reading, MA: Addison Wesley Pub. Co.

Dement, W. C. (1994). *The Principles and Practices of Sleep Medicine.* Philadelphia, PA: Saunders.

Ellman, S. & Antrobus, J. (Eds.) (1991). *Mind in Sleep: Psychology and Psychophysiology.* New York: Wiley.

Gazzaniga, Michael.(1988). *Mind Matters: How Brain and Mind Interact to Create Our Conscious Lives.* Boston: Houghton Mifflin. Insights from the field of neuropsychology can help us better understand the nature of consciousness.

Hartmann, Ernest.(1984). *The Nightmare: The Psychology and Biology of Terrifying Dreams.* New York: Basic Books. Who has nightmares? Why do they happen, and what do they mean? Hartmann looks at the psychological, social, and biological aspects of bad dreams.

Hobson, J. Allen. (1988). *The Dreaming Brain.* New York: Basic Books.

LaBerge, Stephen. (1986). *Lucid Dreaming.* New York: Ballantine Books. Can we learn to control our dreams? LaBerge discusses lucid dreaming as a skill that can be taught.

Sacks, Oliver. (1983). *Awakenings.* New York: Dutton. A great sleeping sickness epidemic 50 years ago left many with a bizarre and debilitating disease. A new "miracle drug" allowed them to wake, but the process of recovery was far from easy. Sacks recounts the fascinating cases of several patients.

<u>**UNIT 14**</u>

THE MIND HIDDEN AND DIVIDED

The mind is the most capricious of insects—flitting, fluttering.

Virginia Woolf

Unit 14 considers the evidence that our moods, behavior, and even our health are largely the result of multiple mental processes, many of which are out of conscious awareness. It also looks at some of the most dramatic phenomena in psychology: hypnosis, multiple personality disorder, and the division of human consciousness into "two minds" when the brain is split in half by surgical intervention.

Objectives

After viewing the program and completing the assigned reading, you should be able to:

1. Describe hypnotic techniques, experiences, and applications

2. Identify the factors that influence a person's susceptibility to hypnosis

3. Explain the difference between psychological dependence and physical addiction

4. Define the major drug categories, and compare the effects of specific drugs such as stimulants and depressants

5. List and describe the characteristics of the various extended states of consciousness such as lucid dreaming, hypnosis, meditation, hallucinations and drug use.

Reading Assignment

After viewing Program 14, review pages 101-136 in *Psychology and Life*.

Key People and Terms

To review textbook terms, refer to Key People and Terms in Unit 13.

The following terms and people are used in Program 14 but are not defined in your text.

posthypnotic amnesia—forgetting selected events by suggestion

F.W. Putman-expert on Multiple Personality Disorder (MPD)

Michael Gazzaniga-conducts research on the psychological study of split brain phenomena

Program Summary

Is it possible to "know thyself"? Evidence suggests both that a lot of important mental activity occurs outside our conscious awareness and that unconscious experiences can significantly alter our moods, behavior, and health. This is the subject of Program 14.

In one experiment, patients under anesthesia were given negative and positive information about their condition. Patients who received positive messages felt better, required less medication, and were discharged earlier than those who overheard upsetting news. This suggests that the unconscious brain processes stimuli and receives messages. Although the patients claimed not to be aware of what was said, many did recall the messages under hypnosis.

How does the unconscious influence our thoughts, moods, and behavior? Neuroscientists theorize that our brains are organized into separate minibrains, or modules. Each is designed to do a specific job, such as speaking or reading; there is really no single, all-powerful command center.

Since the earliest times, people have been fascinated with the idea that human behavior could be taken over by hidden identities or unknown parts of themselves. The transformation of identity is one of the major themes in world literature and myth; recall Robert Louis Stevenson's famous story *The Strange Case of Dr. Jekyll and Mr. Hyde* and Franz Kafka's *The Metamorphosis*.

We do know that there are many ways the mind can be transformed. Psychoactive drugs can change how the mind functions and how personality is expressed. Studies of different cultures reveal rituals and many other forms of altering consciousness, including drugs, fasting, and meditation.

Consciousness can also be altered by mental illness. The multiple personality is a dramatic example of dissociation in which several distinct personalities develop in the same individual. F. W. Putnam, an expert in this field, explains that the typical profile of a multiple personality is that of a woman who shut out the reality of sexual and physical childhood abuse by mentally escaping into dissociative states. The alternate personalities exist in the unconscious, often unaware of one another.

According to Freud, our most traumatic feelings are bound and gagged in the unconscious. Unacceptable desires, urges, and painful memories are hidden by the process he called repression. Freud interpreted anxiety as the alarm that warns when these feelings are about to break through into consciousness. Dreams, errors, and slips of the tongue reveal some of these otherwise repressed aspects of unconscious activity.

Hypnosis is another window into the unconscious. Under hypnosis, some people act unconsciously on ideas, thoughts, and feelings. Suggestions can direct behavior afterward, altering memory, the perception of pain, even influencing decisions about smoking and eating.

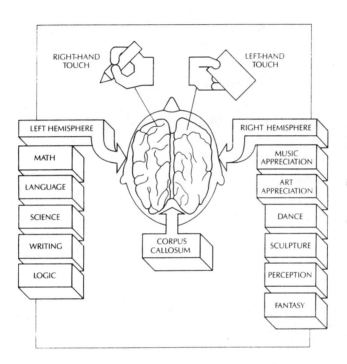

Left Brain/Right Brain Abilities
In this diagram, the differences between the left and right brain are exaggerated. In general, however, the left hemisphere is more involved with logic and reasoning, and the right hemisphere is more concerned with emotions and imagination.

The notion that part of the mind can function separately is difficult for many people to accept. But we can't deny the evidence. Supporting data about the behavior of the divided brain come from studies of patients whose corpus callosum, the connecting nerves between the two hemispheres of the brain, has been cut to prevent epileptic seizures from spreading across both hemispheres. Although the behavior of these patients appears normal, tests of eye-hand coordination show that each hemisphere receives and processes only certain information. The right brain is better at solving perceptual problems, pattern recognition, and spatial relationships; the left excels in language and logical analysis (see figure).

A final study suggests that the left brain is the "social brain" and that each person's unique consciousness is a product of this interpretive left hemisphere. The idea that the brain has many semi-independent modules or highly specialized multiminds is supported by research with split-brain and brain lesion patients. Modularity has a real anatomical base.

Review Questions

Program Questions

1. Which of the following is an example of a circadian rhythm?

    a. Eating three meals a day at approximately the same time
    b. Experiencing alternate periods of REM and non-REM sleep
    c. Having systematic changes in hormone levels during 24 hours
    d. Having changes in fertility levels during a month

2. How normal is it to experience alternate states of consciousness?

    a. It happens to most people, mainly in times of stress.
    b. It is something we all experience every day.
    c. It is rare and generally indicates a mental disorder.
    d. It is common in childhood and becomes rarer with age.

3. In the program, the part of the brain that is identified as the "interior decorator" imposing order on experience is the

    a. pons.
    b. hippocampus.
    c. limbic system.
    d. cerebral cortex.

4. Which of the following is an example of the lower-level processing of sensory input that is nonconscious?

    a. Recognizing a friend's face
    b. Detecting edges
    c. Working on an assembly line
    d. Noticing something tastes good

5. Edward Titchener was the leader of structuralism in the United States. What aspect of the concept of consciousness interested him?

    a. The contents of consciousness
    b. The material repressed from conscious awareness
    c. The uniqueness of consciousness
    d. He viewed consciousness as a scientifically worthless concept.

6. In Donald Broadbent's research, what happened when subjects heard two stories but were asked to attend to only one?

    a. They comprehended both stories.
    b. They comprehended only the attended story.
    c. They wove bits of the unattended story into the attended story.
    d. They were not able to follow either story.

7. What is a positive function of daydreaming?

    a. It focuses attention on a task.
    b. It reduces demands made on the brain.
    c. It enables us to be mentally active when we are bored.
    d. It provides delta wave activity normally gotten only in sleep.

8. Ernest Hartmann points out the logic behind Shakespeare's description of sleep. According to Hartmann, a major function of sleep is that it allows the brain to

    a. process material too threatening to be dealt with consciously.
    b. integrate the day's events with previously learned material.
    c. make plans for the day ahead.
    d. discharge a buildup of electrical activity.

9. According to Freud, dreams are significant because they

    a. permit neurotransmitters to be regenerated.
    b. reveal unconscious fears and desires.
    c. forecast the future.
    d. supply a story line to patterns of electrical charges.

10. According to McCarley and Hobson's activation synthesis theory of dreams, what activates dreams?

   a.   The needs of the dreamer's unconscious
   b.   The sending of electrical charges to the forebrain
   c.   The memories contained in the cerebral cortex
   d.   The synthesis of chemicals needed for brain function

11. In his work on lucid dreaming, why does LaBerge use a flashing light?

   a.   So subjects are consciously aware of their dream and can control it
   b.   So subjects can incorporate the light itself into their dream narrative
   c.   So subjects get feedback about where they are in the REM sleep cycle
   d.   So measurements can be made of physiological response

12. In the experiment described in the program, patients under anesthesia were exposed to a positive or negative message. What effect did getting a positive message have?

   a.   It meant less anesthesia was needed.
   b.   It shortened patients' hospital stays.
   c.   It created more positive attitudes toward surgery.
   d.   Positive messages had no effect because patients were unaware of them.

13. Which phrase sums up the traditional image of the brain in Western culture?

   a.   "Master of all it surveys"
   b.   "The slave of the passions"
   c.   "The tip of the iceberg"
   d.   "Battleground of hostile armies"

14. When societies around the world were studied, what proportion of them practiced some culturally patterned form of altering consciousness?

   a.   Practically none
   b.   About a third
   c.   About half
   d.   The vast majority

15. Harriet is a young woman with a multiple personality disorder. What was her childhood probably like?
   a.   She suffered from severe abuse.
   b.   She was under strong pressure to excel.
   c.   She was an only child whose mother died.
   d.   She had an unusually tranquil childhood.

16. According to Freud, how do we feel when painful memories or unacceptable urges threaten to break into consciousness?

    a. Relieved
    b. Guilty
    c. Sad
    d. Anxious

17. What do Freudian slips reveal?

    a. What we have dreamed about
    b. How we really feel
    c. Who we would like to be transformed into
    d. Why we make certain choices

18. What happens when a hypnotized subject smells ammonia when he expects to smell cologne?

    a. The ammonia smell wakes him from the trance.
    b. He recognizes the ammonia smell, but he remains hypnotized.
    c. He interprets the ammonia smell as a musky cologne.
    d. He overgeneralizes and finds the cologne smells like ammonia.

19. Imagine you see something with your right eye. Where is the information routed in your brain?

    a. To both hemispheres simultaneously
    b. To the right hemisphere
    c. To the left hemisphere
    d. Where it is routed depends on what kind of thing is seen.

20. Michael Gazzaniga has worked with "broken-brain" patients. What has this led him to believe about our individuality?

    a. It comes from an interpreter in the left hemisphere.
    b. It is an illusion based on our emotional needs.
    c. It derives from our unique set of independent mind-modules.
    d. It is located in the corpus callosum.

Textbook Questions

21.   Dualist is to monist as

    a.   behaviorist is to psychoanalyst.
    b.   physiological is to cognitive psychologist.
    c.   neuroscientist is to behaviorist.
    d.   humanist is to neuroscientist.

22.   The selective storage function of consciousness is performed by the

    a.   cognitive register.
    b.   short-term memory.
    c.   decision-making function.
    d.   selective attention monitor.

23.   Nonconscious processes include such things as

    a.   repressed feelings of jealousy.
    b.   the name of your kindergarten teacher.
    c.   orientation of the body with respect to gravity.
    d.   the sound of an air conditioner or heater.

24.   The purpose of the dichotic listening task is to

    a.   bring repressed material into consciousness.
    b.   understand the mental strategies used in problem solving.
    c.   study subconscious awareness.
    d.   determine the contents of consciousness.

25.   Singer's Imaginal Processes Inventory is used to study

    a.   the latent content of daydreams.
    b.   different types of daydreamers.
    c.   the effect of the P-300 wave form.
    d.   circadian rhythms.

26.   Which statement about the sleep cycle is true?

    a.   As you move from stage 1 to stage 4, brain wave activity increases.
    b.   Sleep spindles appear during REM sleep.
    c.   The length of REM periods increases as you move through the cycle.
    d.   NREM dreams are shorter and more bizarre.

27. All of the following statements about REM sleep are true EXCEPT

    a. REM is related to the cyclical release of neurotransmitters such as serotonin.
    b. REM deprivation on one night leads to increased REM the next night.
    c. REM sleep may establish neuromuscular pathways in the eyes among infants.
    d. REM plays a role in moods and emotions.

28. All of the following researchers have contributed to our understanding of sleeping and dreaming EXCEPT

    a. R. W. McCarley and J. A. Hobson.
    b. W. C. Dement.
    c. R. D. Cartwright.
    d. J. Singer.

29. Raymond experiences irresistible urges to fall asleep at various times during the day. A likely diagnosis is

    a. sleep apnea.
    b. epilepsy.
    c. narcolepsy.
    d. cataplexy.

30. Why do we typically forget even our most vivid and bizarre dreams?

    a. The censor inhibits transfer of the latent content to consciousness.
    b. The absence of serotonin and norepinephrine prevent transfer to long-term memory.
    c. Distributed activation leads to inhibition of the memory cortex.
    d. The positive activation system inhibits memory processing.

31. A practical application of hypnosis is in the area of

    a. trance induction.
    b. pain control.
    c. automatic writing.
    d. psychoanalytic training.

32. Many drugs alter consciousness by

    a. stimulating the pituitary gland.
    b. regulating blood flow to the cortex.
    c. blocking ion flow in the neurons.
    d. controlling synaptic transmission.

33.   A person is said to be addicted to a substance when

    a.   hallucinations occur.
    b.   withdrawal symptoms occur.
    c.   psychological dependence occurs.
    d.   powerful cravings occur.

34.   In the United States the greatest number of fatalities occur from the use of

    a.   alcohol and tobacco.
    b.   amphetamines and barbiturates.
    c.   heroine and cocaine.
    d.   tobacco and cocaine.

35.   If you were a supporter of the emergent-interaction theory of mind-brain relationships, with which statement would you agree?

    a.   All behavior can be explained in terms of neuronal activity.
    b.   Brain activities lead to but are not the same as mental states.
    c.   It is more important to evaluate overt, external behavior.
    d.   Introspection is the most efficient way of studying the activity of the mind and brain.

36.   The term "consciousness" refers to all of the following EXCEPT

    a.   feelings such as guilt, remorse, and so on.
    b.   all that we are aware of at a particular moment.
    c.   a general state of mind.
    d.   our sense of self-awareness.

37.   Our physiological functions operate on a 25-hour cycle known as

    a.   diurnal rhythm.
    b.   circadian rhythm.
    c.   paradoxical rhythm.
    d.   the sleep-wake cycle.

38.   It has been suggested that the benefits of REM sleep include

    a.   maintaining muscle tone during sleep.
    b.   storing and organizing memories.
    c.   improving creativity.
    d.   solving ongoing problems and concerns.

39. Short-sleepers are to long-sleepers as

  a. intelligent is to artistic.
  b. creative is to energetic.
  c. worrisome is to creative.
  d. extroverted is to nonconforming.

40. For Sigmund Freud, dreams were

  a. primarily a correlate of gender differences.
  b. an expression of nonconscious processes.
  c. the result of random brain activity.
  d. points of access to the unconscious.

41. According to Freud, the forbidden thoughts and impulses of the unconscious are transformed into acceptable images and actions through

  a. wish fulfillment.
  b. dream work.
  c. latent content.
  d. activation-synthesis.

42. According to the activation-synthesis theory of dreaming, dreams begin with

  a. massive inhibition of sensory input.
  b. unfulfilled wishes.
  c. random brainstem activity.
  d. left hemispheric processing.

43. Which term is the most accurate description of hypnosis?

  a. Hallucinatory state
  b. Deep sleep
  c. High suggestibility
  d. Mind control

44. Depressant is to stimulant as

  a. heroin is to cannabis.
  b. barbiturate is to alcohol.
  c. alcohol is to cocaine.
  d. LSD is to amphetamine.

45.   The effects of stimulants may include all of the following EXCEPT

a.   euphoric mood.
b.   paranoid delusions.
c.   hyperalertness.
d.   deep relaxation.

Questions to Consider

1.   Changes in perceptions, time sense, memory, feelings of self-control, and suggestibility are aspects of an altered state of consciousness. Would you consider illness, love, or grief to be altered states of consciousness?

2.   Psychoactive drugs are only partially responsible for the changes in the drug taker's consciousness. Mental sets, expectations, and the context in which the drugs are taken can also have a significant influence. What are the implications for alcohol and drug education and treatment?

3.   Do you consider television a mind-altering influence? What does TV have in common with other mind-altering substances or experiences? Are children more susceptible to TV's effects than adults?

Optional Activities

1.   Use this visualization technique to achieve a state of relaxation and, perhaps, alter your consciousness. Select a quiet place where you won't be interrupted. Choose a scene in which you have been very relaxed. To help you create a good mental picture, recall all the sensations that enhance in you a feeling of deep calm. Focus on the scene for 15-30 minutes. Practice this visualization exercise several times over a period of a few weeks. With practice, calling up the visual image may trigger a sensation of calm whenever you want it to.

2.   Try to think of a time when you surprised yourself by having a very strong feeling in response to an incident that didn't seem to warrant such a strong response. Could nonconscious factors have played a role in your response? What did you think about your response at the time? What did you think about it later?

Additional Resources

Books and Articles

Dennett, D. (1991). *Consciousness Explained.* Boston: Little Brown & Co.

Freud, Sigmund.(1923). *The Ego and the Id.* Edited by Joan Riviere, New York: Norton. Freud divides the human mind into three categories: id, ego, and superego. He discusses these three elements and theorizes about conscious and unconscious processes.

Gazzaniga, Michael. (1985). *The Social Brain.* New York: Basic Books. The study of split-brain patients has enlightened our understanding of the human brain. Gazzaniga deems the left side of the brain "the social brain"—the interpretive, meaning-making hemisphere.

Grinspoon, L. & Bakalar, J. (1979). *Psychedelic Drugs Reconsidered.* New York: Basic Books. A thoughtful scientific treatment of issues surrounding psychedelic drugs.

Hilgard, Ernest R. (1986). *Divided Consciousness: Multiple Controls in Human Thought and Action.* New York: Wiley. Examines how hypnosis can bring out information that seems hidden from the conscious mind.

Kabat-Zinn. (1994). *Wherever You Go, There You Are.* New York: Hyperion. The best, most accessible book available on learning the practice of mindfulness meditation.

Moore, Thomas. (1992). *Care of the Soul: A Guide For Cultivating Depth and Sacredness in Everyday Life.* New York: HarperCollins. Beautifully written guide on how to increase meaning in life through mindfulness.

Moore, Thomas. (1994). *Soul Mates: Honoring the Mysteries of Relationship.* New York: HarperCollins. Further exploration of the use of mindfulness in producing more meaningful relationships.

Films

Sybil. Directed by Daniel Petrie; starring Sally Field. 1976. Emmy Award-winning study of a woman who, after being terribly abused as a child, develops 17 different personalities. Based on the book about a true story.

The Three Faces of Eve. Directed by Nunnally Johnson. 1957. Joanne Woodward, in an Academy Award-winning role, plays a Southern housewife with multiple personalities. Adapted from the 1957 book by two doctors, C. H. Thigpen and H. M. Cleckley.

UNIT 15

THE SELF

[There is need] to discover that we are capable of solitary joy and having experienced it, know that we have touched the core of self.

Barbara Lazear Ascher

What makes each of us unique? What traits and experiences make *you*? Unit 15 describes how psychologists systematically study the origins and development of self-identity, self-esteem, and other aspects of our thoughts, feelings, and behaviors which make up our personalities.

Objectives

After viewing the television program and completing the assigned reading, you should be able to:

1. Define *personality*

2. Compare idiographic and nomethetic approaches to the study of personality

3. Compare type and trait theories of personality

4. List and describe "The Big Five" dimensions of personality

5. Describe Freud's theory of personality development and the role of the id, ego, and superego in the conscious self

6. Describe how post-Freudian theories differ from Freudian theories

7. Describe the major humanistic theories and their contribution

8. Describe social learning and cognitive theories and their contribution

9. List the five most important differences in assumptions about personality across theoretical perspectives

Reading Assignment

After viewing Program 15, read pages 507-540 in *Psychology and Life*.

Key People and Terms

As you watch the program and read the assignment, pay particular attention to these people and terms. People and terms defined in the text will be found on the given page numbers.

aggregated case study (510)
analytic psychology (524)
anxiety (522)
archetype (524)
case study (510)
collective unconscious (524)
consistency paradox (516)
ego (521)
ego defense mechanisms (521)
Eros (518)
five-factor model (514)
id (520)
idiographic approach (509)
libido (518)
nomothetic approach (510)
observational learning (530)
personal construct (528)
personality (508)
personality types (511)
possible selves (535)
psychic determinism (519)
psychobiography (526)
psychodynamic personality theories (518)
reciprocal determinism (530)
repression (521)
self-actualization (524)
self-efficacy (531)
self-esteem (536)
self-handicapping (536)
social intelligence (532)
superego (520)
Thanatos (518)
traits (512)
unconscious (520)

Alfred Adler (523)
Gordon Allport (512)
Albert Bandura (530)
Nancy Cantor (5302
Hans Eysenck (513)
Sigmund Freud (518)
Hippocrates (511)
William James (534)
Carl Jung (524)
George Kelly (528)
Hazel Markus (535)
Walter Mischel (528)
Carl Rogers (525)
William Sheldon (511)
Mark Snyder (537)

The following terms and people are used in Program 15 but are not defined in the text.

reference standard—a norm or model of behavior that we use to decide how to behave in a situation

shyness—a form of social anxiety caused by the expectation of negative social evaluation *status transaction*—a form of interpersonal communication in which we establish relative degrees of social status and power

Teresa Amabile-studies the psychology of creativity

Patricia Ryan-studies the nuances of status presentations in American culture through her work in theatre

Program Summary

How do you know who you are? Are you the same person when you are alone as you are in public? Who is the real you? In Program 15 we'll find out how we develop our concept of self—the consciousness of our own identities.

Through the ages philosophers have tried to solve the puzzle of identity—to explain the consistencies and differences in human behavior that result in individual character and personality. In 1890, William James differentiated three aspects of identity: our awareness of the world, our awareness of ourselves as thinkers, and our awareness of the impression we make on others.

Maslow's Hierarchy of Needs
Humanist psychologist Abraham Maslow believed that human behavior is motivated by a hierarchy of needs. Once basic needs are met, we move on to higher needs, finally reaching self-actualization, fulfillment of our unique potential.

For much of the twentieth century, the concept of the self was considered too "fuzzy" for the behaviorists who dominated American psychology. Even Freud did not consider the conscious self to be as important as either our moral conscience or our primitive unconscious. Today, however, many psychologists are dedicated to explaining our needs, fears, wishes, decisions, and expectations in an attempt to understand how self-concept affects behavior and, conversely, how behavior influences our sense of self.

The humanist movement of the 1940s, led by Carl Rogers, concentrated on the conscious self, characterizing it as a striver for personal fulfillment (see Figure). Rogers believed that a positive self-image enhanced personal development.

Other psychologists use the term *self-concept* to refer to an individual's awareness of a continuous identity. The self-concept shapes behavior by acting as a self-monitor and regulating behavior according to an inner standard. According to this approach, we organize our knowledge into clusters, or schemas, and make adjustments to match the way we think things ought to be. If our self-concept is good, we try to live up to our ideal standard. If it is bad, we behave and feel badly.

Still other psychologists theorize that we present ourselves so others will see us the way we see ourselves. We act and react to each other, creating and confirming the person we believe ourselves to be. Some research suggests that that's why depressed people are often treated as if they were inadequate and why happy people tend to elicit positive responses from others.

Shy people vividly illustrate this process. Typically, they feel inadequate and anticipate failure and rejection. When they get negative reactions, their self-doubts are reinforced. Their low self-esteem makes them anxious in circumstances in which they may be judged—in meetings, at parties, or in other social and business situations.

People who fear failure need to protect their self-esteem; thus they develop strategies to avoid challenges. They also protect their self-image with cover-ups to avoid blaming themselves for failure. They tend to procrastinate, forget to show up for important appointments, even abuse alcohol or drugs to excuse poor performance or to dull the pain caused by it.

Although people sometimes handicap themselves, society can be a handicapper too. Racism, sexism, and social prejudice discourage and inhibit a positive self-image and good behavior. Consider the high rate of alcoholism and suicide among Native Americans and the perpetual despair and rage in our urban ghettos.

On a more hopeful note, another element of personality—the creative self—testifies to our ability to invent new realities. In every civilization, men and women have left their stamp of individuality on anything that can be shaped, decorated, colored, or rearranged. Just as Carl Rogers believed that people naturally move toward fulfillment, Alfred Adler has called this phenomenon our inner striving for superiority.

But social evaluation can undermine creativity. Researcher Teresa Amabile has found that 7- to 11-year-olds were less creative when they expected their work to be judged by others. To be truly creative, people need a sense of self-esteem independent of social approval. They need the freedom to experience the world in new, unusual, and unconventional ways.

Review Questions

Program Questions

1. What name did William James give to the part of the self that focuses on the images we create in the mind of others?

   a. The material self
   b. The spiritual self
   c. The social self
   d. The outer self

2. Gail is a toddler who is gradually separating from her mother. This process is called

   a. identification.
   b. individuation.
   c. self-presentation.
   d. self-consciousness.

3. In Freudian theory, the part of the person that acts as a police officer restraining drives and passions is called the

    a. superego.
    b. ego.
    c. id.
    d. libido.

4. Which statement reflects the humanistic view of the self described by Carl Rogers?

    a.   Our impulses are in constant conflict with society's demands.
    b.   We have a capacity for self-direction and self-understanding.
    c.   We form an image of ourselves that determines what we can do.
    d.   Our views of ourselves are created by how people react to us.

5. When we characterize self-image as a schema, we mean that

    a.   we use it to organize information about ourselves.
    b.   other people see us in terms of the image we project.
    c.   it is a good predictor of performance in specific situations.
    d.   we rationalize our behavior to fit into an image.

6. In Albert Bandura's research, subjects were given the task of improving production at a model furniture factory. Subjects performed the best when they believed that performance

    a.   depended on their intelligence.
    b.   related mainly to how confident they felt.
    c.   would be given a material reward.
    d.   was based on learning an acquirable skill.

7. Which of the following behaviors signals low status in a status transaction?

    a.   Maintaining eye contact
    b.   Using complete sentences
    c.   Moving in slow, smooth way
    d.   Touching one's face or hair

8. According to the principles of behavioral confirmation, what reaction do people generally have to a person who is depressed?

    a.   People sympathetically offer help to the person.
    b.   People regard the person as inadequate.
    c.   People act falsely cheerful to make the person happy.
    d.   People treat a depressed person the same as anybody else.

9. Which statement about shyness is true?

    a.   It is an uncommon condition.
    b.   It can be overcome by anticipating negative consequences.
    c.   It is a form of social anxiety.
    d.   It accompanies an honest acceptance of oneself

10. Peter is worried about a report. He keeps putting off doing it until the last minute. When he is told that the report is poor, he says that he needed more time. What name do psychologists give to this phenomenon?

   a. Self-efficacy
   b. Self-handicapping
   c. Confirmatory behavior
   d. Status transaction

11. In Teresa Amabile's work on creativity, how did being in a competitive situation affect creativity?

   a. It reduced creativity.
   b. It increased creativity.
   c. Its effects varied depending on the innate creativity of the subject.
   d. There was no effect.

Textbook Questions

12. According to Freud, _____, (the drive related to sexuality), was fueled by the _____.

   a. unconscious; Eros
   b. Eros; libido
   c. Eros; thanatos
   d. ego; Eros

13. According to Freud the part of the personality that leads you to run all your charge accounts up to their limit buying things you really don't need is

   a. the id.
   b. the ego.
   c. the superego.
   d. the libido.

14. All of the following statements summarize criticisms of Freudian personality theory EXCEPT

   a. There is no observable evidence for unconscious motivation.
   b. No predictions are possible, based on the theory.
   c. There is little recognition of the influence of current life situations.
   d. There are no operational definitions for his concepts.

15. In their theories, post-Freudians have

   a. put more emphasis on the influence of social variables.
   b. put less emphasis on functions of the ego.
   c. expanded the concept of libidinal energy.
   d. done all of the above.

16. Although there are several humanistic theories of personality, one factor they all have in common is

   a. acknowledgement of the importance of models and free will in personality development.
   b. an insistence that all behavior is learned and can therefore be unlearned.
   c. an emphasis on the collective nature of our unconscious.
   d. a focus on the more positive growth oriented aspects of functioning.

17. Humanistic theories are not dispositional in the same way trait theories are dispositional because humanistic theories see dispositions as

    a. static and interacting.
    b. temporary and situationally determined.
    c. unstable and goal oriented.
    d. independent and potentially conflicting.

18. Social learning and cognitive theories of personality differ from type and trait, psychodynamic, and humanistic theories in their emphasis on

    a. free will and personal responsibility.
    b. personal history as a determinant of personality.
    c. situational determinants of behavior.
    d. individual differences.

19. Which category of personality theory most strongly supports the idea that personality can change over time?

    a. Trait theories
    b. Typology theories
    c. Learning theories
    d. Psychoanalytic theories

20. All of the following serve as sources of data for personality researchers EXCEPT

    a. simulation data.
    b. specific behavioral data.
    c. physiological data.
    d. observer report data.

21. For your recently created theory of personality to be well regarded or considered useful, it must

    a. have a firm physiological basis.
    b. make use of traits, temperament, and a comprehensive typology.
    c. deal with the structure and functioning of a particular personality.
    d. involve accurate factor analysis of major and minor traits.

22. All of the following personality theorists developed typological theories EXCEPT

    a. Jung.
    b. Adler.
    c. Hippocrates.
    d. Sheldon.

23. A major criticism of trait and type theories has been that they fail to

    a. correlate characteristics and behaviors.
    b. explain the consistency paradox.
    c. explain the causes of behavior or the development of personality.
    d. describe the uniqueness of individuals.

24. Pleasure principle is to reality principle as

    a. id is to superego.
    b. ego is to superego.
    c. superego is to id.
    d. id is to ego.

25. One of the major differences between Freudian and post-Freudian theories of personality is that the latter

    a. expanded the importance of sexuality in personality development.
    b. emphasized the importance of infancy compared to childhood in general.
    c. stressed the importance of ego functioning and social   variables.
    d. eliminated the more sexist aspects of psychoanalytic theory.

26. The idea that people are involved in a life-long process of overcoming feelings of inferiority is most associated with

    a. Sigmund Freud.
    b. Carl G. Jung.
    c. Alfred Adler.
    d. A. Maslow.

27. A likely title for a lecture by Carl Rogers is

    a. "The Mother Archetype in American Poetry."
    b. "Ego Defense Mechanisms and the Urge to Create."
    c. "Self-Actualization in Early Childhood."
    d. "Increasing Unconditional Positive Regard in Marriage."

28. Freud and behaviorists Dollard and Miller would agree that

    a. imitation of parental models is critical in personality development.
    b. tension is motivating and tension reduction is pleasurable.
    c. most important behavior is motivated by unconscious forces.
    d. reciprocal determinism helps explain the choices made by adults.

29. All of the following concepts are associated with Bandura's social learning theory EXCEPT

    a. vicarious learning.
    b. self-efficacy.
    c. self-concept.
    d. reciprocal determinism.

30. According to critics of cognitive personality, an important factor missing from such theories is

    a. emotion.
    b. attention to unconscious motives.
    c. the personal self.
    d. expectations about the impact of decisions made.

Questions to Consider

1. What is your impression of the speaker in the following poem? How would you describe her? What is the poet's level of self-esteem? Do you think it is better to be a somebody or a nobody?

    > I'm nobody! Who are you?
    > Are you—Nobody—Too?
    > Then there's a pair of us!
    > Don't tell! they'd advertise—you know!
    >
    > How dreary—to be—Somebody!
    > How public—like a Frog—
    > To tell one's name—the livelong June—
    > to be an admiring Bog!

    (Emily Dickinson, poem no. 288, from *The Complete Poems of Emily Dickinson*, edited by Thomas H. Johnson. Copyright © 1914, 1929, 1935, 1942 by Martha Dickinson Bianchi; © renewed 1957, 1963 by Mary L. Hampson. Reprinted by permission of Little, Brown and Company.)

2. How is Seligman's concept of pessimism related to shyness?

3. What are some of the positive and negative aspects of the id, according to Freud?

4. Do you have higher self-esteem in some situations than in others? How do different environments and conditions affect you? Do you think that self-esteem is constant or variable?

5. Consider the Barnum effect and the techniques astrologers use to describe personality. Why are people so easily impressed?

Optional Activities

1. How do you recognize extroverts and introverts? Observe people on television, in a public place, or at home. Rate their behavior on a continuum between the opposites of extravert and introvert. How helpful is the distinction? Do these qualities seem to be a primary dimension of personality?

2. Describe yourself by highlighting your special abilities, admirable qualities, and accomplishments. Write a brief description of your spouse, children, or a close friend. Consider how often you appreciate the positive aspects of your own or another's personality and how often you focus on the negatives. How does your focus affect your own self-esteem and your relationships?

3. Create three groups of statements about yourself which illustrate William James's three aspects of the self.

Additional Resources

Books and Articles

Amabile, Teresa M. (1983). *The Social Psychology of Creativity*. New York: Springer-Verlag. A sense of self-esteem not based on social approval seems critical to creativity. Students not focused on the imminent evaluation of judges perform more creatively.

Bandura, Albert. (1995). *Self-Efficacy in Changing Societies*. Cambridge: Cambridge University Press.

Ellison, Ralph. (1982). *Invisible Man.* New York: Random House. This landmark novel illustrates how prejudice can cripple the self-concepts of minority individuals and lead to learned helplessness.

Goffman, Erving.(1959) *The Presentation of Self in Everyday Life.* Garden City, NY: Doubleday. Are we performers constantly managing how we present our "selves" to others? Goffman, a sociologist, uses metaphors of the theater to describe how people "act" in social situations.

Goleman, Daniel.(1992). *Creative Spirit*. New York: Dutton.

Goleman, Daniel. (1985). *Vital Lies, Simple Truths*. New York: Simon & Schuster.

Rogers, Carl. (1961). *On Becoming a Person*. Boston, MA: Houghton-Mifflin.

Snyder, Mark. (1987). *Public Appearances, Private Realities*. New York: W.H. Freeman.

UNIT 16

TESTING AND INTELLIGENCE

Intelligence is not something possessed once and for all. It is in constant process of forming, and its retention requires constant alertness in observing consequences, an open-minded will to learn and courage in readjustment.

John Dewey

Just as no two fingerprints are alike, no two people have the same set of abilities, aptitudes, interests, and talents. Unit 16 explains the tools psychologists use to measure these differences. It also describes the long-standing controversy over how to define intelligence and how IQ tests have been misused and misapplied.

Is it wise, accurate, or fair to reduce intelligence to a number? Researchers arc currently debating the value of intelligence and personality tests.

Objectives

After viewing the television program and completing the assigned reading, you should be able to:

1. Define *assessment*

2. Describe several ways to measure the reliability and validity of a psychological test

3. Identify the contributions of Galton, Binet, Terman and Weschler to the science of measuring intelligence

4. Explain how IQ is computed

5. Explain Howard Gardner's theory of multiple intelligences

6. Summarize the evidence for the genetic and environmental bases of intelligence

7. List the four methodological techniques used to gather information on a person

8. Describe the major objective and projective personality tests

9. Discuss creativity's link to intelligence and madness

10. Explain the function of vocational interest tests

Reading Assignment

After viewing Program 16, read pages 541-582 in *Psychology and Life*.

Key People and Terms

As you watch the program and read the assignment, pay particular attention to these people and terms. People and terms defined in the text will be found on the given page numbers.

achievement test (577)

aptitude test (577)

chronological age (CA) (552)

construct validity (547)

creativity (567)

criterion (predictive) validity (546)

crystallized intelligence (555)

divergent thinking (568)

eugenics (543)

face validity (546)

fluid intelligence (555)

formal assessment (545)

halo effect (551)

heritability estimate (561)

intelligence (551)

intelligence quotient (IQ) (553)

interjudge reliability (551)

internal consistency (545)

interview (549)

job analysis (578)

life history source/archival data (549)

mental age (MA) (552)

norms (548)

observer report methods (550)

parallel forms (545)

personality inventory (571)

personology (576)

projective test (574)

psychological assessment (542)

psychological test (549)

psychometrics (544)

reliability(545)

self-report methods (549)

situational behavior observations (549)

split-half reliability (545)

standardization (548)

stereotype effect (551)

test retest reliability (545)

validity (546)

Alfred Binet (552)
Raymond Cattell (555)
Sir Francis Galton (543)
Howard Gardner (558)
Henry Goddard (559)
Harrison Gough (573)
Stephen Jay Gould (562)
JP Guilford (556)
Richard Herrnstein (566)
Earl Hunt (556)
Juke Family (560)
Kallikak Family (560)
Charles Murray (566)
Henry Murray (575)

Hermann Rorschack (575)
Charles Spearman (555)
Robert Sternberg (557)
Harold Stevenson (567)
Edward Strong (577)
Lewis Terman (553)
David Wechsler (554)
Robert Weisberg (570)

The following person is used in Program 16 but is not defined in the text.

W. Curtis Banks-an expert on psychological testing

Program Summary

From nursery school through college, in business and the military, tests are used to label and classify each of us. Information about our academic achievements and failures, personality traits, and mental health is collected in an effort to predict how we will perform in the classroom, on the job, or in society.

Defining and measuring intelligence is perhaps the best-known but most elusive goal of psychometricians, the scientists who specialize in psychological testing. Since the turn of the century when the Englishman Sir Francis Galton devised a set of mental tests, there has been an ongoing debate about what intelligence is, how to measure it, and how much heredity and environment contribute to it.

In 1905, in France, Alfred Binet set out to replace teachers' subjective opinions with an objective way to identify children who needed special help in school. His procedure included testing children individually on various reasoning tasks, then comparing each child to the average performance of children in the same age group.

In 1916, Lewis Terman of Stanford University adapted Binet's test for American schools and introduced the concept of the intelligence quotient. Terman came to believe that intelligence was an inner quality reflecting inherited differences and an unchangeable aspect of a person's makeup.

Terman's test became popular in the United States. The time was ripe for an efficient and inexpensive way to test and categorize large numbers of children. There were millions of new immigrants to be educated and a flood of army recruits enlisting for service in World War I. Assessing mental ability seemed a good way to impose order on this social chaos. Many people accepted the idea that intelligence tests could identify special abilities. Test results seemed to support the idea that there were racial and ethnic differences in intelligence.

But critics protested that intelligence tests depended too much on language ability and could not measure the competencies of non-English speakers and young children. In 1939, David Wechsler developed test problems that did not depend on English skills, a major milestone in intelligence testing.

Today, psychological testing is big business. Psychologist William Curtis Banks explains the criteria used to judge whether a test does what it is supposed to do. First, a test must predict what it was designed to predict. If it helps to identify those who will get the highest grades in the future, then it is valid as a grade predictor. Second, the test must demonstrate over time that its results are consistent. Third, everyone taking or scoring the test must do it according to the same rules. But how objective are these tests? Are they the unbiased, objective assessment device that Binet had imagined?

Banks points out that tests and testing practices can be used to discriminate against minorities in school and in the workplace. Cultural biases in many tests overlook important differences in experience and only measure attributes such as verbal ability or social conformity without acknowledging the importance of creativity, common sense, and other important skills. Some personnel screening tests are used to reject or exclude people although the tests have nothing to do with skills required for success on the job. The most serious misuse of tests is rooted in the mistaken belief that an intelligence test can somehow reveal basic unchanging qualities of mind and character. Some people have even used test results to claim that entire races are inferior.

In addition to challenging how tests are constructed and how results are used, psychologists define intelligence in different ways. Some psychometricians believe they are measuring a single ability or trait called intelligence. But recently cognitive psychologists have provided alternative views on the subject.
  Howard Gardner of Harvard University theorizes that there are at least seven different kinds of abilities and that it is society or culture that decides the value of a particular ability (see figure). Western cultures prize verbal skills and logical thinking; in Bali, physical grace and musical talent are highly coveted skills.

Some neurologists completely bypass the complications of mind and culture. They measure brain waves to detect differences in how people react and adjust to surprises. They assume that the smart brain has characteristic reaction patterns. Whether these measures are valid and what purpose they serve is not yet known. And the controversies will likely continue.

1. Linguistic ability

2. Logical-mathematical ability

3. Spatial ability—navigating in space; forming, transforming, and using mental images

4. Musical ability—perceiving and creating pitch patterns

5. Bodily-kinesthetic ability—skills of motor movement, coordination

> 6. Interpersonal ability—understanding others
>
> 7. Intrapersonal ability—understanding one's self, developing a sense of identity

Gardner's Seven Intelligences
According to cognitive psychologist Howard Gardner, intelligence can be identified as seven different abilities, the value of which are culturally determined.

Review Questions

Program Questions

1. What is the goal of psychological assessment?

   a. To derive a theory of human cognition
   b. To see how people vary in ability, behavior, and personality
   c. To measure the stages of growth in intellectual abilities
   d. To diagnose psychological problems

2. You are taking a test in which you are asked to agree or disagree with statements such as "I give up too easily when discussing things with others." Which test would this be?

   a. The Scholastic Aptitude Test
   b. The Rorschach test
   c. The Strong Interest Inventory
   d. The Minnesota Multiphasic Personality Inventory

3. What was Binet's aim in developing a measure of intelligence?

   a. To identify children in need of special help
   b. To show that intelligence was innate
   c. To weed out inferior children
   d. To provide an empirical basis for a theory of intelligence

4. How were the results of Binet's test expressed?

    a. In terms of general and specific factors
    b. As an intelligence quotient
    c. As a mental age related to a norm
    d. As a percentile score

5. What formula did Terman create to express intelligence?

    a. $MA/CA = IQ$
    b. $MA \times CA = IQ$
    c. $CA/MA \times 100 = IQ$
    d. $MA/CA \times 100 = IQ$

6. In 1939, David Wechsler designed a new intelligence test. What problem of its predecessors was the test designed to overcome?

    a. Bias against minority groups
    b. Unreliable scores
    c. Dependence on language
    d. Norms based on a restricted population

7. A test for prospective firefighters has been shown to predict success on the job. Which statement about the test is true?

    a. The test is reliable.
    b. The test is valid.
    c. The test is standardized.
    d. The test is unbiased.

8. Cultural biases in tests can lead to the overvaluing of some attributes and the undervaluing of others. Which of the following is likely to be overvalued?

    a. Common sense
    b. Motivation
    c. Creativity
    d. Verbal ability

9. Imagine that anyone who wants a job as a hospital orderly has to take a test. The test is valid for its norm group, white men. Imagine a black woman is taking the test. Which statement about the woman's score is most likely to be accurate?
    a. It will accurately predict her job performance.
    b. It will be lower than that of white men.
    c. It may indicate she is not capable when she in fact is capable.
    d. It cannot indicate anything about her because there were no blacks or women in the norm group.

10. What new perspective does Howard Gardner bring to the study of intelligence?

    a. He wants to redefine intelligence as "practical intelligence."
    b. He wants to expand intelligence to include other dimensions.
    c. He hopes to find a biological basis for describing intelligence in terms of brain waves.
    d. He believes that the term *intelligence* should be abolished.

11. Robert Sternberg has devised a test for managers. How does its prediction of success compare with predictions from a standard IQ test?

    a. They predict equally well and are not correlated.
    b. They predict equally well, probably because they are measuring the same thing.
    c. Sternberg's test predicts twice as well as IQ and is not correlated with IQ.
    d. Sternberg's test predicts twice as well as IQ and is moderately correlated with IQ.

12. The attempt by neuroscientists to find biologically based measures of intelligence rests on the assumption that intelligence involves

    a. multiple factors.
    b. cultural learning.
    c. speed of adaptation.
    d. high excitability.

Textbook Questions

13. The area of psychological assessment differs from most other areas of psychology in its emphasis on

    a. prediction.
    b. quantification.
    c. individual differences.
    d. empiricism.

14. If Earl Hunt were coming to speak to your psychology class, a likely title for his talk might be:

    a. "Individual Styles of Problem Solving."
    b. "One-hundred Fifty Ways to Be Intelligent."
    c. "Increasing Your Crystallized Intelligence."
    d. "Types of Intelligences Valued by Preliterate Societies."

15. Most definitions of intelligence specify that intelligence is

    a. modifiable by environmental circumstances.
    b. the ability to use symbols.
    c. specific to a situation.
    d. all of the above.

16. An important goal of Simon and Binet's first intelligence test was to

    a. test their theory of innate intelligence in a practical setting.
    b. better fit children to the French public school curriculum.
    c. identify children who needed special education to help them perform well.
    d. select intellectually gifted children for advanced learning.

17. Psychologists Terman, Thorndike and Yerkes made a major contribution to the course of American history by

    a. creating an instrument that could quickly classify military recruits in terms of ability.
    b. standardizing intelligence tests so that they no longer discriminated against immigrant groups.
    c. updating the Simon–Binet test to select gifted as well as retarded children.
    d. distinguishing between crystallized and fluid intelligence.

18. If you were to choose a person at random from the English-speaking population of the United States, the best prediction you could make would be that the person has an IQ of

    a. 90.
    b. 100.
    c. 110.
    d. No prediction can be made.

19. Immense controversy over the use of IQ scores began when

    a. Thorndike and other psychologists stated that the lower scores of blacks on IQ tests indicated racial inferiority.
    b. psychologists such as Goddard advocated exclusion of immigrants on the basis of their scores on IQ tests.
    c. Gardner argued that Western civilization was limiting in the types of intelligence it valued.
    d. the family histories of the Jukes and Kallikaks became public.

20. IQ scores have been found to accurately predict all of the following factors EXCEPT
    a. high school and college grades.
    b. entrepreneurial achievement.
    c. performance in certain jobs.
    d. job status.

21. All of the following are strengths of the MMPI-2 EXCEPT

   a. it can be used as a measure of personality in nonclinical populations.
   b. researchers may refer to a large multicultural and international data archive.
   c. it has established reliability and validity.
   d. researchers can use it to create new scales of measurement.

22. The value of any test or assessment instrument is its ability to

   a. predict future performance.
   b. select individuals who would score poorly on similar tests.
   c. point out those individuals unsuited.
   d. validate selection of those already judged suitable for a job or school.

23. The most serious criticism of psychological tests has been that such tests

   a. depend on specific learned material.
   b. are not objective assessments of abilities and capacities.
   c. are susceptible to practice effects.
   d. discriminate against the poor and disadvantaged.

24. All of the following terms are associated with the work of Sir Francis Galton EXCEPT

   a. environmental influence.
   b. correlations.
   c. eugenics.
   d. objective measurement of intelligence.

25. Estimates of the reliability of a test can be adversely affected by

   a. inconsistent scoring.
   b. changes in internal states of test takers.
   c. variations in motivation.
   d. all of the above.

26. To establish the construct validity of a new test designed to measure "risk taking" as a personality trait, one might

   a. examine the relationship between test scores and the subject's activities and attitudes.
   b. administer the test to the same subjects six months later.
   c. ask a panel of experts of evaluate the items on the test.
   d. administer the test to a randomly selected group from another population.

27. All of the following are techniques of data collection in psychological assessment EXCEPT

    a. tests.
    b. situational observation.
    c. neurometric analysis.
    d. interviews.

28. The term IQ or intelligence quotient is most associated with the work of

    a. Charles Spearman.
    b. Alfred Binet.
    c. Lewis Terman.
    d. David Wechsler.

29. The intellectual abilities that are measured by the Binet and Wechsler tests are most similar to what Robert Sternberg calls _____ intelligence.

    a. interpersonal.
    b. experiential.
    c. contextual.
    d. componential.

30. According to Howard Gardner, the types of intelligences valued by our culture are

    a. interpersonal ability and spatial ability.
    b. logical-mathematical ability and linguistic ability.
    c. linguistic ability and interpersonal ability.
    d. interpersonal ability and spatial ability.

Questions to Consider

1. Does evidence of a genetic basis for intelligence mean that intelligence is unchangeable?

2. What would happen if everyone knew everyone else's IQ scores? How might it affect decisions about whom to marry or hire?

3. How can standardized test numbers affect you? If you took a test that indicated you were a genius, how would it change your life? If after a year, you were notified that you had been given someone else's results by mistake and that your score was lower than average, what difference would it make?

4. How are projective tests, such as the Rorschach inkblot test and the Thematic Apperception Test, related to intelligence? How are intelligence and creativity related?

5. What are some of the ethical questions related to intelligence testing and psychological assessment?

Optional Activities

1. Pick a special interest of yours, such as cooking, baseball, woodworking, dancing, or traveling. Design a test that includes both questions and tasks that measure knowledge and ability in that area. How would you ensure the test's validity?

2. Consider the possibility that intelligence could be improved. Design a one-year plan to improve your intelligence. What would be the most important components of your plan?

Additional Resources

Books and Articles

Coleman, Andrew. (1987). *Facts, Fallacies, and Frauds in Psychology.* London: Hutchinson. In Chapter 2, Coleman critically examines the concept of IQ and looks at the nature-nurture debate. Chapter 3 explores the racism behind attempts to show scientifically that intelligence is determined by genetics.

Fraser, Steven. (Ed.) (1995). *Bell Curve Wars: Race, Intelligence and the Failure of America.* New York: Basic Books.

Gardner, Howard.(1983). *Frames of Mind: The Theory of Multiple Intelligences.* New York: Basic Books. The definition of "intelligence" varies from culture to culture. Gardner suggests that intelligence can be understood as an array of seven different capacities, including a sense of music and a sense of oneself.

Gould, Stephen Jay. (1981). *The Mismeasure of Man.* New York: Norton. Does the size and shape of your head mark you as a genius or a fool? Some scientists of the past believed so. Gould recounts incredible and often shocking stories of the measure—and mismeasure—of people.

Herrnstein, Richard & Murray, Charles. (1995). *The Bell Curve.* New York: Free Press.

Herrnstein, R. J. (1971). "IQ." *Atlantic Monthly* 228, 43-64. The debate over "Jensenism" (that is, that racial differences in IQ scores are inherited and not a bias of the test) can be explored in the charges and counter-charges reviewed in this work.

Keyes, D. (1966). *Flowers for Algernon.* New York: Harcourt, Brace and World. A fictitious experiment changes a man from retarded to gifted and back.

McKean, Kevin.(1985, October). "Intelligence: New Ways to Measure the Wisdom of Man." *Discover*, 25-41. An excellent, entertaining review of the history of IQ testing and of recent attacks on this limited measure of intelligence. Profiles the work of Howard Gardner and others currently attempting to redefine intelligence.

Sternberg, Robert.(1985). *Beyond IQ*. Cambridge: Cambridge University Press. In this exploration of human intellectual capacities, Sternberg outlines cognitive processes used in problem solving.

Film

Stand and Deliver. Directed by Ramon Menendez. 1987. Math teacher Jaime Escalante prepares Hispanic students from the barrios of East Los Angeles to pass the Advanced Placement calculus test and convinces the Educational Testing Service that the results are valid.

UNIT 17

SEX AND GENDER

Different though the sexes are, they intermix. In every human being a vacillation from one sex to the other takes place, and often it is only the clothes that keep the male or female likeness, while underneath the sex is the very opposite of what it is above.

Virginia Woolf

Unit 17 looks at the similarities and differences between the sexes resulting from the complex interaction of biological and social factors. It contrasts the universal differences in anatomy and physiology with those learned and cultural, and it reveals how roles are changing to reflect new values and psychological knowledge.

Objectives

After viewing the television program and completing the assigned readings, you should be able to:

1. Define and compare the difference between the terms *sex, gender, gender identity,* and *gender role*

2. Explain the role of pheromones in sexual arousal

3. Describe evolutionary theory as it applies to sexual behavior

4. Describe the similarities in and differences between males and females in the sexual response cycle and mating

5. Summarize current research on homosexuality

Reading Assignment

After viewing Program 17, read pages 197-198 and 440-449 in *Psychology and Life*.

Key People and Terms

As you watch the program and read the assignment, pay particular attention to these people and terms. People and terms defined in the text will be found on the given page numbers.

date rape (447)

fetish (445)

gender (197)

gender identity (197)

gender roles (198)

parental investment (442)

pheromones (442)

sexual arousal (445)

sex differences (197)

sexual scripts (447)

Jeanne Block (198)

David Buss (442)

Virginia Johnson (444)

Alfred Kinsey (446)

Eleanor Maccoby (198)

William Masters (444)

The following terms and person are used in the program but are not defined in the text.

androgynous—having both masculine and feminine traits

cognitive developmental theory—the theory stating that children use male and female as fundamental categories and actively sex-type themselves to achieve cognitive consistency

developmental strategies—behaviors that have evolved to conform to the sex roles typical of the adult members of a species

sex typing—the psychological process by which boys and girls become masculine or feminine

social learning theory—the theory stating that children are socialized by observing role models and are rewarded or punished for behaving appropriately

stereotype—the belief that all members of a group share common traits

Michael Meaney-developmental neuroscientist who studies the interaction of biology and psychology in the development of sex differences

Program Summary

From the first breath a baby takes, sex determines how he or she will be treated throughout life. Being male or female means we inhabit very different biological, psychological, and social environments. Program 17 looks at sex, the biologically based characteristic that distinguishes males from females, and gender, the cultural category that includes the psychological and social characteristics of being male or female.

From birth, life is full of gender messages and lessons that shape behavior. Boys and girls learn which behaviors are appropriate for their gender group and act accordingly. In our culture, they also dress differently, act differently, and often develop different interests and goals. These categories exist in the home, in school, in social situations, and in the workplace.

Although gender roles are often portrayed as polar opposites, psychologist Sandra Bem argues that people have both masculine and feminine characteristics, and, in fact, this blend of traits she calls psychological androgyny often results in greater behavioral adaptiveness.

Scientists have discovered that there are some universal behavioral differences between the sexes. Male children tend to engage in more rough play and gross motor activities. Female children are more likely to play mother, groom baby dolls, and engage in fine motor activities. This is true of people as well as other animals.

Neuroscientist Michael Meany explains that these sex differences in social play are evidence of how biology and psychology influence each other. Sex-role behaviors have evolved because different activities stimulate different brain regions. And the hormones affect the brain during prenatal development, causing sex-linked preferences to certain social activities. Another example of the interaction of biology and psychology in sex differences is physical health. Because men are more likely to drink, smoke, use weapons, and work in hazardous environments, they are more vulnerable to certain diseases, such as lung cancer, bronchitis, emphysema, and heart disease.

One example of sex-role behavior that has no biological basis is crying. It is acquired as part of the socialization process. Of course, both male and female babies cry. But as they grow, boys learn to hold back their tears while girls learn that crying is acceptable.

According to psychologist Jeanne Block, social gender messages affect the way children think about themselves and the world. Girls' activities are more supervised, structured, and restricted. They are raised to stay close to home, while boys are typically given more freedom to roam and discover the world.

But children also participate in shaping their own social environment. Eleanor Maccoby has studied how young boys and girls use sex as a basic category to sort themselves. In the classroom and on the playground, each group seems to have a distinct culture and style, including different language patterns. Gender identification serves as a powerful organizer of their social lives. Girls play house and boys play army. Girls play with dolls and boys play with trucks. These differences are apparent as early as nursery school.

There are positive and negative consequences to gender differences. Males have the freedom to innovate and explore, but their independence may cost them a sense of family intimacy or the security of belonging to a community. Females have the freedom to express their feelings and build a social support network, but they suffer social constraints on their intellectual and individual development. And a greater focus on their feelings and moods makes them more susceptible to depression.

Despite traditional gender stereotypes, researchers have never been able to link different social roles to innate sex differences. Any differences are more a matter of degree than a difference in kind. For example, in physical ability and sports, male and female performances overlap when their training is comparable.

It is important to recognize that our gender categories heavily influence our expectations, judgments, and behavior. These gender stereotypes narrow the options available to us. In fact, women and men are more similar than different in almost all psychological traits and abilities.

Review Questions

Program Questions

1. According to research by Zella Lurin and Jeffrey Rubin, the difference in the language parents use to describe their newborn sons or daughters is primarily a reflection of

   a. actual physical differences in the newborns.
   b. differences in the way the newborns behave.
   c. the way the hospital staff responds to the babies.
   d. the parents' expectations coloring their perceptions.

2. What is gender?

   a. The biologically innate differences between male and female
   b. The psychological and social meanings attached to male and female
   c. The interplay between biologically based and psychologically based definitions of male and female
   d. The blend of masculine and feminine characteristics within an individual person

3. Which set of adjectives best characterizes the feminine gender role in the United States?

   a. Gentle, emotional, dependent
   b. Creative, intelligent, attractive
   c. Aggressive, independent, dominant
   d. Industrious, nurturing, ambitious

4. Which difference between the ways in which boys and girls play seems linked to sex hormones?

   a. Girls play with dolls.
   b. Boys engage in rough and tumble play.
   c. Boys play in larger groups than girls do.
   d. Girls build rooms, and boys build towers.

5. Michael Meany attributes the differences in the behavior of male and female rats to the fact that these behaviors "feel good" to the animals. The reason for this is that the behaviors

   a. increase hormone production.
   b. prepare the organism for its life tasks.
   c. stimulate certain brain regions.
   d. fit the preferred pattern of motor activity.

6. How does the health of men compare with the health of women through the life cycle?

   a. Men are more vulnerable throughout the life cycle.
   b. Women are more vulnerable throughout the life cycle.
   c. Women are more vulnerable only during their childbearing years.
   d. There is no consistent sex difference in health.

7. Which learned behavior in the masculine gender role poses a health risk?

   a. Having recessive genes
   b. Relying on social networks
   c. Being active in sports
   d. Drinking alcohol

8. According to Professor Zimbardo, what is the source of the behavioral difference between the sexes regarding crying?

   a. It is an innate difference.
   b. Initial innate differences are reinforced by parents.
   c. It is learned during the socialization process.
   d. We do not know the source.

9. What typically happens when a girl behaves in gender-inappropriate ways?

   a. She feels uncomfortable.
   b. She is praised.
   c. She is scolded.
   d. The behavior is not noticed.

10. According to Jeanne Block, the sociopsychological contexts for boys and girls tend to be different. One such difference is that the context for girls tends to be more

   a. home centered.
   b. achievement oriented.
   c. filled with risk.
   d. involved with same-sex peers.

11. What is one of the negative consequences of the masculine gender role?

    a. It makes men more vulnerable to depression.
    b. It imposes limits on intellectual development.
    c. It provides little sense of belonging.
    d. It encourages risk-taking behaviors.

12. According to Eleanor Maccoby, at about what age do children begin to prefer same-sex playmates?

    a. 2 years old
    b. 3 years old
    c. 4 years old
    d. 5 years old

13. Which sentence is more characteristic of girls' speech patterns than of boys'?

    a. "I can do it better than you can."
    b. "Do you want to come over to my house?"
    c. "Mr. Clark is the world's worst teacher."
    d. "Let's have a picnic."

14. Which statement about sex differences in psychological traits and abilities is best supported by research?

    a. There are no identifiable differences.
    b. The differences that exist are more a matter of degree than a difference in kind.
    c. The differences are the result of differences in brain chemistry and organization.
    d. The differences are arbitrary because they are the result of social learning.

Textbook Questions

15. Sex is unique among biological motivations because

    a. it has less reinforcement power compared to food or water.
    b. it involves arousal rather than reduction of tension.
    c. it does not involve higher brain structure such as the cortex.
    d. it does not contribute to survival of the individual.

16. A major gender difference in the sexual response cycle is

    a. men respond to different sources of arousal.
    b. women have an extended plateau period.
    c. men become more aroused for a longer period of time.
    d. men do not experience a refractory period.

17. David Buss believes that men and women have evolved different mating strategies because

    a. women make a greater prenatal investment.
    b. men seek mates who will be most successful at producing healthy offspring.
    c. women seek mates who will stay committed to the care and protection of offspring.
    d. men seek mates who will be more exciting sexual partners.

18. Research regarding why a minority of individuals prefer homosexuality to heterosexuality

    a. concludes there is a hormonal basis for this.
    b. demonstrated poor or harsh fathering to be important.
    c. offered evidence that there is a genetic basis for such preferences.
    d. is inconclusive.

19. The term satyriasis refers to

    a. compulsive male sexual behavior.
    b. promiscuous female behavior.
    c. a sexually transmitted disease.
    d. a type of male impotence.

20. An evolutionist believes we probably developed the capacity for orgasm

    a. to increase the likelihood we would engage in sexual reproduction.
    b. to make up for our loss of instincts.
    c. to promote the physical health and well-being of the reproducing individual.
    d. to encourage good caretaking of infants.

21. Human sexuality is largely under the control of

    a. hormonal factors.
    b. psychological factors.
    c. socioeconomic factors.
    d. biological factors.

22. Masters and Johnson included all of the following in their model of human sexual response EXCEPT

    a. plateau.
    b. orgasm.
    c. desire.
    d. resolution.

23. There are dramatic vascular changes in the body during the _____ phase of the sexual response cycle.

   a. excitement
   b. plateau
   c. orgasm
   d. resolution

24. A study of patterns of date rape found unwanted sex was associated with a view of male–female relationships best described as

   a. competitive.
   b. adversarial.
   c. cooperative.
   d. driven by hormones.

25. What is the current attitude of the American Psychological Association towards homosexuality?

   a. There is a growing preference for homosexual behavior.
   b. Homosexuality is considered a moral and not a psychological problem.
   c. Homosexuality is not considered a disorder.
   d. Homosexuality is considered a deviant sexual orientation.

Questions to Consider

1. People organize their perceptions, expectations, and judgments around social schemas and scripts. How are sexual scripts related to gender roles?

2. How does gender-typing influence perceptions?

3. How do young children show that they are aware of their gender identity?

4. Research suggests that androgynous people are better adjusted than those who are traditional sex-role stereotyped. But critics contend that the masculine traits lead to higher self-esteem and better adjustment than does a combination of masculine and feminine traits. How can having masculine traits enhance a woman's self-esteem?

5. Many women writers have published under masculine-sounding names. Does the sex of the writer make a difference? Should it?

Optional Activity

Pick three close relatives or friends. How would your relationship with them be different if you were of the opposite sex? Which aspects of your personal identity and behavior would change? Which would stay the same?

Additional Resources

Books and Articles

Bem, Sandra. (1993). *The Lenses of Gender*. Hew Haven, CT: Yale University Press.

Benderly, Beryl L.(1987). *The Myth of Two Minds: What Gender Means and Doesn't Mean*. Garden City, NY: Doubleday. Science writer Benderly set out to write a book on current research backing a biological basis for gender differences. Her findings, though, led her to conclude that most gender differences are rooted in cultural influences, not genes. A good synthesis of recent work on sex and gender.

Buss, David. 1994). *The Evolution of Desire: Strategies of Human Mating*. New York: Basic Books.

Fout, J. & Tantillo, M. (1993). *American Sexual Politics: Sex, Gender, and Race Since the Civil War*. Chicago, IL: University of Chicago Press.

Gilligan, Carol.(1982). *In a Different Voice*. Cambridge, MA: Harvard University Press. Why do women tend to see moral dilemmas differently than men do? Are women weaker or less capable of seeing things logically? Gilligan's important work traces the moral voices of men and women to their different psychological development.

Kohn, Alfie. (1988, February). "Girl Talk, Guy Talk: How Speaking Patterns Reveal Our Gender." *Psychology Today*, 65-66. Why do men and women speak in distinctly different styles? Is it because they relate to others and think about themselves in different ways?

Masters, W., Johnson, V. & Kolodny. R. (1988). *Human Sexuality*. 3rd Ed. Glenview, IL: Scott Foresman.

Michael, R, Gagnon, J., Laumann, E. & Kolata, G. 1994. *Sex in America: A Definitive Survey*. New York: Time Warner.

Miller, Jean Baker.(1986). *Toward a New Psychology of Women*. 2d ed. Boston: Beacon Press. A book attempting to reinterpret the "weaknesses" of women as strengths.

Money, John. (1988). *Gay, Straight and In-Between: The Sexology of Erotic Orientation*. New York: Oxford University Press.

Reinisch, J. with Beasley, R. Kent, D. (Ed.) (1990). *The Kinsey Institute's New Report on Sex: What You Must Know to Be Sexually Literate*. New York: St. Martin's Press.

Tannen, Deborah.(1990). *You Just Don't Understand: Women and Men in Conversation*. New York: Ballantine. Study of gender differences in communication.

Tannen, Deborah. (1994). *Gender and Discourse*. New York: Oxford University Press.

Unger, R. & Crawford, M. (1992). *Women and Gender: A Feminist Psychology*. New York: McGraw-Hill.

Films

Mona Lisa. Directed by Neil Jordan; starring Bob Hoskins, Cathy Tyson. 1986. A moving drama that explores the darker side of sexuality: the underworld of prostitution.

The Pinks and the Blues. NOVA #709, Time-Life Video. 1980. From moments after birth, baby boys and girls are treated differently. This film explores how environmental influences affect gender.

Tootsie. Directed by Sydney Pollack; starring Dustin Hoffman, Jessica Lange. 1982. An actor who disguises himself as a woman to get work sees himself and the world in a different light. Illustrates how both sexes can play both gender roles.

Victor/Victoria. Directed by Blake Edwards; starring Julie Andrews. 1982. Role-reversal, the other way round. Andrews masquerades as a man masquerading as a woman and becomes the toast of the town in 1930s Paris.

UNIT 18

MATURING AND AGING

As a man advances in life he gets what is better than admiration—judgement to estimate things at their own value.

Samuel Johnson

Thanks to growing scientific interest in the elderly, research on aging, has replaced many myths arid fears with facts. Unit 18 focuses on what scientists are learning about life cycle development as they look at how aging is affected by biology, environment, and life-style.

Objectives

After viewing the television program and completing the assigned readings, you should be able to:

1. Describe Erikson's eight psychosocial stages

2. Discuss the lifespan theories of Jung and Neugarten

3. List the physical changes associated with aging

4. Summarize the tasks of adolescence

5. Discuss the central concerns of adulthood

6. List the strengths and weaknesses of Kohlberg's cognitive approach to moral development, and describe the controversies around the issues of gender differences in moral judgement and the distinction between moral behavior and moral judgement.

7. Identify cultural factors that place youth at risk for healthy development

8. Discuss the importance of attachment in social development

10. List the biological and social factors that can affect health and sexuality in later life

11. Describe the risk factors for an elderly person in a nursing home

Reading Assignment

After viewing Program 18, read pages 181-197 and 199-214 in *Psychology and Life*.

Key People and Terms

As you watch the program and read the assignment, pay particular attention to these people and terms. People and terms defined in the text will be found on the given page numbers.

ageism (207)
attachment (190)
contact comfort (195)
empathy (212)
generativity (193)
hospice approach (208)
imprinted (190)
initiation rites (199)
intimacy (203)
morality (209)
parenting practices (192)
parenting style (192)
psychosocial dwarfism (196)
psychosocial stages (183)
selective social interaction (205)
socialization (188)

Mary Ainsworth (191)
John Bowlby (191)
Ruth Benedict (200)
Laura Carstensen (205)
Alison Clarke-Stewart (194)
Erik Erikson (182)
Anna Freud (200)
Carol Gilligan (211)
G. Stanley Hall (200)
Henry Harlow (195)
Martin Hoffman (212)
Carl Jung (185)
Jerome Kagan (190)
Lawrence Kohlberg (209)
Elisabeth Kubler-Ross (208)
Konrad Lorenz (190)
Margaret Mead (200)
Pat Moore (journalist) (207)
Bernice Neugarten (185)
Alison Clarke Steward
Steven Suomi (190)
George Vaillant (205)

The following term and people are used in Program 18 but is not defined in the text.

senile dementia—biochemical and neuronal changes in the brain that lead to a gradual reduction in mental efficiency

Dan Levinson-studies the life course as a sequence of developmental experiences

Werner Schaie-studies long term effects of aging

B.F. Skinner-prominent example of a psychologist who remains very active mentally and physically in later life

Sherry Willis-uses new educational training methods to help elderly function more effectively

Diana Woodruf-Pak-studies the physiology of memory loss

Program Summary

Until recently, many psychologists believed that there were few important developmental changes after adolescence. However, beginning in the 1950s, research on aging began to expose many myths about the extent of deterioration and despair among the elderly.

The concept of life-cycle development was created by psychologist Erik Erikson. His framework describes eight psychosocial developmental stages in which individuals face specific conflicts that require balancing two opposite demands. Failure to resolve these conflicts can lead to isolation, feelings of unfulfillment, even despair (see figure).

Approximate Age	Crisis	Adequate Resolution	Inadequate Resolution
0–1½	Trust vs. mistrust	Basic sense of safety	Insecurity, anxiety
1½–3	Autonomy vs. self-doubt	Perception of self as agent capable of controlling own body and making things happen	Feeling of inadequacy to control events
3–6	Initiative vs. guilt	Confidence in oneself as initiator, creator	Feelings of lack of self-worth
6–puberty	Competence vs. inferiority	Adequacy in basic social and intellectual skills	Lack of self-confidence, feelings of failure
Adolescent	Identity vs. role confusion	Comfortable sense of self as a person	Sense of self as fragmented; shifting, unclear sense of self
Early adult	Intimacy vs. isolation	Capacity for closeness and commitment to another	Feeling of aloneness, separation; denial of need for closeness
Middle adult	Generativity vs. stagnation	Focus of concern beyond oneself to family, society, future generations	Self-indulgent concerns; lack of future orientation
Later adult	Ego-integrity vs. despair	Sense of wholeness, basic satisfaction with life	Feelings of futility, disappointment

Figure 11: Erikson's Psychosocial Stages
According to Erik Erikson, certain conflicts must be resolved at each stage in the life cycle in order for people to meet the demands of the next life stage.
(Based on Erikson, 1963; from Zimbardo Psychology and Life, *Scott Foresman and Co., 11th ed., 1985)*

Dan Levinson, another developmental psychologist, studies the life course of adults as a sequence of developmental stages. He has identified age-linked developmental periods and transition periods that coincide with specific age ranges.

Until we are old, most of us will have little understanding of what it is like to be old, and we rarely consider how society treats its elderly citizens. Social responses to the elderly range from indifference to fear to hostility. But although the processes of biological aging are inevitable,variables such as life-style, diet, and exercise, can influence when and how fast they occur. Whether or not a person lives in a supportive community or has a sense of control over his or her life can also influence self-concept and attitude toward aging. Mental strategies may also increase an individual's self-worth and optimism.

Recent studies have shown that psychological deterioration is the exception, not the rule, of old age when there is no physical illness. Specialists have developed new strategic training methods to teach the elderly to recover earlier levels of inductive reasoning, spatial orientation, and attention. Behaviorist B. F. Skinner also believes that behavioral problems associated with aging can be overcome by learning specific strategies.

Though some problems can be overcome with training, brain injury and dementia are often permanent disabilities with devastating consequences. But they occur much less frequently than people generally think. Contrary to another popular myth, depression and anxiety are not more common among the elderly. In fact, the elderly do not show an increase in stress-related disorders despite an increase in stressful life events. And, if a person remains in good health, there is no decline in the ability to enjoy sex either.

If the latest research findings are generally optimistic about the state of the elderly, why does the stereotype of deterioration and despair persist? It may be because of the availability heuristic. Dramatic or vivid negative images are overrepresented in our memory so that we get a falsely exaggerated picture despite many examples of outstanding accomplishment and self-satisfaction among the elderly.

But there is also a very sad side of growing old in the United States. As the number of older people in the population increases, the percentage of those living in nursing homes will increase too. In many nursing homes, unfortunately, people suffer significant losses and are subjected to conditions that accelerate their physical deterioration, even death.

As we learn more about the elderly, we discover that many of those problems can be ameliorated by education, training, and environmental changes. We can also work on improving our attitudes toward aging and the elderly.

The first step is dispelling the myths and changing our culture's negative stereotypes about the elderly. Second, it is important to redesign the environment and health care delivery systems to make them more accessible and accommodating to the needs of those with limitations. Third, an early intervention program that identifies those with psychological and behavioral problems and provides psychotherapy and behavioral therapy is needed.

As older people become an increasingly powerful force in the population, we can expect the "Graying of America" to bring about many positive changes.

Review Questions

Program Questions

1. How has research on life-span development changed our idea of human nature?

   a. We see development as a growth process of early life.
   b. We see that a longer life span creates problems for society.
   c. We view people as continuing to develop throughout life.
   d. We regard development as a hormonally based process.

2. What does the term *psychological adolescing* mean?

   a. Coming into conflict with parents
   b. Entering into a senile state
   c. Being swept by emotional conflicts
   d. Developing to our full potential

3. What personal experience does Erik Erikson cite as leading to his redefinition of himself?

   a. Having a religious conversion
   b. Being an immigrant
   c. Surviving a major illness
   d. Getting married

4. According to Erikson, the young adult faces a conflict between

   a. isolation and intimacy.
   b. heterosexuality and homosexuality.
   c. autonomy and shame.
   d. wholeness and futility.

5. Which statement sounds most typical of someone in the throes of a midlife crisis?

   a. "I enjoy my connections with other people."
   b. "I'd like to run off to a desert island."
   c. "My work is my greatest source of satisfaction."
   d. "I accept the fact that I've made some bad decisions."

6. Daniel Levinson divides the life cycle into a series of eras. For which era is a major problem the hazard of being irrelevant?

    a. Childhood
    b. Early adulthood
    c. Middle adulthood
    d. Late adulthood

7. In her work, Diana Woodruf-Pak is studying the eyelid response and its changes in aging rabbits and people. Why has she chosen to study this particular response?

    a. The brain circuit involved is well mapped.
    b. It is typical of the cognitive deficits that occur with aging.
    c. Memory loss in this area is highly correlated with other forms of memory loss.
    d. Changes occur progressively, beginning in midlife.

8. When Pat Moore transformed herself into an 85-year-old woman, she was surprised by the

    a. compassion with which others treated her.
    b. lack of facilities designed to accommodate the aged.
    c. extent of ageism in our society.
    d. poverty faced by many older people.

9. How do psychosomatic symptoms tend to change with age?

    a. People develop more of them.
    b. The ones people develop are more severe.
    c. They tend to be more related to sleeping and less related to eating.
    d. They are less common.

10. What has Sherry Willis found about the abilities of older people with regard to spatial orientation tasks?

    a. Irreversible decline is inevitable.
    b. Training programs yield improved skills.
    c. Skills can be maintained but not improved.
    d. If memory loss occurs, other skills deteriorate.

11. About what percent of people over 65 suffer from senile dementia?

    a. 5 percent
    b. 15 percent
    c. 25 percent
    d. 40 percent

12. Assuming that a person remains healthy, what happens to the ability to derive sexual pleasure as one ages?

    a. It does not change.
    b. It gradually diminishes.
    c. It abruptly ceases.
    d. It depends on the availability of a suitable partner.

13. In general, how does the view of the elderly among the population at large compare with the actuality?

    a. It is more negative.
    b. It is more positive.
    c. It is generally accurate.
    d. It is more accurate for men than for women.

14. The results of the long-term study by Werner Schaie suggest that the people who do best in the later stages of life are people with

    a. high incomes.
    b. advanced degrees.
    c. flexible attitudes.
    d. large, close-knit families.

15. In nursing homes, the staff often behave in ways that treat the elderly like children. What is the effect of this treatment on most older people?

    a. It makes them feel more secure.
    b. It makes them behave in dependent, childlike ways.
    c. It increases their sense of autonomy and control.
    d. It improves their health by reducing their stress levels.

Textbook Questions

16. Your text discusses three tasks of adolescence. These are

    a. gender identity, values, and goals.
    b. sexuality, social roles, and occupation.
    c. family relationships, peer relationships, and education.
    d. self-acceptance, sexuality, and peer relationships.

17. Almost all theorists of adult development agree that adulthood is characterized by needs for

    a. success and power.
    b. emotional connection and successful achievement.
    c. economic stability and meaningful social roles.
    d. physical attractiveness and sexual intimacy.

18. What is the correct order of successful adult development according to Erikson?

    a. Identity, intimacy, generativity
    b. Intimacy, competence, integrity
    c. Intimacy, generativity, transition
    d. Identity, security, generativity

19. In order to avoid loss of cognitive functioning, elderly people should

    a. reduce sensory overload.
    b. pursue high levels of stimulation.
    c. increase sexual experience.
    d. avoid tasks involving short-term memory.

20. Memory loss in old age primarily affects

    a. sensory memory.
    b. language memory.
    c. short-term memory.
    d. long-term memory.

21. Alzheimer's disease is a type of

    a. depression.
    b. dementia.
    c. personality disorder.
    d. alcohol-related syndrome.

22. Elisabeth Kübler-Ross has contributed to our understanding of

    a. changes in fluid and crystallized intelligence.
    b. the psychology of dying and death.
    c. selective social interaction among the elderly.
    d. disengagement theory and other socioemotional declines.

23. Carl Jung differed sharply from Sigmund Freud on the importance of
    a. intimacy rather than competence.
    b. adulthood rather than childhood.
    c. adolescence rather than infancy.
    d. the conscious rather than unconscious.

24. A serious criticism of Kohlberg's theory of moral development is that

    a. emotion rather than cognition is at the root of morality.
    b. he had no place in the theory for empathy.
    c. he does not distinguish between moral reasoning and moral behavior.
    d. research does not support the stage order he proposes.

25. One cognitive ability that improves with aging is

    a. memory.
    b. wisdom.
    c. fluid intelligence.
    d. classical conditioning.

Questions to Consider

1. Define normal aging. How has science helped to differentiate between the normal processes of aging and the effects of illness?

2. What are the psychological themes unique to the middle years, sometimes called the midlife crisis?

3. How does intelligence change in the later adult years?

4. How do changing social patterns affect adult life patterns?

5. How do social conditions help create the characteristics of adolescence and adulthood in the human life cycle?

6. How does becoming a parent help define the developmental stages of adulthood?

Optional Activities

1. At what age will you consider yourself to be "old"? Define your personal concept of old age, and describe what you expect your life to be like. Describe the health status, activities, satisfactions, and concerns you anticipate in your late adult years.

2. Keep track of the images of people over 60, over 70, and over 80 that you encounter during an average day. Notice how older adults are depicted in television programs and advertisements. What conclusions can you draw about how popular images reflect the characteristics, abilities, concerns, and diversity of the over-60 population? What stereotypes persist? Is there evidence that images are changing?

3. Make a list of the labels used to describe people at various stages of life from infancy to old age. Which age group has the most labels? Compare the synonyms and modifiers for childhood to the words that help define adulthood. What might explain the difference?

4. Tape record an oral history interview of a person over age 75, perhaps someone in your own family. (Be sure to obtain the person's permission for the taping.) Ask for comments about the technological and social changes he or she has observed. Ask about memories of important community, national, and global events. What have you learned that you did not know before?

Additional Resources

Books and Articles

Berren, J. & Schaie, Werner. (Ed.) (1990). *Handbook of the Psychology of Aging.* 3rd Ed. San Diego, CA: Academic Press.

Blythe, R. (1979). *The View in Winter: Reflections on Old Age.* New York: Harcourt Brace Jovanovich. First-person accounts of how individuals experience the process of aging.

Daniels, P. & Weingarten, K. (1982). *Sooner or Later: The Timing of Parenthood in Adult Lives.* New York: Norton. The characteristic issues, advantages, and drawbacks of having children at different stages of adult life.

Erikson, Erik.(1981). *The Life Cycle Completed: A Review.* New York: Norton. A compact explanation of Erikson's psychosocial theory.

Erikson, Erik, Erikson, J. & Kivirich, H. (1986). *Vital Involvement in Old Age.* New York: Norton. Interviews with older people show that vitality is possible in the last stage of psychosocial development.

Kidder, Tracy. (1993). *Old Friends.* Boston, MA: Houghton-Mifflin.

Kubler-Ross, Elisabeth. (1969). *On Death and Dying.* New York: MacMillan.

Kübler-Ross, Elisabeth. (1975). *Death: The Final Stage of Growth.* New York: Simon & Schuster. Why is death treated as a taboo subject? How do we accept the deaths of those close to us—or prepare for our own? This book explores how different cultures answer such universal questions.

Levinson, D. (1978). *Seasons of a Man's Life.* New York: Knopf. Presents a stage theory of adult development through individual case studies.

Lowenthal, M. & Chiribaga, D. (1990). *Change and Continuity in Adult Life.* San Francisco, CA: Jossey-Bass Publishers.

Moore, Pat.(1985). *Disguised.* Waco, TX: Word Books. The true story of a young reporter who assumed various disguises in order to study the obstacles and frustrations experienced by old women.

Neugarten, Bernice, & Neugarten, D. (1987, May). "The Changing Meanings of Age." *Psychology Today*, 29-33. What does it mean to "act your age"? Past assumptions about aging are being challenged.

Sheehy, Gail.(1976). *Passages: Predictable Crises of Adult Life.* New York: Dutton. A book based on interviews that reveal the life patterns of adult men and women.

Films

To Live Until You Die: The Work of Elisabeth Kübler-Ross. *NOVA* #1013, distributed by Time-Life Video. 1983. A profile of Elisabeth Kübler-Ross, a psychiatrist who challenges prevalent attitudes about aging and death.

The following popular films illustrate the diversity and vitality of older people:

Cocoon. Directed by Ron Howard. 1985.

Harold and Maude. Directed by Hal Ashby. 1972.

On Golden Pond. Directed by Mark Rydell. 1981.

The Trip to Bountiful. Directed by Peter Masterson. 1985.

The Whales of August. Directed by Lindsay Anderson. 1987.

Driving Miss Daisy. Directed by Bruce Beresford. 1989.

UNIT 19

THE POWER OF THE SITUATION

This man is dangerous. He believes what he says.
Joseph Goebbels on Adolf Hitler

Is everyone capable of evil? Unit 19 investigates the social and situational forces that influence our individual and group behavior and how our beliefs can be manipulated by other people.

Objectives

After viewing Program 19 and completing the assigned reading, you should be able to:

1. Describe Philip Zimbardo's prison experiment and his conclusions about how people are trapped by roles and rules

2. Describe Solomon Asch's experiment and his conclusions on the conditions that promote conformity

3. Compare the major leadership styles in Lewin's experiment and describe their effects on each group of boys

4. Describe Stanley Milgram's obedience experiments and his conclusions about conditions that promote blind obedience

5. Describe the phenomenon of bystander intervention and how it reflects another aspect of situational forces.

6. Describe Serge Moscovici's work on the influence of the minority on the majority

7. Discuss the Bennington study and how its findings might help develop strategies to promote more responsible decisionmaking

Reading Assignment

After viewing Program 19, read pages 583-604 and pages 615-626 in *Psychology and Life*.

Key People and Terms

As you watch the program and read the assignment, pay particular attention to these people and terms. People and terms defined in the text will be found on the given page numbers.

autokinetic effect (588)
bystander intervention (600)
conformity (587)
demand characteristics (598)
informational influence (588)
group dynamics (594)
norm crystallization (588)
normative influence (588)
prejudice (615)
reference groups (589)
rules (585)
social categorization (616)
social norms (588)
social role (585)
total situation (590)

Elliot Aronson (617)
Solomon Asch (591)
John Darley (601)
Kenneth Clark (615)
Allen Funt (604)
Bibb Latane (601)
Kurt Lewin (594)
Stanley Milgram (596)
Serge Moscovici (593)
Theodore Newcomb (589)
Muzifer Sherif (588)

The following terms are used in Program 19 but are not defined in the text.

autocratic—governed by one person with unlimited power

democratic—practicing social equality

laissez-faire—allowing complete freedom, with little or no interference or guidance

legitimate authority—a form of power exercised by someone in a superior role such as a teacher or president

Program Summary

During the 1930s and 1940s, evil seemed to have taken over much of the world. Millions of ordinary people became willing agents of fascist governments dedicated to genocide. The Holocaust took place almost 50 years ago, but accounts of massacres, terrorism, torture, and cruelty are still in the news every day. Are these horrors the work of sadists and madmen? Or are they perpetrated by ordinary people, people like us? Program 19 attempts to provide some answers to these questions.

While most of psychology tries to understand the individual, social psychology looks at human behavior within its broader social context. Efforts to understand how dictators mold the behavior of individuals gave birth to this field. Its practitioners began to analyze how leaders, groups, and culture shaped individual perceptions, attitudes, and actions.

One group of social psychologists began by studying the power of persuasive speeches. Another group looked at the nature of prejudice and the authoritarian personality. A third team, headed by Kurt Lewin, studied how leaders directly influence group dynamics. Lewin's team trained men to lead groups of boys, using one of three styles of leadership: autocratic, laissez-faire, and democratic. The results suggested that the leader's style, not personality, determined how the boys behaved.

Understanding conformity is another important goal of social psychologists. In a series of visual perception tests, Solomon Asch discovered that nearly a third of the subjects were willing to go along with the majority's wrong judgment to avoid seeming "different" (see figure).

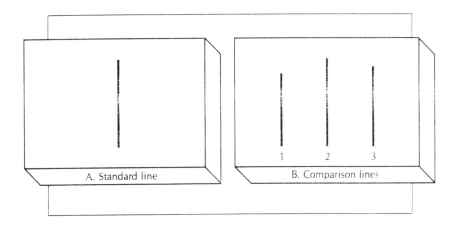

Asch's Study on Conformity
When test subjects were asked which line on Card B was the same length as the line on Card A, nearly a third chose a line that was obviously incorrect to avoid seeming different from the group.

Another researcher, Stanley Milgram, concluded that virtually all of us are capable of blind obedience to authority. In various versions of an experiment, hundreds of subjects—men and women, young and old—delivered what they believed were severe shocks to innocent people rather than disobey authority. Milgram demonstrated that anyone has the capacity for evil if the situation is powerful enough.

Philip Zimbardo's Stanford prison experiment also demonstrated the effect of social situations on human behavior. In the study, college students were assigned to play the roles of either prison guards or prisoners. The situation was so powerful that these bright, healthy students actually took on the personalities of sadistic guards and despondent prisoners. In fact, the experiment, which was meant to last two weeks, had to be terminated after six days because of the extremely disturbing results.

Social influence can be positive as well. Researcher Tom Moriarity showed how apathy can be turned into action simply by asking for assistance from another person, even a total stranger. And Ellen Langer, in her experiments with ROTC cadets training to be fighter pilots, demonstrated that treating people with greater respect and professionalism can actually improve their performance on a visual task.

Clearly, manipulating even small or seemingly minor aspects of social situations can bring out the best or worst in human nature. But most of us are too quick to blame people for their problems and to give them credit for their successes. We tend to overemphasize the importance of personality traits and to discount how easily people are influenced by the power of situations.

The experiments in Program 19 reveal much about human nature, but they also raise an important ethical question: how far can researchers go when a study calls for deceiving, manipulating, or humiliating their subjects? Research goals and procedures must meet ethical standards to protect study participants from distress or unnecessary deception. They must also maintain the integrity of psychological research. Many of the experiments in this program would not be permitted under today's strict guidelines.

Review Questions

Note: Review Questions for Units 19 and 20 are provided in Unit 20.

Questions to Consider

1. Some psychologists have suggested that Milgram's subjects must have suffered guilt and loss of dignity and self-esteem, although they were told later that they hadn't actually harmed the learner. Follow-up studies to the prison experiment revealed that the subjects had not suffered long-term ill effects. What psychological principle might explain these outcomes? Did the value of the research outweigh the risks for the subjects? Would you participate in such experiments?

2. The doctor-patient relationship is one in which many people feel trapped by situational power. The idea of patients playing a more active role in their own medical care threatens the power of many doctors and contradicts the stereotype of the patient who passively obeys orders. Think about the relationship you have with your doctor. Imagine a situation in which you would question your doctor's authority. How would you do it? How would you feel about it? What might inhibit you? And how might you overcome your hesitations?

3. In Zimbardo's prison experiment, students were randomly assigned the role of guard or prisoner. All participants in the study were surprised when the true identities of the guards and prisoners

were erased during the course of the experiment. Each of us plays many roles: child, spouse, friend, student, parent, boss, employee, citizen, consumer, sibling. Do you feel that any of the roles you play conflict with your "true identity"? How do you know what your true identity is?

4. Think about your own experiences in school, at work, and in group situations. Consider which factors bring out the best and worst in you. Recall and compare examples of how teachers, bosses, or leaders brought out positive and negative aspects of your personality.

5. What is the difference between respect for authority and blind obedience? How do you tell the difference? How would you explain the difference to a child?

Optional Activities

1. Architects and interior designers use specific elements—furnishings, lighting, color, seating arrangements—to encourage certain behaviors and to discourage others. Compare the comfort level of chairs in various public places. Which chairs are designed to encourage lingering or to discourage loitering? What types of people use the spaces? What physical changes would influence who uses the space and how they behave there?

2. Norms of social behavior include "social distances" that we place between ourselves and friends, acquaintances, and strangers. Observe and compare the social distance you maintain between yourself and family members, friends, and strangers. Purposely change how close to them you would normally stand. Observe their responses. Does anyone mention it? Do others adjust their positions to achieve normal distances?

Additional Resources

Books and Articles

Aronson, Eliott. (1992). *The Social Animal.* 6th Ed. New York: W.H. Freeman and Co.

Festinger, L., H. Riecken, and S. Schachter.(1956). *When Prophecy Fails.* Minneapolis: University of Minnesota Press. What happens to a follower's faith when a leader's predictions fail to come true? This analysis of fanatical followings reads like a novel.

Kelman, H. C., and V. L. Hamilton.(1989). *Crimes of Obedience.* New Haven: Yale University Press. Explores examples of the tendency both of people to commit illegal or immoral acts when so ordered by authority and of others later to excuse them. Includes discussion of the My Lai massacre, Watergate, and the Iran-contra affair.

Langer, Ellen.(1989). *Mindfulness.* Reading, MA: Addison-Wesley. Causes and consequences of "mindlessness," with implications for mindful alternatives. Includes study done on ROTC cadets' vision.

Lewin, Kurt. (1951). *Field Theory in Social Science.* New York: Harper.

Milgram, Stanley. (1974). *Obedience to Authority.* New York: Harper & Row.Further exploration of obedience which discusses factors that might encourage or discourage blindly obedient behavior.

Ross, L. & Nisbett, R. (1991). *The Person and the Situation: Persepctives of Social Psychology.* New York: McGraw-Hill.

Films

The Great Dictator. Directed by and starring Charlie Chaplin. 1940. The theme of murder on a grand scale contrasted with individual crime. Is murder by a government normal and legal? Chaplin challenges us to question accepted definitions of "crime," "normality," and "insanity."

Lacombe Lucien. Directed by Louis Malle. 1974. A chilling investigation of the banality of evil. A rough farm boy becomes a vicious brute—a Nazi collaborator who casually tortures people.

Trading Places. Directed by John Landis; starring Dan Ackroyd and Eddie Murphy. 1983. This popular movie is another version of the prince and the pauper reversal. Will heredity and character or environment prove to be the major influence?

UNIT 20

CONSTRUCTING SOCIAL REALITY

Everything that deceives may be said to enchant.

Plato

Unit 20 explores our subjective view of reality and how it influences social behavior. It reveals how your perceptions and reasoning ability can be influenced in positive and negative ways, and it increases our understanding of how psychological processes govern interpretation of reality.

Objectives

After viewing the television program and completing the assigned reading, you should be able to:

1. Explain the Fundamental Attribution Error

2. Describe Attribution theory

3. Explain Self-perception theory

4. Summarize Rosenthal's experiment that demonstrates the Pygmalion effect and explain its relation to self-fulfilling prophecies

5. Describe the effect of cognitive dissonance on behavior and attitude change

Reading Assignment

After viewing Program 20, review pages 604-615 in *Psychology and Life*.

Key People and Terms

attitude (612)

attribution theory (606)

behavioral confirmation (612)

cognitive dissonance (613)

covariation principle (607)

fundamental attribution error (608)

self-fulfilling prophecies (610)
self-perception theory (614)
self-serving bias (609)
social perception (606)

Daryl Bem (614)
Robert Cialdini (605)
Leon Festiger (612)
Fritz Heider (606)
Harold Kelley (607)
Joan Miller (609)
Robert Rosenthal (610)
Lee Ross (608)
Mark Snyder (611)

To review additional textbook terms, refer to the Key People and Terms in Unit 19. The following terms and people are used in Program 20 but are not defined in the text.

cognitive control—the power of beliefs to give meaning to a situation

Pygmalion effect—the effect of positive and negative expectations on behavior

Elliot Aronson-helped change the way students saw themselves and others in terms of cooperation and not competition through creating the "Jigsaw classroom" with *Alex Gonzalez*

Jane Elliott-conducted an experiment where she induced prejudice in third graders based   on blue-eyed versus brown-eyed children

Program Summary

In 1978, nearly 900 members of a religious cult committed murder and mass suicide in a remote jungle settlement in Jonestown, Guyana. What kind of people would participate in a mass suicide? What kind of people would murder their own children? Beware of making the fundamental attribution error! Program 20 explains how social forces can distort reality and exert tremendous power on apparently rational people. So the question "What kind of people?" may not be the right question.

Our beliefs can be so powerful that they can, in fact, influence our perceptions and interpretation of reality. The power to create subjective realities is known to psychologists as cognitive control. When individuals and nations believe that their own perception is the only valid one, hostility and prejudice can result and an "us versus them" mentality develops.

Even our most minor differences can trigger prejudice, as we see in Jane Elliot's fourth-grade classroom experiment. Elliot demonstrated how easy it is to alter reality by providing an arbitrary reason to think in adversarial terms. She divided the children into two groups: the "inferior" brown-eyed students and the "superior" blue-eyed ones. This superficial difference provided the basis for institutionalizing discrimination. Those who were seen as inferior began to feel and act that way. And the blue-eyed students took on superior airs.

Another classroom experiment demonstrated that positive expectations can dramatically influence perceptions and behavior. When psychologist Robert Rosenthal and school principal Lenore Jacobson randomly labeled some students as academically superior, those students were given more attention, support, and praise by their teachers. They had created a climate of approval and acceptance that transformed ordinary kids into extraordinary students. The teachers' expectations became a self-fulfilling prophecy.

Both classroom experiments illustrate how social feedback influences the way we see ourselves and the way we behave. In another school, Elliot Aronson and Alex Gonzales created the "Jigsaw Classroom," a class divided into several expert groups that reported on specific topics. Aronson and Gonzales wanted to test their theory that cooperation, not competition, increases achievement and instills self-esteem in all students. The Jigsaw Classroom proved to be a great success, demonstrating that situational forces include not only objective characteristics but the participants' subjective realities too.

Manipulating our perceptions is also the specialty of advertising professionals. They are experts in manipulating the decisions we make as consumers and voters. Their goal is to get us to say yes to their products without thinking or critically evaluating what we are doing.

Psychologist Robert Cialdini has studied thousands of tactics used by salespeople, fund-raisers, public relations practitioners, and advertisers. Their tactics fell into categories, each governed by a basic psychological principle (see figure). Cialdini's research shows how easy it is for us to behave in conforming, prejudiced, or competitive ways. Social psychologists hope to use these same principles of influence to develop new strategies that will help people become more independent, more tolerant, and more cooperative.

1.   *Commitment–Consistency*—Public commitment engages the need to be or appear consistent with others and/or oneself.

2.   *Authority–Credibility*—Conferring authority status on others by virtue of their roles and appearances simplifies information processing by increasing credibility.

3.   *Obligation–Reciprocity*—When someone does us a favor or gives us a gift or compliment, a context of obligation is created which induces a social need to respond politely-to reciprocate.

4.   *Scarcity–Competition*—When anything is perceived as scarce, demand for it escalates, and individuals will compete against potential rivals to get it.

5.   *Social Validation–Consensus*—We use the behavior of similar others or the majority as guidelines for what we do, especially in novel or ambiguous situations.

6.   *Friendship–Liking*—Contexts that encourage the perception of familiarity and similarity increase liking and effectiveness.

Cialdini's Six Influence Strategies

Psychologist Robert Cialdini of Arizona State University spent three years examining advertising strategies and tactics as a professional in the field. He found six central categories of influence strategies, each based on a basic psychological principle.

Review Questions

Program Questions

1. What do social psychologists study?

    a. How people are influenced by other people
    b. How people act in different societies
    c. Why some people are more socially successful than others
    d. What happens to isolated individuals

2. What precipitated Kurt Lewin's interest in leadership roles?

    a. The rise of social psychology
    b. The trial of Adolf Eichmann
    c. Hitler's ascent to power
    d. The creation of the United Nations after World War II

3. In Lewin's study, how did the boys behave when they had autocratic leaders?

    a. They had fun but got little accomplished.
    b. They were playful and did motivated, original work.
    c. They were hostile toward each other and got nothing done.
    d. They worked hard but acted aggressively toward each other.

4. In Solomon Asch's experiments, about what percent of subjects went along with the group's obviously mistaken judgment?

    a. 30 percent
    b. 50 percent
    c. 70 percent
    d. 90 percent

5. Before Stanley Milgram did his experiments on obedience, experts were asked to predict the results. The experts

    a. overestimated the subjects' willingness to administer shocks.
    b. underestimated the subjects' willingness to administer shocks.
    c. gave accurate estimates of the subjects' performance.
    d. believed most subjects would refuse to continue with the experiment.

6. Which light did Milgram's experiment shed on the behavior of citizens in Nazi Germany?

    a. Situational forces can bring about blind obedience.
    b. Personal traits of individuals are most important in determining behavior.
    c. Cultural factors unique to Germany account for the rise of the Nazis.
    d. Human beings enjoy being cruel when they have the opportunity.

7. Which statement most clearly reflects the fundamental attribution error?

    a. Everyone is entitled to good medical care.
    b. Ethical guidelines are essential to conducting responsible research.
    c. People who are unemployed are too lazy to work.
    d. Everyone who reads about the Milgram experiment is shocked by the results.

8. Why did the prison study conducted by Philip Zimbardo and his colleagues have to be called off?

    a. A review committee felt that it violated ethical guidelines.
    b. It consumed too much of the students' time.
    c. The main hypothesis was supported so there was no need to continue.
    d. The situation that had been created was too dangerous to maintain.

9. How do you imagine Lewin's reaction to his experimental results compared to Professor Zimbardo's reaction to the results of the prison study?

    a. Both men were pleased that their ideas were confirmed.
    b. Both men were disappointed by the subjects' performance.
    c. Lewin was pleased, but Zimbardo was shocked.
    d. Lewin was disappointed, and Zimbardo felt neutral.

10. How did Tom Moriarity get people on a beach to intervene during a robbery?

    a. By creating a human bond through a simple request
    b. By reminding people of their social responsibility
    c. By making the thief look less threatening
    d. By providing a model of responsible behavior

11. How did the situation of being involved in an active flight simulation affect the vision of the Air Force ROTC cadets that Ellen Langer studied?

    a. It made them so nervous they saw less well.
    b. It stimulated them to see better.
    c. It had no effect.
    d. It improved the performance of female cadets but not male cadets.

12. According to the program, the behavior of the people who died in Jonestown was a function of

    a. their mental state, as created by Jim Jones.
    b. their moral weakness in getting involved in a cult.
    c. the situation in which they found themselves.
    d. the human tendency toward self-destruction.

13. Psychologists refer to the power to create subjective realities as the power of

    a. social reinforcement.
    b. prejudice.
    c. cognitive control.
    d. the Pygmalion effect.

14. When Jane Elliot divided her classroom of third-graders into the inferior brown-eyed people and the superior blue-eyed students, what did she observe?

    a. The students were too young to understand what was expected.
    b. The students refused to behave badly toward their friends and classmates.
    c. The boys tended to go along with the categorization, but the girls did not.
    d. The blue-eyed students acted superior and were cruel to the brown-eyed students, who acted inferior.

15. In the research carried out by Robert Rosenthal and Lenore Jacobson, what caused the performance of some students to improve dramatically?

   a. Teachers were led to expect such improvement and so changed the way they treated these students.
   b. These students performed exceptionally well on a special test designed to predict improved performance.
   c. Teachers gave these students higher grades because they knew the researchers were expecting the improvement.
   d. The students felt honored to be included in the experiment and so were motivated to improve.

16. Imagine you are a teacher who wants to use the results of the Rosenthal study to improve the performance of your students. What step would be in line with the study results?

   a. Praise students no matter how they do.
   b. Provide differentiated feedback.
   c. Keep the input as simple as possible.
   d. Provide for more group response and less individual response.

17. What happens to low-achieving students in the Jigsaw Classroom?

   a. They tend to fall further behind.
   b. They are given an opportunity to work at a lower level, thus increasing the chance of success.
   c. By becoming "experts," they improve their performance and their self-respect.
   d. By learning to compete more aggressively, they become more actively involved in their own learning.

18. When Robert Cialdini cites the example of the Hare Krishnas' behavior in giving people at airports a flower or other small gift, he is illustrating the principle of

   a. commitment.
   b. reciprocation.
   c. scarcity.
   d. consensus.

Textbook Questions

19. The Stanford prison study described in the opening of the chapter demonstrated

   a. the power of social roles in determining behavior.
   b. how certain jobs exaggerate the character flaws of individuals.
   c. that personality factors can lead to mental disturbance.
   d. that some of us will behave like criminals for no apparent reason.

20. The "social context" includes

    a. the expectations and norms that govern behavior.
    b. the real or imagined presence of others.
    c. the features of the environment in which behavior occurs.
    d. all of the above.

21. Formal and informal groups that a person values and identifies with are called

    a. reference groups.
    b. in-groups.
    c. social models.
    d. norm sources.

22. Which of the following is a "total institution"?

    a. Fort Shape-Up Military Boot Camp
    b. Knowitall University
    c. First Presbyterian Church of Boston
    d. Veterans of Foreign Wars

23. Asch is to Sherif as

    a. norm is to role.
    b. normative influence is to informational influence.
    c. independence is to conformity.
    d. conformity is to group norms.

24. All of the following factors have been found to increase the degree of conformity EXCEPT

    a. increasing the size of the group.
    b. the ambiguity of the task.
    c. increasing the cohesiveness of the group.
    d. making one's responses public, rather than private.

25. Which of the following social psychologists has studied how minority dissent reduces conformity?

    a. Solomon Asch
    b. Muzafer Sherif
    c. Norman Triplett
    d. Serge Moscovici

26. The author of your text observed that the minority members of a society tend to be

    a. radical and disruptive.
    b. idealistic and independent.
    c. supporters of innovation and change.
    d. defenders of the status quo.

27. Lewin found that autocratic leaders produced groups that were

    a. consistently high in productivity.
    b. low in hostility and aggression.
    c. highly independent.
    d. low on creativity and originality.

28. According to Stanley Milgram, what factor best predicts whether a person will engage in harmful, cruel behavior toward another human being?

    a. A deviant personality
    b. Childhood history of physical abuse
    c. The social situation
    d. Mental disorder and low self-esteem

29. Milgram found all of the following factors increased obedience EXCEPT

    a. the victim demands to be shocked.
    b. an obedient peer model.
    c. distance or separateness from the victim.
    d. direct surveillance by the authority.

30. What was found to be the critical factor that determines whether or not someone assists another person who needs help?

    a. How easily help was available
    b. The nature of the help that was needed: strength, medical, technical, etc.
    c. The age and gender of the person needing help
    d. The number of other people present

31. The Good Samaritan study also identified _____ as an important variable predicting whether or not someone helps.

    a. familiarity with environment
    b. time pressures
    c. the presence of an authority
    d. the demands of the "subject" role

32. Which of the following statements best represents the "motivation-tactician thinker" as described by Fiske and Taylor?

    a. "I rated the guys I've dated on a number of attributes and decided that I should be nicest to Alvin."
    b. "It bothers me that I love my mother but I don't enjoy having her visit us."
    c. "I visited seven countries in 13 days, and I can tell you that the Italians are the best cooks in Europe."
    d. "I try to wear clothes that are appropriate for the place, the people and the occasion."

33. According to Daryl Bem's self-perception theory, we

    a. infer our attitudes from our behavior.
    b. change our behavior if it is not consonant with our attitudes.
    c. are all naive scientists in social relationships.
    d. all differ in our social reality.

34. All of the following are principles of Kelley's covariation theory EXCEPT

    a. consistency.
    b. comparison.
    c. consensus.
    d. distinctiveness.

35. All of the following are major themes or directions for social psychological research EXCEPT

    a. people respond in terms of their subjective reality, not the objective features of a situation.
    b. situational factors can be more powerful than personality factors.
    c. large groups or collectives have their own culture.
    d. application of the knowledge gained from research applied to solving social problems.

36. Norman Triplett found that the mere presence of other people influenced performance. This phenomenon is called

    a. social loafing.
    b. social co-action.
    c. social comparison.
    d. social facilitation.

37. Newcomb's classic Bennington College study demonstrated

    a. how political views change as one gets older.
    b. that women are very susceptible to political persuasion.
    c. how group norms can shift due to changing reference groups.
    d. that failure to adhere to campus norms can lead to the 3 R's.

38. One juror does not agree that the defendant has been shown to be "guilty beyond a reasonable doubt." Studies using the Asch paradigm suggest that the juror is less likely to conform to the verdict of the majority if

    a. the dissenter is persistent.
    b. one other juror decides the dissenter is right.
    c. the dissenter has high status.
    d. the dissenter is a male.

39. The study done by Kurt Lewin and his colleagues showed that the most important variable in determining the manner in which groups functioned was the

    a. personality of the leader.
    b. style of leadership.
    c. cohesiveness of the group.
    d. size of the group.

40. Lewin's experimentation in group dynamics led to the conclusion that

    a. laissez-faire groups were the most consistently creative.
    b. democratic groups were the most productive.
    c. autocratic leaders were the most respected.
    d. democratic groups were the least efficient.

41. Which phrase best captures the essence of Milgram's research?

    a. Conformity to groups that are perceived as powerful
    b. Perceived role requirements overshadowing individual factors
    c. The influence of reference groups on social behavior
    d. Obedience to perceived legitimate authority

42. How were Milgram's findings tested outside the laboratory?

    a. Psychiatrists were asked to predict the performance of subjects.
    b. Nurses were ordered by an unfamiliar physician to administer an unusually large dose of a drug, and most obeyed.
    c. College students disobeyed orders to harm a puppy.
    d. Witnesses to a harmful procedure intervened to stop the harmful activity.

43. The text reports a study of bystander intervention on a New York subway train. The independent variable in the study was

    a. the time of day.
    b. whether people were going to work or coming home from work.
    c. characteristics of the victim.
    d. characteristics of the passengers.

44. Which of the following is an example of social reality?

    a. All the employees of the Burton Button Company think Mr. Burton is mean and stingy.
    b. The people of a small religious group believe that the San Francisco earthquake was punishment for sexual misconduct.
    c. Before World War II, the U.S. military thought the Japanese were too nearsighted to fly airplanes and drop bombs accurately.
    d. All of the above are examples of social reality.

45. What was the effect on children of being members of the "out-group" in Jane Elliot's study involving third grade children?

    a. There was an increase in aggressive behavior.
    b. There was a decline in their academic performance.
    c. There was an increase in group solidarity and cooperation.
    d. Knowledge of their supposed inferiority motivated them to strive harder.

Questions to Consider

1. How do social power and personal power contribute to behavior?

2. How is nationalism used to structure social reality?

3. Would Rosenthal's experiment meet today's ethical standards?

4. What do dissonance reduction, the self-serving bias, and the defense mechanism of rationalization all have in common?

5. How do programs on television construct a distorted reality for children?

Optional Activities

1. Look for editorials, news stories, or political cartoons that portray an international situation. Which words, labels, and images promote "us versus them" thinking? How might someone with opposite views have written the articles or drawn the cartoons differently?

2. Think of norms of proper dress or social behavior that you can violate. For example, what would happen if you wore shorts to a formal gathering? Or asked a stranger an extremely personal question? Or arrived at work in your bedroom slippers? Pay attention to your feelings as you think about carrying out these activities. What fears or inhibitions do you have? How likely is it that you could actually carry out these activities?

Additional Resources

Books and Articles

Bettelheim, Bruno.(1979). *Surviving and Other Essays.* New York: Vintage Books. Beautifully written and insightful essays by a psychologist who survived life in a concentration camp. Some of the essays deal with how both prisoners and persecutors behave in extreme situations.

Cialdini, Robert.(1993) *Influence: Science and Practice.* Revised Edition. Glenview, IL: Scott, Foresman. An engaging book that describes six central strategies of influence and their application in advertising and other arts of persuasion.

Festinger, Leon (1957). *A Theory of Cognitive Dissonance.* Evanston, IL: Row Peterson.

Goffman, Erving.(1966). *Behavior in Public Places.* New York: Free Press of Glencoe. Uncovers the behavioral order found in all peopled places, whether an organized social occasion or merely a routine social setting.

Goffman, Erving. (1990). *Asylums.* New York: Doubleday.

Hassan, Steven. *Combatting Cult Mind Control.* Rochester, VT: Park St. Press.

Heider, Fritz. (1958). *The Psychology of Interpersonal Relations.* New York: Wiley.On "perceiving the other person" and other topics of interpersonal relationships.

Orwell, George.(1949). *1984.* New York: Harcourt Brace and World. Imagine if every aspect of your life were planned for you and every move you made were watched by a "Big Brother." Orwell's frightening vision of the future shows how behavior can be molded in a totalitarian society.

Osherow, N. (1981). "Making Sense of the Nonsensical: An Analysis of Jonestown." In *Readings About the Social Animal,* edited by E. Aronson. San Francisco: Freeman. How can we begin to understand the tragic mass suicide led by Jim Jones? This article tries to piece together and explain what happened.

Reaves, Dick. (1995). *Ashes of Waco.* New York: Simon & Schuster.

Rosenthal, Robert, and Lenore F. Jacobson.(1968). *Pygmalion in the Classroom.* New York: Holt, 1968. Classroom studies show that the expectations teachers have about their students greatly influence how the students perform.

Tabor, James. (1995). *Why Waco?* Berkeley, CA: University of California Press.

Turnbull, C. M.(1972). *The Mountain People.* New York: Simon & Schuster. Social crises and the breakdown of social structures can be devastating to individuals. In one African tribe, conditions of extreme deprivation led to drastic changes in personality and behavior.

Film

Twelve Angry Men. Directed by Sidney Lumet; starring Henry Fonda. 1957. The jury deliberations in a murder case illustrate principles of social influence, conformity, and persuasion.

UNIT 21

PSYCHOPATHOLOGY

Life begins on the other side of despair.
Jean-Paul Sartre

Unit 21 describes the major types of mental illnesses and some of the factors that influence them—both biological and psychological. It also reports on several approaches to classifying and treating mental illness and explains the difficulties of defining abnormal behavior.

Objectives

After viewing the television program and completing the assigned readings, you should be able to:

1. Identify the seven criteria commonly used to determine abnormal behavior

2. Describe the *Diagnostic and Statistical Manual of Mental Disorders* and how it is used

3. Explain how psychological disorders are classified

4. List and describe the major types of psychological disorders

5. List the biological and psychological approaches to studying the etiology of psychopathology

6. Summarize the genetic and psychosocial research related to the origins of schizophrenia, including subtypes and etiology

7. Identify sources of error in judgments of mental illness

Reading Assignment

After viewing Program 21, read pages 627-670 in *Psychology and Life*.

Key People and Terms

As you watch the program and read the assignment, pay particular attention to these people and terms. People and terms defined in the text will be found on the given page numbers.

abnormal psychology (629)
agoraphobia (642)
antisocial personality disorder (639)
anxiety disorders (642)
biological marker (662)
bipolar disorder (649)
comorbidity (638)
delusions (657)
diathesis-stress model (662)
dissociative amnesia (640)
dissociative disorder (639)
dissociative identity disorder (DID) (640)
dopamine hypothesis (662)
double bind (663)
drapetomania (666)
DSM-IV (636)
etiology (633)
explanatory style (653)
fear (643)
generalized anxiety disorder (642)
hallucinations (656)
histronic personality disorder (639)
hysteria (630)
insanity (665)
interactionist perspective (635)
learned helplessness (653)
manic episode (649)
mood disorder (648)
narcissitic personality disorder (639)
neurotic disorders (636)

obsessive-compulsive disorder (644)
panic disorders (642)
paranoid personality disorder (639)
personality disorders (639)
phobia (643)
posttraumatic stress disorder (PTSD) (645)
psychological diagnosis (635)
psychopathological functioning (629)
psychotic disorders (637)
schizophrenic disorders (656)
social phobia (643)
specific phobias (644)
stigma (668)
unipolar depression (648)

Gregory Bateson (663)
Aaron Beck (652)
Jean Charcot (632)
Sigmund Freud (634)
Irving Gottesman (660)
Emil Kraeplin (632)
Teresa LaFromboise (656)
R.D. Laing (667)
Brendan Maher (664)
Franz Mesmer (632)
Susan Nolen-Hoeksema (654)
Philippe Pinel (632)
David Rosenhan (666)
Martin Seligman (653)
Edwin Shneidman (655)
Thomas Szasz (667)

The following people are used in Program 21 but at not defined in the text:

Hans Strupp-argues that psychological factors are of primary importance in the origin of schizophrenia

Fuller Torrey-studies the psychology and biology of schizophrenia

Program Summary

Hearing voices, fear of public places, and pervasive feelings of inadequacy are just a few examples of how the powers of the brain distort our perceptions, thoughts, and feelings. Psychopathology, the subject of Program 21, is the study of these distortions, the mental disorders that affect personality and normal functioning.

One in every five Americans suffers from some form of mental disorder. It is difficult to measure the true extent of the problem because many mental disorders resemble typical everyday problems that we all experience. Mental health specialists trained to make these judgments rely on observations of behavior, diagnostic tests, and complaints from the individual who is suffering and from others.

Mental illnesses need to be classified for many different reasons. When a problem is identified and classified, appropriate treatment can be planned. Mental health and stability can also have important legal implications. For example, a psychiatric diagnosis may determine whether a person is able to stand trial. Classification also aids research, furthering the study of pathology and the effectiveness of various treatments. And insurance companies need classification for economic reasons; they provide payments based on the type of mental disorder and its accepted treatment.

Years ago, people with psychological problems were lumped with society's outcasts and punished without compassion. In the eighteenth century, Phillippe Pinel, a French physician, suggested that mental problems should be viewed as sickness. The treatment of people with mental disorders has changed and continues to improve—but not fast enough.

Psychiatrist Thomas Szasz argues that mental illness is a myth used as an excuse for authorities to repress people who violate social norms. It has been used by the Soviet Union to justify imprisoning social and political dissidents. It was also used to justify the treatment of slaves in the United States.

Stanford psychologist David Rosenhan explains that behavior is always interpreted within a context. In an experiment, he and seven other sane people gained admission to a mental hospital, having convinced authorities that they were suffering from hallucinations. Although they behaved normally once they were admitted, virtually everything they did was interpreted as abnormal. His experiment teaches us that virtually anyone can be diagnosed as mentally ill in certain situations.

But mental illness is not simply a social label. Anxiety disorders such as phobias, affective disorders such as depression of mania, and schizophrenia account for an estimated 25 million cases in the United States.

Freud labeled anxiety states *neuroses,* a term considered too general today. He believed that neurotic individuals, unaware of the underlying infantile conflicts, showed a pattern of self-defeating behavior. According to his theory, the difference between neurotic and normal behavior is one of degree.

Although almost everyone has been depressed at one time or another, an individual with extreme and chronic depression may require hospitalization and drug therapy. In fact, depression accounts for most mental hospital admissions. But about 80 percent of those suffering from clinical depression never receive any treatment.

The label *psychosis* describes a class of disorders that are not on the continuum of normal behavior. People with psychotic disorders suffer from impaired perception, thinking, and emotional responses. Schizophrenic disorders, a major subclass, are characterized by a complete break with reality.

The two primary approaches to understanding schizophrenia are biological and psychological. The biological approach traces the disorder to abnormal brain structure or functioning. The psychological approach assumes that the key to understanding lies in the patient's personal experiences, traumas, and conflicts.

Because schizophrenia and depression are so varied, most researchers believe that the disorders are the result of complex interactions between biological and psychosocial factors. Irving Gottesman, a leading expert on the genetics of schizophrenia, concludes that there is a genetic path for some forms of the disease. The results of his research with pairs of identical twins who are discordant for schizophrenia sheds light on other psychosocial factors, such as family communication patterns and social isolation.

Other scientists, such as Teresa La Framboise, are trying to understand the origins of psychopathology by looking at cultural factors in the Native American population. La Framboise explains that because Native American values conflict with those that predominate in the culture around them, mental problems have become common in their culture.

Mental illness may be caused by a combination of physical and psychological variables, and its diagnosis may be biased by cultural or social factors. But the suffering of the afflicted is real.

Review Questions

Program Questions

1. Psychopathology is defined as the study of

   a. organic brain disease.
   b. perceptual and cognitive illusions.
   c. clinical measures of abnormal functioning.
   d. mental disorders.

2. What is the key criterion for identifying a person as having a mental disorder?

   a. The person has problems.
   b. The person's functioning is clearly abnormal.
   c. The person's ideas challenge the status quo.
   d. The person makes other people feel uncomfortable.

3. Frannie is a mental health specialist who has a Ph.D. in psychology. She would be classified as a

    a. psychiatrist.
    b. clinical psychologist.
    c. social psychologist.
    d. psychoanalyst.

4. What happened after David Rosenhan and his colleagues were admitted to mental hospitals by pretending to have hallucinations and then behaved normally?

    a. Their sanity was quickly observed by the staff.
    b. It took several days for their deception to be uncovered.
    c. In most cases, the staff disagreed with each other about these "patients."
    d. Nobody ever detected their sanity.

5. Olivia is experiencing dizziness, muscle tightness, shaking, and tremors. She is feeling apprehensive. These symptoms most resemble those found in cases of

    a. anxiety disorders.
    b. affective disorders.
    c. psychoses.
    d. schizophrenia.

6. Agoraphobia is the most common of the phobias. What does a person with this condition fear?

    a. Being at the top of a tall building
    b. Going out in public
    c. Being violently attacked
    d. In this condition, people have a generalized fear of experience.

7. When Freud studied patients with anxiety, he determined that their symptoms were caused by

    a. childhood abuse, both physical and sexual.
    b. imbalances in body chemistry.
    c. childhood conflicts that had been repressed.
    d. cognitive errors in the way patients viewed the world.

8. Vincent Van Gogh's paintings reflect his mental disorder. He suffered from

    a. alternate episodes of mania and depression.
    b. an anxiety state unrelated to any specific phobia.
    c. an extreme fear of open spaces.
    d. impaired perception, thinking, and emotion.

9. What happens to most people who are suffering from serious clinical depression?

    a. They commit suicide.
    b. They are hospitalized.
    c. They receive treatment outside a hospital.
    d. They receive no treatment at all.

10. People lose touch with reality in cases of

    a. neurosis but not psychosis.
    b. psychosis but not neurosis.
    c. both psychosis and neurosis.
    d. all psychoses and some neuroses.

11. When Hans Strupp speaks of the importance of psychological factors in schizophrenia, he specifically cites the role of

    a. feelings of inadequacy.
    b. antisocial personality.
    c. delayed development.
    d. early childhood experiences.

12. Irving Gottesman and Fuller Torrey have been studying twins to learn more about schizophrenia. If the brain of a twin with schizophrenia is compared with the brain of a normal twin, the former has

    a. less cerebrospinal fluid.
    b. larger ventricles.
    c. a larger left hemisphere.
    d. exactly the same configuration as the latter.

13. For Teresa La Framboise, the major issue in the treatment of mental disorders among Native Americans is

    a. the prevalence of genetic disorders.
    b. alcohol's impact on family structure.
    c. the effect of imposing white American culture.
    d. isolation due to rural settings.

Textbook Questions

14. For a person's behavior to be considered "abnormal"
    a. his or her behaviors or characteristics must be statistically rare.
    b. the person must be very unhappy.
    c. two or more of the "behavioral indicators" need to be applicable.
    d. others cannot understand what is causing a person to behave a certain way.

15. To say that a disorder has a psychological or functional basis means

    a. the disorder is caused by a malfunctioning nervous system.
    b. there is no organic basis for the disorder.
    c. disturbed cognitions are the sole basis for the disorder.
    d. hypnosis would have a positive impact on the disorder.

16. According to the psychodynamic model, all of the following are involved in mental disorder EXCEPT

    a. nervous system abnormalities.
    b. unconscious conflict.
    c. childhood trauma.
    d. overwhelming anxiety.

17. You go to a behavioral therapist for help with some personal problems. This type of therapist will look for the origin of your problems in

    a. current situations or conditions.
    b. childhood trauma.
    c. self-defeating thoughts.
    d. neurotransmitter level disturbances.

18. A weakness of the classification system used by mental health researchers is

    a. that it makes the creation of treatment plans very difficult.
    b. the great disagreement about the etiology of disorders.
    c. an absence of agreed upon terminology.
    d. a bias toward the behavioral perspective in labeling disorders.

19. Obsessions are to compulsions as

    a. thoughts are to acts.
    b. ideas are to concepts.
    c. behaviors are to thoughts.
    d. fears are to reckless acts.

20. What is the outstanding characteristic of bipolar affective disorder?

    a. periods of calmness alternating with periods of anxiety.
    b. alternating episodes of obsessiveness and compulsive behavior.
    c. times of amnesia alternating with full remembrance.
    d. periods of mania alternating with depression.

224 Unit 21: Psychopathology

21. Clinical depression is characterized by all of the following symptoms EXCEPT

    a. dysphoria.
    b. insomnia or hypersomnia.
    c. mania.
    d. motor retardation or agitation.

22. All of the following substances have been identified as factors in the biology of depression EXCEPT

    a. dopamine.
    b. serotonin.
    c. norepinephrine.
    d. cerebral glucose.

23. A hormone called melatonin appears to be involved in

    a. unipolar depression.
    b. bipolar depression.
    c. catatonic schizophrenia.
    d. seasonal affective disorder.

24. Gregory Bateson used the term "double bind" to describe a type of _____ that may be involved in the etiology of schizophrenia.

    a. deviant communication
    b. family milieu
    c. interpersonal relationship
    d. motivational conflict

25. The confinement of Rosenhan and his colleagues in psychiatric hospitals demonstrated that

    a. context affects judgments of abnormality.
    b. patients in mental hospitals are treated as if they were inmates in penal institutions.
    c. drugs are overused in institutions as a convenience to the staff.
    d. patients are better diagnosticians than professionals.

26. Who developed the first classification system for psychological disorder?

    a. Phillippe Pinel
    b. Sigmund Freud
    c. Jean Charcot
    d. Emil Kraepelin

27. One can think of any addiction as

    a. a phobia.
    b. a compulsive behavior.
    c. a dissociative state.
    d. a mood disorder.

28. In their explanations of depression, both Aaron Beck and Martin Seligman include

    a. a negative interpretation of life events.
    b. lack of positive reinforcement.
    c. paralysis.
    d. an internal locus of control.

29. Paranoid schizophrenia is to catatonic schizophrenia as

    a. delusions of persecution are to bizarre positions.
    b. delusions of reference are to inappropriate giggling.
    c. word salad is to stupor.
    d. waxy flexibility is to negativity.

30. Unusually elevated levels of which neurotransmitter have been associated with the presence of schizophrenia?

    a. Dopamine
    b. Serotonin
    c. Norepinephrine
    d. Noradrenaline

Questions to Consider

1. Is the insanity defense legitimate?

2. Why has the DSM been criticized?

3. Is homosexuality a deviant behavior?

4. Are standards for psychological health the same for men and women? Why are most patients women?

5. How can you tell whether your own behavior, anxieties, and moods are within normal limits or whether they signal mental illness?

6. Explain why the term *split personality* is not an accurate way to describe schizophrenia.

Optional Activities

1. Collect the advice columns in the daily papers for a week or two (such as "Dear Ann Landers" or "Dear Abby"). What kinds of problems do people write about? How often does the columnist refer people to a psychologist, psychiatrist, or other professional for counseling? Why do people write to an anonymous person for advice about their problems?

2. Ask several people (who are not psychology professionals) to define the terms *emotionally ill, mentally ill, crazy, insane,* and *mad.* Ask them to describe behaviors that characterize each term. Do some terms indicate more extreme behavior than others? How do their definitions compare with the ones in your text? What can you conclude about the attitudes and understanding of mental illness shown by the people you interviewed?

Additional Resources

Books and Articles

Burns, David. (1980). *Feeling Good.* New York: Morrow.

Capote, Truman.(1966). *In Cold Blood.* New York: Random House. Murder is often thought of as a crime of hot-blooded passion. This gripping novel tells the true story of two psychopathic men who commit a set of senseless murders without remorse.

Gottesman, Irving. (1982). *Schizophrenia.* Cambridge: Cambridge University Press.
Discusses evidence that there is a genetic transmission path for some forms of schizophrenia.

Green, H. (1964). *I Never Promised You a Rose Garden.* New York: Holt, Rinehart & Winston. A based-on-fact account of a young woman's experience with a schizophrenic disorder. Includes descriptions of her inner world and an account of her psychotherapy.

Kaufman, Barry. (1977). *Son Rise.* New York: Warner Books. Moving account of parents who seek to treat their son's autism by unconventional means, and achieve surprising success.

Laing, R.D. (1965). *The Divided Self.* Baltimore, MD: Penguin Books.

Peterson, C., Maier, S. & Seligman, Martin. 1993). *Learned Helplessness.* New York: Oxford University Press.

Rosenhan, David L.(1973). "On Being Sane in Insane Places." *Science* 179, 250-58. Rosenhan and several colleagues gained admission to mental hospitals by feigning mental illness. Their subsequent "sane" behavior was interpreted within a context of illness.

Rubin, Theodore I. (1961). *Lisa and David*. New York: Macmillan. A love story about two troubled adolescents, one suffering from multiple personality disorder, the other fearing the slightest human touch. Together they develop a trusting relationship that helps them recover.

Sheehan, Susan.(1982). *Is There No Place on Earth for Me?* Introduction by Robert Coles. New York: Vintage Books. This biography of a young schizophrenic woman offers insights both into the disease and the mental health care system. A moving novel that won the Pulitzer Prize for nonfiction.

Szasz, Thomas. (1964). *The Myth of Mental Illness*. New York: Harper & Row. Controversial argument that the labeling of mental illness is done merely to justify the repression or individuals deviating from social norms.

Styron, William. (1990). *Darkness Visible*. New York: Random House.

Vonnegut, Mark.(1975). *The Eden Express*. New York: Praeger. An autobiographical account of the author's schizophrenic breakdown and recovery.

Winokur, G.(1981). *Depression: The Facts*. New York: Oxford University Press. A thorough summary of the issues of and research on depression.

Films

Best Boy. Directed by Ira Wohl. 1979. A poignant documentary about the director's 52-year-old, mentally retarded cousin Philly. It illustrates the many struggles faced by 19 mentally impaired people and their families.

I Never Promised You a Rose Garden. Directed by Anthony Page. 1977. The story of a young schizophrenic, focusing on her relationship with one dedicated psychiatrist. Based on the book by Hannah Green.

In Cold Blood. Directed by Richard Brooks. 1967. A gripping adaptation of Truman Capote's novel about two methodical murderers.

One Flew over the Cuckoo's Nest. Directed by Milos Forman; starring Jack Nicholson. 1975. This Oscar award-winning adaptation of Ken Kesey's novel takes a critical look at mental institutions. When a high-spirited—but hardly mentally ill—individual is admitted for treatment, he enlightens fellow patients to paths of recovery. His help, though, is considered a threat to the system.

Rain Man. Starring Dustin Hoffman and Tom Cruise. 1988. Dustin Hoffman accurately and sensitively portrays an individual with a remarkable mental disorder. While able to perform extraordinary feats of memorization and mental arithmetic, he cannot process simple information necessary for functioning alone in the outside world.

Silent Snow, Secret Snow. (Macmillan, 20 min.) An adaptation of Conrad Aiken's short story about a little boy's gradual descent into schizophrenia.

Fisher King. Directed by Terry Gilliam. 1991. Jeff Bridges as a cynical disk jockey and Robin Williams as a delusional homeless man who help each other overcome guilt and mental illness.

UNIT 22

PSYCHOTHERAPY

To say that a particular psychiatric condition is incurable or irreversible is to say more about the state of our ignorance than about the state of the patient.
Milton Rokeach

Unit 22 looks at the field of psychotherapy and therapists, the professionals trained to help us solve some of our most critical problems. You will learn about different approaches to the treatment of mental, emotional, and behavioral disorders and the special kind of helping relationships that therapists provide.

Objectives

After viewing the television program and completing the assigned reading, you should be able to:

1. Describe early approaches to identifying and treating mental illness

2. Identify the major approaches to psychotherapy

3. Describe how psychiatrists, psychoanalysts, and clinical psychologists differ in their training and therapeutic orientation

4. Identify the major features of psychoanalysis and explain the purposes of each

5. Explain the goals of various behavior therapies

6. Summarize the major rationale behind all types of cognitive therapy

7. Summarize the main features of person-centered therapy and Gestalt therapy and how these reflect the existential-humanistic perspective.

8. Describe the use of psychosurgery and electroconvulsive shock in the treatment of mental illness

9. Identify the common forms of drug therapy and how they have changed the mental health system

10. Summarize research on the effectiveness of psychotherapy

Reading Assignment

After viewing Program 22, read pages 671-712 in *Psychology and Life*.

Key People and Terms

As you watch the program and read the assignment, pay particular attention to these people and terms. People and terms defined in the text will be found on the given page numbers.

aversion therapy (685)
behavior modification (682)
behavior therapy (682)
behavioral contract (686)
behavioral rehearsal (689)
biomedical therapies (673)
catharsis (680)
client (674)
clinical ecology (709)
clinical psychologist (675)
clinical social worker (675)
cognitive behavior modification (692)
cognitive therapy (691)
contingency management (686)
counseling psychologists (674)
counterconditioning (683)
countertransference (680)
dream analysis (680)
electroconvulsive therapy (ECT) (701)
eye movement desensitization and
         reprocessing (EMDR) (685)
free association (679)
flooding (684)
Gestalt therapy (696)
human potential movement (695)
implosion therapy (684)
insight therapy (678)
meta-analysis (706)
participant modeling (689)
pastoral counselor (675)
patient (674)
person-centered therapy (695)
placebo therapy (706)

prefrontal lobotomy (701)
psychiatrist (675)
psychoanalytic therapy (677)
psychoanalyst (675)
psychopharmocology (702)
psychosurgery (700)
psychotherapy (673)
rational-emotive therapy (694)
resistance (680)
ritual healing (677)
shamanism (677)
social-learning therapy (687)
spontaneous remission effect (6705)
symptom substitution (681)
systematic desensitization (683)
transference (680)

Albert Bandura (687)
Aaron Beck (693)
Clifford Beers (676)
Joseph Breuer (679)
Albert Ellis (694)
Hans Eysenck (705)
Sigmund Freud (677)
J.C. Heinroth (676)
Karen Horney (681)
Mary Cover Jones (683)
Heinz Kohut (682)
Rollo May (694)
Egao Moniz (701)
Fritz Perls (697)
Philippe Pinel (676)

Bertha Pappenheim (679)
Carl Rogers (695)
Virginia Satir (699)
Francine Shapiro (685)
B.F. Skinner (686)
Henry Stack Sullivan (681)
Joseph Wolpe (683)

The following terms and people are used in Program 22 but are not defined in the text.

biological biasing—a genetic predisposition that increases the likelihood of getting a disorder with exposure to prolonged or intense stress

genetic counseling—counseling that advises a person about the probability of passing on defective genes to offspring

time-limited dynamic psychotherapy—a form of short-term therapy

Enrico Jones-investigates which type of treatment is best for which type of problem

Hans Strupp-psychodynamic therapist

Program Summary

When you have a problem, to whom do you turn for comfort and advice? For most of us, the answer is a family member or a friend. But when problems cause prolonged or severe distress, friends and relatives may not have the interest or skills to help us resolve them. Then it may be time to seek professional help. Program 22 considers the range of treatments available, how they developed, and the types of problems they are effective in treating.

Therapies can be divided into two major groups: biomedical therapies, which focus on physical causes, and psychological therapies, which focus on helping us to change the way we think, feel, and behave.

The biomedical approach looks at mental disorders as the result of biochemical events that disrupt the delicate ecology of the mind. Psychiatrists and neurobiologists specialize in identifying disease states or syndromes believed to underlie the disorders.

One of the most radical biomedical treatments is psychosurgery. The prefrontal lobotomy, used only in extreme cases, cuts the nerve fibers connecting the brain's frontal lobes. Although the operation eliminates agitated schizophrenia or extreme compulsions, many people consider the cure to be worse than the illness. After a lobotomy, the patient cannot remember clearly or plan ahead and may no longer feel the normal range of emotions.

Electroconvulsive shock therapy, which alters the brain's electrical and chemical activity, is also controversial. Its proponents claim that, for depressed patients who can't tolerate medication, it can be an effective treatment. But its misuse has prompted legal restrictions in many states.

The real revolution in biomedical therapy began in the 1950s with the use of tranquilizing and antipsychotic drugs. Drug therapies not only relieved suffering but also made psychotherapy possible. The danger with drugs, however, is that they may be misused by overworked or poorly trained hospital staff or by patients overmedicating themselves.

Another great revolution in biomedical therapy is currently under way. Scientists are already making significant breakthroughs in identifying genetic sources of schizophrenia, depression, and Alzheimer's disease. They are also learning how these genetic predispositions interact with environmental influences to affect the development of the disease.

Psychotherapists deal with psychological problems in very different ways. Although there are at least 250 different approaches, they can be divided into four general categories. Psychodynamic (or psychoanalytic) therapy sees all behavior as being driven by inner forces, including early life traumas and unresolved conflicts. This perspective was developed by Sigmund Freud around the turn of the century.

In psychoanalysis, the patient's therapy is based on talking things out. Change comes from analyzing and resolving unconscious tensions by using various techniques, including free association, dream analysis, achieving insight and ultimately catharsis.

Over the years, psychoanalysts have modified Freud's techniques, but the goal has always been to change the patient's personality structure, not just to cure the symptoms. It can take years and requires a lot of participation by the patient. Shorter, time-limited, and less intensive treatment can also be effective in helping many patients.

Another approach, behavior therapy, ignores unconscious motives, the past, and personality, and instead concentrates on problem behaviors. Behavior therapists apply principles of conditioning and reinforcement in an effort to eliminate symptoms and teach patients new and healthier behaviors.

Cognitive therapists teach their clients how to change problem attitudes, irrational beliefs, and negative thoughts that trigger anxiety or low self esteem. They also teach clients to change the way they perceive significant life events. In rational-emotive therapy, a form of cognitive therapy developed by Albert Ellis in the 1960s, the therapist teaches clients to recognize the "shoulds," "oughts," and "musts" that control them so that they can choose the life they wish to lead.

In contrast to the therapies that focus on problem behaviors and psychological disorders, humanistic therapies focus on normal people who wish to be more productive, creative, or fulfilled. They emphasize the psychological growth of the total person in the social context and have expanded treatment to include therapy for groups, couples, and families.

Review Questions

Program Questions

1. What are the two main approaches to therapies for mental disorders?

   a. The Freudian and the behavioral
   b. The client-centered and the patient-centered
   c. The biomedical and the psychological
   d. The chemical and the psychosomatic

2. The prefrontal lobotomy is a form of psychosurgery. Though no longer widely used, it was at one time used in cases in which a patient

   a. was an agitated schizophrenic.
   b. had committed a violent crime.
   c. showed little emotional response.
   d. had a disease of the thalamus.

3. Elinor had electroconvulsive shock therapy a number of years ago. She is now suffering a side effect of that therapy, What is she most likely to be suffering from?

   a. Tardive dyskinesia
   b. The loss of her ability to plan ahead
   c. Depression
   d. Memory loss

4. Vinnie suffers from manic-depressive disorder, but his mood swings are kept under control because he takes the drug

   a. chlorpromazine.
   b. lithium.
   c. Valium.
   d. tetracycline.

5. The Woodruff family is receiving genetic counseling because a particular kind of mental retardation runs in their family. What is the purpose of such counseling?

   a. To explain the probability of passing on defective genes
   b. To help eliminate the attitudes of biological biasing
   c. To repair specific chromosomes
   d. To prescribe drugs that will keep problems from developing

6. In psychodynamic theory, what is the source of mental disorders?

    a. Biochemical imbalances in the brain
    b. Unresolved conflicts in childhood experiences
    c. The learning and reinforcement of nonproductive behaviors
    d. Unreasonable attitudes, false beliefs, and unrealistic expectations

7. Imagine you are observing a therapy session in which a patient is lying on a couch, talking. The therapist is listening and asking occasional questions. What is most likely to be the therapist's goal?

    a. To determine what drug the patient should be given
    b. To change the symptoms that cause distress
    c. To explain how to change false ideas
    d. To help the patient develop insight

8. Rinaldo is a patient in psychotherapy, The therapist asks him to free associate. What would Rinaldo do?

    a. Describe a dream
    b. Release his feelings
    c. Talk about anything that comes to mind
    d. Understand the origin of his present guilt feelings

9. According to Hans Strupp, what is an important way in which psychodynamic therapies have changed?

    a. Less emphasis is now placed on the ego.
    b. Patients no longer need to develop a relationship with the therapist.
    c. Shorter courses of treatment can be used.
    d. The concept of aggression has become more important.

10. In the program, a therapist helped a girl learn to control her epileptic seizures. What use did the therapist make of the pen?

    a. To record data
    b. To signal the onset of an attack
    c. To reduce the girl's fear
    d. To reinforce the correct reaction

11. When Albert Ellis discusses with the young woman her fear of hurting others, what point is he making?
    a. It is the belief system that creates the "hurt."
    b. Every normal person strives to achieve fulfillment.
    c. Developing a fear-reduction strategy will reduce the problem.
    d. It is the use of self-fulfilling prophecies that cause others to be hurt.

12. What point does Enrico Jones make about investigating the effectiveness of different therapies in treating depression?

    a.   All therapies are equally effective.
    b.   It is impossible to assess how effective any one therapy is.
    c.   The job is complicated by the different types of depression.
    d.   The most important variable is individual versus group therapy.

Textbook Questions

13. Although there are many different types of therapy, which of the following represents the most useful general definition of therapy?

    a.   Talking to another person about one's problems
    b.   Intervention into a person's life to improve functioning
    c.   Curing mental disturbance
    d.   Changing a person's environment for the better

14. Which of the following types of therapy attempts to change the "messages" a person sends to him or herself?

    a.   psychoanalysis
    b.   behavior modification
    c.   humanistic therapy
    d.   cognitive therapy

15. Who first used the principles of Behaviorism to treat a problem?

    a.   B. F. Skinner
    b.   Albert Bandura
    c.   C. Margaret Mahler
    d.   Mary Cover Jones

16. The "third-force" in psychology arose in response to

    a.   cognitive and biological approaches.
    b.   behavioral and psychoanalytic perspectives.
    c.   psychoanalytic and existential viewpoints.
    d.   behavioral and social learning therapies.

17. The existential-humanistic approach differs from the psychodynamic, behavioral, and cognitive approaches in its emphasis on the client's

    a. sense of self-worth.
    b. history and background.
    c. false assumptions about reality.
    d. free will and personal responsibility.

18. The human potential movement has spearheaded a major change in the clientele and direction of psychotherapy. Which statement best describes the nature of this change?

    a. New forms of group therapy for schizophrenics
    b. Therapy for the average person aimed at personal growth, interpersonal enrichment, and greater awareness
    c. Expansion of therapy to the more deviant members of our society such as psychopaths and pedophiles
    d. Viewing the family as a whole system rather than a collection of individuals

19. Treatments that alter specific brain functions responsible for the symptoms of psychosis, depression, and anxiety are referred to as

    a. psychosurgery.
    b. chemotherapy.
    c. psychoanalysis.
    d. ECT.

20. The treatment that has had the most dramatic impact on reducing long-term hospitalization for mental problems and given mental patients real relief from their symptoms has been

    a. psychoanalysis.
    b. ECT.
    c. chemotherapy.
    d. behavior therapy.

21. Which statement best summarizes the conclusions of the NIMH study on treatment for depression?

    a. Patients in the placebo group improved as much as those in the treatment group.
    b. Patients receiving chemotherapy only improved the most.
    c. Patients receiving Imipramine showed improvement faster compared to the psychotherapy-only groups.
    d. Severely depressed patients improved the most with psychodynamic therapy.

22. Self-help groups such as Alcoholics Anonymous take _____ in treating alcoholism.

    a. an abstinence approach
    b. a controlled drinking approach
    c. a biomedical approach
    d. a prevention approach

23. Thoughts are to cognitive therapists as _____ are to existential-humanistic therapists.

    a. goals
    b. values
    c. barriers
    d. conflicts

24. Systematic desensitization, flooding, and implosion are all examples of

    a. exposure therapy.
    b. cognitive behavior therapy.
    c. psychoanalytic therapy.
    d. biomedical therapy.

25. The rational-emotive therapy of Albert Ellis is similar to the person-centered therapy of Carl Rogers in the goal of helping clients

    a. cultivate a social support network.
    b. learn to use intrinsic rewards.
    c. use problem-focused coping strategies.
    d. increase their sense of self-worth.

26. The terms nondirective, unconditional positive regard, and self-actualization are associated with which therapeutic approach?

    a. Freud's psychoanalytic therapy
    b. Bandura's social learning therapy
    c. Kohut's object relations therapy
    d. Roger's person-centered therapy

27. The type of therapy that emphasizes "being in the moment", the importance of the "here and now", and the expression of pent-up emotions is

    a. cognitive behavioral therapy.
    b. person-centered therapy.
    c. Gestalt therapy.
    d. social learning therapy.

28. In the past, some schizophrenics and individuals, those suffering with extreme obsessive-compulsive disorder, underwent a type of psychosurgery called

    a. prefrontal lobotomy.
    b. amygdalotomy.
    c. ECT.
    d. chemotherapy.

29. All of the following are undesirable side effects of ECT EXCEPT

    a. impaired language and memory.
    b. impaired personality functioning.
    c. used in "managing" difficult patients.
    d. tardive dyskinesia.

30. A naturally occurring substance found to be helpful in the treatment of bipolar affective disorder is

    a. lithium salt.
    b. chicken soup.
    c. tetracycline.
    d. Valium.

Questions to Consider

1. How do the placebo effect and the spontaneous remission effect make evaluating the success of therapy difficult?

2. Why is it so difficult to evaluate and compare the relative effectiveness of therapies?

3. How does someone decide on an appropriate therapy?

4. Can everyone benefit from psychotherapy, or do you think it is only for people with serious problems?

5. Why is there a stigma sometimes associated with seeking professional help for psychological problems?

Optional Activities

1. Identify the services and resources available in your community in case you ever need emotional support in a crisis, want to seek therapy, or know someone who needs this information. How much do these services cost? Look for names of accredited professional therapists and counselors, support groups, hotlines, medical and educational services, and programs in church and community programs. Is it difficult to find information? How accessible are mental health services?

2. Do you have any self-defeating expectations? Do you feel that you might benefit from cognitive therapy? Write out statements of positive self-expectations. For a week, rehearse them. Then try to use them in situations in which you feel anxious or insecure. Do they have any effect?

3. Speculate on how you would feel upon receiving a computer printout of all your genetic biases.

Additional Resources

Books and Articles

Basch, Michael F.(1988). *Understanding Psychotherapy: The Science Behind the Art.* New York: Basic Books. Through compelling case histories, Basch explores both the processes of psychotherapy and human nature. His perspective draws from many branches and schools of psychology.

Frankl, Victor E. (1963). *Man's Search for Meaning.* New York: Pocket Books. Frankl's brand of therapy, logotherapy, grew out of his experiences in a Nazi death camp. Frankl also discusses several clinical applications of his theory.

Freud, S. (1969). *The Question of Lay Analysis.* New York: Norton. Freud explains psychoanalysis through arguing with an imaginary "impartial person."

Garfield, S. L. & A. E. Bergen. (Eds.). (1994). *Handbook of Psychotherapy and Behavior Change.* 4th ed. New York: Wiley. Contributed chapters review the substantive technical and methodological issues in psychotherapy research.

Horney, Karen. (1939). *New Ways in Psychoanalysis.* New York: W.W. Norton.

Kohut, Heinz. (1984). *How Does Analysis Cure?* Chicago, IL: University of Chicago Press.

Mahoney, Michael. (1991). *Human Change Processes.* New York: Basic Books.

Maslow, Abraham. (1964). *Religions, Values, and Peak Experiences.* New York: Viking. Conveys Maslow's humanistic approach to psychology.

May, Rollo. (1955). *Psychotherapy and Counseling*. New York: The Academy.

Rogers, Carl. (1942). *Counseling and Psychotherapy*. Boston, MA: Houghton-Mifflin.

Satir, Virginia. (1967). *Conjoint Family Therapy.* Palo Alto, CA: Ballantine Books.

Sullivan, Harry Stack. (1972). *Personal Psychopathology*. New York: Norton.

Wolpe, Joseph. (1982). *Practice of Behavior Therapy.*3rd Ed. New York: Permagon Press.

UNIT 23

HEALTH, MIND, AND BEHAVIOR

Suffering isn't enabling, recovery is.

Christiaan Barnard

A profound rethinking of the relationship between mind and body has led to the holistic concept in which mental and physical processes are seen as constantly interacting. Unit 23 looks at what health psychologists know about the factors that increase our chances of becoming ill and what we can do to improve and maintain our health.

Objectives

After viewing the television program and completing the assigned readings, you should be able to:

1. Define *stress* and list the major sources of stress

2. Describe the role of cognitive appraisal in stress

3. Describe the major physiological stress reactions including the general adaptation syndrome

4. Explain the relationship between stress and illness

5. Describe various kinds of events that can lead to psychological stress

6. Describe the roles of coping strategies in coping with stress

7. Explain the mind-body relationship in terms of the biopsychosocial model of health and illness

8. Describe biofeedback, how it works, and its role in behavioral medicine

9. Discuss how personality types relate to different health outcomes

10. List some things you can do to reduce your stress level and promote your health

Reading Assignment

After viewing Program 23, read pages 472-506 in *Psychology and Life*.

Key People and Terms

As you watch the program and read the assignment, pay particular attention to these people and terms. People and terms defined in the text will be found on the given page numbers.

acute stress (473)
acquired immune deficiency syndrome (AIDS) (496)
anticipatory coping (486)
biofeedback (500)
biopsychosocial model (492)
chronic stress (473)
cognitive appraisal (477)
coping (486)
"fight-or-flight" syndrome (473)
general adaptation syndrome (475)
hardiness (485)
health (491)
health promotion (492)
health psychology (491)
hozho (491)
human immunodeficiency virus (HIV)(496)
job burnout (503)
life change units (LCU) (478)
perceived control (488)
posttraumatic stress disorder (482)
primary appraisal (478)
pscyhoneuroimmunology (476)
psychosomatic disorders (475)
relaxation response (499)
residual stress pattern (482)

secondary appraisal (478)
social support (489)
stress (472)
stress moderator variables (477)
stressor (472)
Type-A behavior pattern (502)
Type B (502)
Type C (503)
wellness (492)

Thomas Coates (497)
Norman Cousins (501)
Suzanne Kobasa (485)
Christina Maslach (503)
Donald Meichenbaum (488)
Neal Miller (500)
James Pennebaker (500)
Martin Seligman (503)
Shelley Taylor (490)
Hans Selye (475)

The following terms and people are used in Program 23 but are not defined in the text.

psychic numbing—being emotionally unaffected by an upsetting or alarming event

psychogenic—organic malfunction or tissue damage caused by anxiety, tension, or depression

Judith Rodin-through her study of aging and mind-body relationships, Rodin investigates how subtle psychological factors bring about significant physiological change

Program Summary

Noise, smoke, overcrowding, pollution, divorce, violence—how much can one person tolerate? Program 23 focuses on the work of health psychologists who study the social and environmental conditions that put people at risk for physical and psychological disorders.

The field of health psychology has grown out of a profound rethinking of the mind-body relationship. In contrast to the traditional biomedical model, health psychology is based on a new holistic approach that recognizes each person as a whole system in which the emotional, cognitive, and physical processes constantly interact and affect one another.

Mind and body affect each other in a number of ways. Ulcers and hypertension can be caused by anxiety or depression. Headache and exhaustion may be signs of underlying tension. Evidence suggests that psychological factors may suppress or support the body's immune system. And psychological factors certainly contribute to smoking, drinking, and taking drugs.

Judith Rodin of Yale University studies mind-body relationships in the hope of finding ways to improve our health. Her work reveals the link between a person's sense of control and the functioning of the immune system. Rodin has discovered that psychological factors affect complex biological systems that in turn can affect health, fertility, even the life span.

There are many other ways in which the mind can influence the body. Skin temperature, blood pressure, and muscle tension can be influenced by mere thinking. Psychologist Neal Miller discovered that the mind can have a powerful influence on biological systems. Using the psychology of biofeedback, he has helped many people learn to manage chronic pain and to lower their blood pressure.

Another important area of health psychology is stress control. When we feel stressed, our heart beats faster, and our blood pressure and blood sugar levels change. The physical state of alertness, called the fight-or-flight response, is the body's answer to anything that disturbs our equilibrium or taxes our ability to cope. Any change in our lives, good or bad, causes stress because it demands an adjustment to new circumstances. But even life's little hassles, like sitting in traffic or searching endlessly for a parking space, can create stress (see figure).

As stress accumulates, the chance of becoming ill increases. Some experts believe that stress contributes to more than half of all cases of disease.

The Canadian physician Hans Selye identified two types of stress reactions in animals. One type is a specific response to a specific stressor. Blood vessels constrict in response to cold, for example. The second type is a pattern of responses known as the general adaptation syndrome, which begins with the body's alarm reaction, mobilizing the body's ability to defend itself. In the resistance stage, hormonal secretions are activated, and the body seems to return to normal. Finally, the body may express a state of exhaustion caused by chronic stress.

Selye's work helped point out the role stress plays in the origin of many disorders. However, because he worked mainly with animals, he neglected one factor—how individuals perceive and interpret an event is often more important than the event itself. We know that what one person perceives as a stressful situation another person may consider to be a challenge. Richard Lazarus calls this personalized perception of stress "cognitive appraisal."

As relative newcomers to the field, health psychologists help people develop strategies for coping with stress, preventing illness, and promoting good health. They teach behaviors that encourage wellness and help condition our bodies to be less vulnerable to disease.

One illness combines psychological and medical issues in an explosive way: AIDS. Thomas Coates is part of a health psychology team studying the AIDS epidemic from the psychological

Life Event	Life-Change Units
Death of one's spouse	100
Divorce	73
Marital separation	65
Jail term	63
Death of a close family member	63
Personal injury or illness	53
Marriage	50
Being fired at work	47
Marital reconciliation	45
Retirement	45
Change in the health of a family member	44
Pregnancy	40
Sex difficulties	39
Gain of a new family member	39
Business readjustment	39
Change in one's financial state	38
Death of a close friend	37
Change to a different line of work	36
Change in number of arguments with one's spouse	35
Mortgage over $10,000*	31
Foreclosure of a mortgage or loan	30
Change in responsibilities at work	29
Son or daughter leaving home	29
Trouble with in-laws	29
Outstanding personal achievement	28
Wife beginning or stopping work	26
Beginning or ending school	26

Change in living conditions	25
Revision of personal habits	24
Trouble with one's boss	23
Change in work hours or conditions	20
Change in residence	20
Change in schools	20
Change in recreation	19
Change in church activities	19
Change in social activities	18
Mortgage or loan of less than $10,000*	17
Change in sleeping habits	16
Change in number of family get-togethers	15
Change in eating habits	15
Vacation	13
Christmas	12
Minor violations of the law	11

Figure 14: Scale of Life-Change Units
Researchers Thomas Holmes and Richard Rahe assigned units to both positive and negative life changes. They found that people who accumulated more than 300 units within a year were at greater risk for illness. Source: Holmes and Rahe (1967).

*This figure was appropriate in 1967, when the Life-Change Units Scale was constructed. Today, sad to say, inflation probably puffs this figure up to at least $50,000.

perspective. He calls for combining medical, epidemiological, psychological, and social knowledge to improve what we know about risk factors, incidence, and progression of the disease. Health psychologists, as scientists and advocates, study how psychological and social processes contribute to disease and then apply their knowledge to the prevention and treatment of illness. Coates emphasizes the need for messages that inform and motivate educational, social, and medical interventions at a variety of levels in the fight against AIDS. It is evident that the role of health psychologists will increase as we acknowledge the importance of psychological factors in health.

Review Questions

Program Questions

1. How are the biopsychosocial model and the Navaho concept of *hozho* alike?

   a. Both are dualistic.
   b. Both assume individual responsibility for illness.
   c. Both represent holistic approaches to health.
   d. Both are several centuries old.

2. Dr. Wizanski told Thad that his illness was psychogenic. This means that

    a. Thad is not really sick.
    b. Thad's illness was caused by his psychological state.
    c. Thad has a psychological disorder, not a physical one.
    d. Thad's life-style puts him at risk.

3. Judith Rodin and Ellen Langer have studied mind-body relationships among older people. What independent variable did they investigate?

    a. The role of exercise
    b. Increased social contacts
    c. Decreased mortality rates
    d. Increased sense of control

4. When Judith Rodin talks about "wet" connections to the immune system, she is referring to connections with the

    a. individual nerve cells.
    b. endocrine system.
    c. sensory receptors.
    d. skin.

5. What mind-body question is Judith Rodin investigating in her work with infertile couples?

    a. How do psychological factors affect fertility?
    b. Can infertility be cured by psychological counseling?
    c. What effect does infertility have on marital relationships?
    d. Can stress cause rejection of in vitro fertilization?

6. When Professor Zimbardo lowers his heart rate, he is demonstrating the process of

    a. mental relaxation.
    b. stress reduction.
    c. biofeedback.
    d. the general adaptation syndrome.

7. Psychologist Neal Miller uses the example of the blindfolded basketball player to explain

    a. the need for information to improve performance.
    b. how chance variations lead to evolutionary advantage.
    c. the correlation between life-change events and illness.
    d. how successive approximations can shape behavior.

8. In which area of health psychology has the most research been done?

    a. The definition of health
    b. Stress
    c. Biofeedback
    d. Changes in life-style

9. Imagine a family is moving to a new and larger home in a safer neighborhood with better schools. Will this situation be a source of stress for the family?

    a. No, because the change is a positive one.
    b. No, because moving is not really stressful.
    c. Yes, because any change requires adjustment.
    d. Yes, because it provokes guilt that the family does not really deserve this good fortune.

10. Which response shows the stages of the general adaptation syndrome in the correct order?

    a. Alarm reaction, exhaustion, resistance
    b. Resistance, alarm reaction, exhaustion
    c. Exhaustion, resistance, alarm reaction
    d. Alarm reaction, resistance, exhaustion

11. What important factor in stress did Hans Selye not consider?

    a. The role of hormones in mobilizing the body's defenses
    b. The subjective interpretation of a stressor
    c. The length of exposure to a stressor
    d. The body's vulnerability to new stressors during the resistance stage

12. Today, the major causes of death in the United States are

    a. accidents.
    b. infectious diseases.
    c. sexually transmitted diseases.
    d. diseases related to life-style.

13. When Thomas Coates and his colleagues studying AIDS carry out interview studies, they want to gain information that will help them

    a. design interventions at a variety of levels.
    b. determine how effective mass media advertisements are.
    c. motivate AIDS victims to take good care of themselves.
    d. stop people from using intravenous drugs.

Textbook Questions

14. The major improvement of the LES over the SRRS is that the LES

    a.   counts more items as life change events.
    b.   is more student oriented.
    c.   measures the personal significance of events.
    d.   deals with more catastrophic events.

15. Recent research suggests that the high incidence of hypertension among Afro-Americans is a result of

    a.   genetic factors.
    b.   interpersonal conflicts.
    c.   low self-esteem.
    d.   chronic stress.

16. Research showed that there is a relationship between passive smoking in spouses of smokers and

    a.   inflammation of epithelial tissue.
    b.   breast and colon cancer.
    c.   heart disease.
    d.   all of the above.

17. Which of the following activities would a Type-T person prefer?

    a.   A chess game with an excellent player
    b.   Shopping for a whole new wardrobe
    c.   Starting a new business
    d.   Skydiving

18. A "weak spot" in our biological or evolutionary heritage is that we

    a.   have inadequate fight-or-flight responses.
    b.   are not well equipped to deal with psychological stressors.
    c.   produce an insufficient amount of "stress hormones" such as ACTH.
    d.   have problems in primary appraisal.

19. When animals experience severe and prolonged stress, _____ may occur.

    a.   bruxism
    b.   learned helplessness
    c.   Type-T
    d.   hardiness

20. In her study of perceived social support provided to cancer patients, Shelley Taylor found that almost all of the patients rejected support that involved

    a. information or advice.
    b. "just being there."
    c. written messages.
    d. forced cheerfulness.

21. David Spiegel's research with cancer patients demonstrated

    a. early detection is a key to longevity.
    b. control is a key factor in recovery from breast cancer.
    c. improving the ratio of health behaviors compared to illness behaviors increased longevity.
    d. group social and therapeutic support increased longevity.

22. A major study was done in three California towns on methods of persuading people to eliminate poor health habits, like smoking. The most effective method combined a media campaign with

    a. peer pressure.
    b. group therapy.
    c. personal instruction.
    d. medical intervention.

23. HIV kills by

    a. gradually weakening and paralyzing the muscles of the body.
    b. causing cancer in the various organs of the body.
    c. weakening the immune system's resistance to harmful agents.
    d. reducing cortical control over behavior.

24. Susan is increasingly annoyed with the patients and other staff members at the nursing home where she works and also with her husband and children at home. She may be developing what Maslach calls

    a. job burnout.
    b. occupational anxiety.
    c. emotional exhaustion.
    d. Type-A behavior syndrome.

25. Researchers who have evaluated the effect of everyday hassles and stress levels have concluded that

    a.   accumulated small frustrations can result in more stress than a large change.
    b.   catastrophic events are more stressful than everyday hassles.
    c.   there are genetic factors involved in our response to stressors.
    d.   daily hassles have little effect on well-being.

26. Alarm, resistance and exhaustion are all aspects of the

    a.   SRRS.
    b.   LES.
    c.   GAS.
    d.   ACTH.

27. Adrienne is a survivor of a hostage situation in which several people were killed or injured. Ten years have passed since then, but she still has sleep problems, difficulty in concentrating, and an exaggerated startle response. A likely diagnosis here is

    a.   PTSD.
    b.   Type-T personality.
    c.   learned helplessness.
    d.   bruxism.

28. Your great-grandfather can no longer be cared for at home. Several members of your family are evaluating various nursing homes for him. What advice can you offer, based on your readings?

    a.   Choose a place that offers cognitive restructuring therapy.
    b.   Choose a place that offers greater decision and behavior control to the residents.
    c.   Choose a place that offers the most up-to-date medical technology.
    d.   Choose a place that offers a staff that makes almost all the decisions for the residents.

29. HIV is passed from person to person in all of the following ways EXCEPT

    a.   exchange of semen and blood products.
    b.   sharing contaminated needles.
    c.   transfusions of contaminated blood.
    d.   contact with contaminated skin or clothing.

30. Type A behavior syndrome was defined because of the belief that it is a factor in the etiology of

    a.   coronary heart disease.
    b.   peptic ulcers.
    c.   alcoholism.
    d.   unipolar depression.

Questions to Consider

1. How can you help another person cope with stress?

2. How can a voodoo curse cause sudden death?

3. How do defense mechanisms help you deal with stress?

4. How can self-deprecating thoughts and behavior increase stress?

5. How might perfectionism lead to stress?

Optional Activities

1. Sort the following behaviors into two categories: Category A, stress warning signals; and Category B, signs of successful coping. (You may add others from your own experience.)

Indigestion	Ability to sleep
Fatigue	Tolerance for frustration
Loss of appetite	Constipation
Indecision	Overeating
Sense of belonging	Overuse of drugs or alcohol
Sense of humor	Adaptability to change
Irritability	Optimism
Reliability	Cold hands
Sexual problems	Ulcers
Frequent urination	Sleep problems
Migraine headaches	Difficulty concentrating
Boredom	Free-floating anxiety
Temper tantrums	Frequent colds

2. Use the Student Stress Scale on page 475 in *Psychology and Life* to rate the stress in your life. Are you at risk for stress-related problems? Do you need to make your life less stressful? What can you do to reduce the amount of stress in your life?

Additional Resources

Books and Articles

Benson, H., and W. Proctor.(1984). *Beyond the Relaxation Response: How to Harness the Healing Power of Your Personal Beliefs.* New York: Times Books. Further advice on managing stress.

Goldberger, L. & Breznitz, S. (1993). *Handbook of Stress.* 2nd ed. New York: Free Press.

Lazarus, R. (1993, May-June). "Coping Theory and Research: Past, Present and Future," *Psychosomatic Medicine*, 3, 234-247.

Monat, A. & Lazarus, R. (1991). *Stress and Coping.* New York: Columbia University Press.

Ornstein, Robert & Sobel, D.(1987, March).   "The Healing Brain." *Psychology Today* 48. Attitudes about ourselves and others may affect our ability to resist disease.

Rodin, Judith.(1988, December). "A Sense of Control." *Psychology Today,* 311-45. A leading figure in the field of health psychology, Rodin discusses the importance of having a sense of control, in everything from losing weight to being productive in old age.

Seligman, Martin. (1991). *Learned Optimism.* New York: A.A. Knopf.

Selye, Hans.(1956). *The Stress of Life.* New York: McGraw-Hill. Explores the stressors that threaten the physiological function of animals and proposes a "general adaptation syndrome."

Taylor, Shelley. (1991). *Health Psychology.* 2nd ed. New York: McGraw-Hill.

Turk, D., Meichenbaum, D. & Genet, M. (1983). *Pain and Behavioral Medicine.* New York: Guilford.

UNIT 24

IN SPACE, TOWARD PEACE

*It will free man from the remaining chains, the chains
of gravity which still tie him to this planet.*
Wernher von Braun

Unit 24 concentrates on how psychologists from a variety of fields put their knowledge, research skills, and insights to work in space travel, arms negotiation, and peacemaking.

Objectives

After viewing Program 24 and completing the assigned reading, you should be able to:

1 Describe how psychologists try to improve the human condition through the application of social psychological principles to social problems

2. Identify at least three important stress factors for space travelers, and discuss how studying those problems can help people on Earth

3. Define *peace psychology*

4. Describe the key issues of environmental psychology

Reading Assignment

After viewing Program 24, read pages 622-625 in *Psychology and Life*.

Key People and Terms

As you watch the program and read the assignment, pay particular attention to these people and terms. People and terms defined in the text will be found on the given page numbers.

environmental psychology (622)
peace psychology (624)

Irving Janis (624)

The following terms and people are used in Program 24 but are not defined in the text:

applied psychology—the practical application of psychological knowledge and principles to concrete problems

virtual reality—a three-dimensional, alternate reality created by special computer technology in which a person wears a mask and gloves that sense the user's movements and play them back, along with other visual information, into a video screen that wraps around his or her head. Developed by NASA as part of the space program, but currently being popularized in science fiction films as the ultimate escape to a new reality.

Max Bazerman-studies how best use negotiators to resolve conflict

Yvonne Clearwater-studies how confinement and isolation affects astronauts

Patricia Cowings-teaches astronauts how to overcome motion sickness with psychological techniques

Millie Hughes-Fulford-biochemist who studies the physiological and psychological responses to space travel

Scott Fisher-develops virtual interactive environmental work stations

John Mack-former director for Psychological Studies in the Nuclear Age; worked to create awareness of what we do as people engaged in group conflict

Program Summary

In the previous programs, we have seen how psychologists study neurons and hormones, motives and needs, perception and decision making, communication, intelligence, creativity, critical thinking, and stress. In Program 24 we see how psychologists put their insights to work to solve global problems and improve the quality of life for individuals and nations.

Two areas of great interest to applied psychologists today are space travel and peacemaking. Both fields incorporate knowledge gleaned from many areas of study, from behavioral and social psychology to biochemistry and environmental engineering.

As the duration of space travel lengthens and the crews become larger and more diverse, psychologists will play an increasingly important role in addressing the psychological and physiological dimensions of space flight. There are a variety of stressors in space that could cause medical and psychological problems such as anxiety, depression, boredom, loneliness, and hostility. These problems threaten the well-being, morale, and performance of astronauts and future space travelers.

The limitations in space are not as much medical as psychological. Taking into account human reactions to the unique features of space travel, psychologists are helping to design the spacecraft environment and to teach personal and group adjustment strategies. Yvonne Clearwater of NASA provides evidence of the many ways confinement and isolation affect astronauts. There is often a rise in stress hormones, some intellectual impairment, a decline in motivation, an increase in tension and hostility, and social withdrawal.

Another psychologist, Pat Cowings, teaches astronauts how to overcome motion sickness in space using individualized psychological techniques. In a laboratory setting, she uses rotating devices and linear accelerators to make them actually sick. Then she shows them how to control voluntarily specific symptoms, such as heart rate, temperature changes, and blood flow.

In order to create a socially comfortable spacecraft environment, psychologists are working on techniques for overcoming the inevitable distortions of voice, facial expression, and movement that affect interpersonal communication. They are also researching techniques to help space travelers overcome boredom. And with larger, more diversified crews on board, they will need to help solve the problems caused by conflicts in professional status, language styles, even cultural differences.

Just as the psychology of space travel brings together many different disciplines, the study of peace demands the involvement of psychologists, sociologists, political scientists, and others concerned with preventing nuclear war and promoting peace among nations. Research ranges from studies of arms negotiations to how people respond to the possibility of nuclear war.

Psychologist Scott Plous, who has explored the attitudes of American and Soviet leaders, has discovered that both sides are suspicious of the other's intentions. Max Bazerman of Northwestern University explains the problems of negotiation when participants mistrust each other. He explores ways of finding areas of shared self-interest that both sides can agree on.

John Mack specializes in understanding the obstacles to international conflict resolution. At his center, researchers study the psychosocial forces that lead many Soviets and Americans to see each other as demons. No matter what the society, nations portray each other in similar, dehumanizing ways. When each side pictures its enemies as monsters, madmen, or vicious animals to be eradicated, preparing for nuclear war seems reasonable and justified. Researchers are now investigating new strategies for changing how people perceive their traditional enemies.

Review Questions
Program Questions

1. Why is there more concern about psychological factors in space flight now than there was several years ago?

   a. Psychologists' shift toward cognitive science has increased interest in what happens in space.
   b. Longer flights and larger crews make greater psychological demands.
   c. The severe psychological problems of previous astronauts has demonstrated the need for more research.
   d. As funding has become available, psychologists have become interested in doing research.

2. Dr. Millie Hughes-Fulford points out that as part of the preselection process potential astronauts are tested for

   a. anxiety disorders.
   b. antisocial personality disorder.
   c. paraphilias.
   d. claustrophobia.

3. What causes the motion sickness astronauts experience?

   a. The speed at which their craft is moving
   b. The restricted diet they eat
   c. The conflict between vision and position
   d. The rotational pattern in which their craft is orbiting

4. What physical problem has emerged on flights of long duration?

   a. Kidney failure
   b. Hearing loss
   c. Hormone imbalances
   d. Bone loss

5. What effect does living in close quarters have on the likelihood of interpersonal conflict?

   a. The likelihood increases.
   b. The likelihood decreases.
   c. The likelihood does not change.
   d. It depends on the nationality of the crew.

6. What is meant by the term *cocooning?*

    a. Making one's living quarters comfortable

    b. Ignoring the demands of the job to concentrate on oneself

    c. Becoming psychologically adjusted to a new environment

    d. Withdrawing from social contacts by creating private space

7. According to Yvonne Clearwater, the people on the submarine may have spent so much of their time alone because of their need to

    a. reflect on their experiences.

    b. get away from an environment that was too stimulating.

    c. limit the possibility of hostile interactions.

    d. escape into books and other forms of entertainment.

8. What is Pat Cowings's purpose in using rotating rooms and linear accelerators to induce motion sickness?

    a. To select as astronauts those least likely to develop motion sickness

    b. To work with exastronauts who suffer from recurrent motion sickness

    c. To find personality variables that are correlated with developing motion sickness

    d. To train potential astronauts to control their motion sickness

9. According to the program, why are astronauts at risk for sleep disorders?

    a. Their circadian rhythms are out of sync with shipboard time.

    b. Their lack of exercise makes it harder for them to fall asleep.

    c. They must be restrained during sleep.

    d. Inner-ear disturbances from lack of spatial orientation disrupt sleep.

10. Scott Fisher takes us on an imaginary escalator ride using the virtual interactive environment work station. What is the purpose of this device?

    a. To generate images of objects astronauts are working with

    b. To provide recreation in a simulated environment

    c. To calculate designs that fit human measurements

    d. To visualize objects hidden in the darkness of space

11. Imagine you are a crew member on a space mission. How would your voice sound?

    a. Higher in pitch

    b. Lower in pitch

    c. As if you had laryngitis

    d. As if you had a cold

12. The program points out that the Soviet ground control monitors cosmonauts' stress levels through

    a. checking blood hormone levels.
    b. recording interactions between cosmonauts.
    c. measuring performance levels.
    d. analyzing speech patterns.

13. Yvonne Clearwater shows us a mock-up of a crew member's living quarters. What is the purpose of the wall treatment?

    a. To cue spatial orientation
    b. To relieve boredom
    c. To create opportunities for individual choice
    d. To lessen muscle fatigue

14. What does research by Scott Plous on the attitude of Soviet and American leaders suggest?

    a. Each side really wants to take advantage of the other.
    b. Each side realizes that the other wants disarmament.
    c. Each side is suspicious of the other's intentions.
    d. Each side believes the other is trustworthy.

15. Max Bazerman cites the example of the recent progress in negotiations between the United States and the Soviet Union as the result of

    a. breaking out of a zero-sum situation.
    b. escalating the level of conflict.
    c. using psychological principles to promote trust.
    d. giving the "enemy" a more human face.

16. What is the effect of portraying enemies as demons, vermin, liars, and rapists?

    a. It makes us fearful enough to take action.
    b. It dehumanizes them so we can kill them.
    c. It projects our own feelings of shame so we feel better about ourselves.
    d. It makes them seem easier to defeat.

17. According to John Mack, one of the aims of the Center for Psychological Studies in the Nuclear Age is to challenge the norm of

    a. accepting war as inevitable.
    b. seeing the other side as people like ourselves.
    c. viewing conflict as the basis of political life.
    d. blaming the enemy.

Questions to Consider

1. Contrast and compare the contributions of basic research with those of applied research.

2. Organizational and industrial psychologists focus on how individuals and organizations influence each other. One of their interests is increasing the compatibility between people and machines. Many computer companies claim their machines and programs are "user friendly." What does that mean?

3. Can psychological principles and knowledge be applied for evil purposes as well as good?

Optional Activities

1. Collect political cartoons and analyze how individuals, countries, and opposition parties are characterized. Do you see any evidence of stereotyping or dehumanizing?

2. Interview a few people about their attitudes about countries in the news. Ask them to give you two or three adjectives to describe the traits they associate with each. Ask your survey participants how they feel their associations have been shaped. By the media? By experience?

Additional Resources

Books and Articles

Fisher, J. (1984). *Environmental Psychology*. New York: Hold, Rinehart & Winston.

Keen, Sam. (1986). *Faces of the Enemy: Reflections on a Hostile Imagination*. San Francisco, CA: Harper & Row. Images of "the enemy" in many countries and throughout history reveal processes of dehumanization.

Rubin, R. (Ed.) (1991). *Psychology of War and Peace*, New York: Plenum.

Stokols, D.& Altman, J. (Eds.) (1987). *Handbook of Environmental Psychology*. New York: Wiley.

Walsh, H., Craik, K. & Price, R. (1992). *Person-Environment Psychology: Models and Perspectives*. Hillsdale, N.J.: L. Erlbaum Associates.

UNIT 25

A UNION OF OPPOSITES

The closing of a door can bring blessed privacy and comfort—the opening, terror. Conversely, the closing of a door can be a sad and final thing—the opening, a wonderfully joyous moment.

Andy Rooney

Unit 25 reviews the psychological principles, studies, and theories that psychologists use in their quest to solve the puzzle of human nature. This knowledge, organized as a set of complementary opposites, helps us make sense of the many approaches to studying the enormous complexity of behavior.

Objectives—Course Review

1. Outline major subfields in the study of psychology and their areas of emphasis

2. Summarize the history of the major theoretical approaches to psychology

3. Identify important milestones in the history of psychology

4. Describe some of the tools that psychologists use to measure behavior

5. Explain how statistics help psychologists describe what they observe and determine the significance of their findings

Reading Assignment

Review the program summaries for each unit and the chapter summaries from each chapter of *Psychology and Life*.

Key People and Terms

As you reexamine the course material, be sure to review the Key People and Terms in each unit. Key People who are reviewed in Program 25 are noted below.

Rene Baillargeon
Tiffany Field
Howard Gardner
Daniel Kahneman
Joe Martinez
Amos Tversky
Saul Schanberg
B.F. Skinner
Steve Suomi
Sherry Willis

Program Summary

Psychologists are trained people watchers dedicated to understanding how we function and why we think, feel, and act as we do. As scientists, they are trained to challenge their assumptions. They analyze common, everyday experiences such as perception, memory, and language and try to make sense of the infinite variations in our everyday functioning.

Not all psychologists work in the same way or come up with the same results. In fact, many studies seem to contradict each other. Program 25 reviews some of the most significant insights and principles of human nature and animal behavior, organizing the various approaches into complementary opposites. Like the Chinese principles of yin and yang, the psychological opposites are inextricably entwined, each influencing the other.

The most basic pair of opposites is nature versus nurture as determinants of behavior. On the side of nature, our genes and brain chemistry exert constraints of what is possible at a given stage of development. Research has made us increasingly aware that much of our behavior is determined by inherited traits. On the other side, we have environmental influences. Nurture—our physical, cultural, and social environment—can be extraordinarily powerful, affecting not only our perceptions and social roles but also our physical growth and even brain chemistry. Understanding how nature and nurture interact to shape human behavior is one of psychology's most important challenges.

Another task is understanding how the physical and conceptual worlds interact. What we think, feel, and know are all products of the complex activities of billions of nerve cells. Our consciousness emerges from these activities. While the brain can control the mind by altering behavior, the mind can also alter the brain by responding to the environment. There is no dualism of brain versus mind but rather a continual interplay of two inseparable systems.

The principles of learning raise another important question: Are we objects of deterministic forces or creators of our own limitless universe? Is our behavior merely a set of conditioned responses, or are we free to make our own choices? Throughout this series we have seen how the same principles of learning that help us profit from experience allow us to create new realities and free us from behavioral constraints.

One of psychology's most rewarding endeavors has been the study of life-span development. Advances in developmental psychology have shown how precocious babies really are and have revealed the wisdom and previously unrecognized abilities of older people. As a result, we have a more sophisticated view of life as a continuum of new challenges. As a society we are able to overcome the myths about youth and aging and have become more responsive to the needs of people at all stages of life.

Cognitive competence and irrationality are another pair of opposites of great interest, especially to cognitive psychologists. The origins of bad decisions, foolish actions, and irrational beliefs are found within the basic processes of the human intellect that ordinarily works so well for us. Clearly, the power and fallibility of the human mind are two sides of the same coin.

Psychologists have discovered the interplay of opposite roles as we function both as individuals and as members of social groups. In Western culture there is an emphasis on individuality and self-reliance. A person earns praise for initiative and accomplishment but also bears the burden of failure alone. In other cultures the group is more important than any one individual. It offers comfort and social support. But its influence can also lead to intolerance and rigid conformity.

Psychologists strive to understand the balance of human needs and the influence of situational forces that can cause us to be gregarious or shy, independent or conforming, selfish or altruistic.

Review Questions

Note: Review Questions for Units 25 and 26 are provided in Unit 26.

Questions to Consider

Note: Because these questions are open-ended and require answers based on your own experience and personal opinions, an answer key has not been included in the Appendix.

1. Apply the nature–nurture dynamic to your own development. In what ways can you contribute to your future identity?

2. Why study human behavior? Why look for understanding and insight into the sources of your own beliefs, motives, and behaviors? Compare your ideas to those expressed in the paragraph below.

For the self-renewing man the development of his own potentialities and the process of self-discovery never end. It is a sad but unarguable fact that most human beings go through their lives only partially aware of the full range of their abilities. As a boy in California I spent a good deal of time in the Mother Lode country, and like every boy of my age I listened raptly to the tales told by the old-time prospectors in that area, some of them veterans of the Klondike gold rush. Every one of them had at least one good campfire story of a lost gold mine. The details varied: the original discoverer had died in the mine, or had gone crazy, or had been killed in a shooting scrape, or had just walked off thinking the mine worthless. But the central theme was constant: riches left untapped. I have come to believe that those tales offer a paradigm of education as most of us experience it. The mine is worked for a little while and the abandoned. (From John W. Gardner, *Self-Renewal*. New York: Harper & Row, 1983, p. 10.)

3. One of the goals of *Discovering Psychology* is to increase our understanding and tolerance of the behavior of others. How can you know whether you have achieved that goal? One way might be to think about the judgments you make about individual differences and the behavior of others. Read the following excerpt from *On Becoming a Person* by Carl R. Rogers (Boston: Houghton Mifflin Sentry Edition, 1961), which suggests that understanding and tolerance come from eliminating those automatic judgments. What other questions might you ask yourself? As you read, consider the contribution that humanism has made to psychology and its impact on society.

Our first reaction to most of the statements which we hear from other people is an immediate evaluation, or judgment, rather than an understanding of it. When someone expresses some feeling or attitude or belief, our tendency is, almost immediately, to feel "That's right" or "That's stupid"; "That's abnormal"; "That's unreasonable"; "That's incorrect"; "That's not nice." Very rarely do we permit ourselves to understand precisely what the meaning of the statement is to him.

I have found that to truly accept another person and his feelings is by no means an easy thing, any more than is understanding. Can I really permit another person to feel hostile toward me? Can I accept his anger as a real and legitimate part of himself? Can I accept him when he views life and its problems in a way quite different from mine? (p. 18)

Optional Activities

1. Identify and analyze the strategies used in a specific political election or an advertising campaign. Does understanding techniques of influence weaken some of their persuasive power? Why or why not?

2. Imagine that you had the chance to live the last 10 years of your life over again. What would you do differently? What different choices would you have made? Discuss how your identity would be different as a result.

UNIT 26

NEW DIRECTIONS

*There's only one corner of the universe you can be
certain of improving, and that's your own self.*

Aldous Huxley

Where is psychology headed? In Unit 26, leading theorists and researchers in many areas of psychology predict future directions for psychological research, theory, and application.

Objectives

After viewing the television program, you should be able to:

1. Describe possible new directions in psychological research

2. Suggest ways in which cognitive science will influence other areas of psychology

3. Describe how new approaches to individual assessment will influence education

4. Discuss the implications of turning from the old emphasis on abnormality and therapy to a new psychology based on a model of health and prevention

5. Cite evidence that psychology can help solve some of society's most perplexing problems and cite evidence to the contrary

Reading Assignment

There is no textbook reading for this unit.

Key People and Terms

As you reexamine the course material, be sure to review the Key People and Terms in each unit. Key People who are reviewed in Program 26 are listed below.

Teresa Amabile
W. Curtis Banks
Jean Berko Gleason
Howard Gardner
E. Roy John
F.W. Putnam
Judith Rodin
David Rosenhan
Martin Seligman
B.F. Skinner
Dan Slobin
Steve Suomi
Richard Thompson

Program Summary

The goals of today's psychological researchers are very much the same as those of their predecessors. Unit 26 presents the views of some of the leading psychologists who are engaged in the effort to explain human nature and behavior. They were asked to speculate on where the field of psychology is headed.

The leading cognitive psychologist Howard Gardner sees increased specialization in the future. He believes that researchers will branch off into areas such as cognitive science and neuroscience, while other psychologists will merge with philosophy, sociology, anthropology, and other disciplines.

Psycholinguist Jean Berko Gleason speculates that psychology will become less fragmented because humans can only be understood as complex systems. Researchers must take into consideration the interactive effects of all the physical and social systems—family, cognitive development, language, sex roles, and so on. In agreement with Gleason, Steven Suomi sees fewer barriers between specific areas and predicts the growing integration of interests.

Richard Thompson anticipates an increased emphasis on the brain. Researchers will not only study the physiology of the brain but will also look at behavior, awareness, and consciousness as expressions of the brain itself. He foresees the increasing overlap of brain science, psychology, and artificial intelligence.

No one model of psychology will dominate the future, predicts Dan Slobin. He points out that psychological research is going on all over the world at hundreds of universities and on all levels. Increased cross-fertilization of ideas and methodologies will likely result.

Behaviorist B. F. Skinner deplores the growth of cognitive psychology, claiming that it will not help us explain anything about the behaving organism. He believes that in forsaking observable behavior in favor of metapsychology, intention, and mental processes, psychology is going down the wrong path.

F. W. Putman, an expert on multiple personality, suggests that there are expanded ways of defining behavioral and mental disorders. He contrasts the concept of the "unified self" with the concept of "separate selves."

Stanford psychologist David Rosenhan sees an increasing sensitivity to the effects of the social environment on individual behavior. This will have implications for how we understand behavior, perception, and judgment.

Teresa Amabile favors a more personal, inward-looking approach that combines cognitive and emotional areas of psychology.

The computer has offered psychology new tools for studying behavior and has also created new areas of interest. E. Roy John discusses how new measurement techniques will contribute original information about the brain and behavior. Jean Berko Gleason points out how computers have provided access to enormous data banks that have revolutionized the amount of information researchers can tap.

Dan Slobin sees increased interest in individual patterns of behavior and styles of learning. Explaining how the complex human machine has such amazing flexibility in response to the environment will be one of the next big challenges in the field.

Testing expert Curtis Banks believes that psychology should assess individuals in more narrow contexts. He points out that individuals within groups, such as blacks or women, must be conceptualized, assessed, and understood on different terms.

A number of psychologists were also asked how psychology will change or improve the quality of life in the future. Judith Rodin predicts an intense collaboration between the geneticists and the environmentalists as the importance of the interaction between biology and environment becomes increasingly recognized.

Martin Seligman contrasts the bywords of the past, "illness and therapy," with those of the future, "health and prevention." The new model will be based on helping people to fulfill their potential. But B. F. Skinner doubts that psychological knowledge will be enough to prevent disasters such as global pollution or nuclear holocaust.

In conclusion, *Discovering Psychology's* host Philip Zimbardo declares his optimism about the future, believing that psychology will help alleviate and even prevent some problems. But he stresses that it must be a new psychology that includes social, economic, and political realities. The psychology of the future must incorporate many complex, interacting factors and go beyond the traditional focus on individual actions and mental processes.

Review Questions

Course Review

1. What is the basic goal of psychology?

    a. To improve human nature by understanding its strengths and weaknesses
    b. To integrate biological and sociological knowledge to form a complete picture of the individual
    c. To determine the relative roles of nature and nurture in shaping a person
    d. To describe, explain, predict, and control behavior

2. In Steven Suomi's work on shyness in monkeys, what seems to be the basis of shyness?

    a. Traumatic experiences in early life
    b. A genetic predisposition
    c. Inadequate mothering
    d. Biological weakness due to prematurity

3. Research on the mother's touch in baby rats has shown that

    a. the need for touch is brain based.
    b. maternal touch is helpful but not essential to development.
    c. sex differences exist in the need for touch.
    d. baby rats use behaviors that trigger maternal touch.

4. Imagine you were studying the biological basis of remembering and forgetting. You would be especially interested in the chemical substances called

    a. androgens.
    b. steroids.
    c. fatty acids.
    d. neurotransmitters.

5. In a perfume ad, a product becomes associated with positive stimuli. This process is most comparable to

    a. classical conditioning.
    b. operant conditioning.
    c. reasoning by representativeness.
    d. consensual validation.

6. How have recent advances in developmental psychology changed the way we view babies?

    a. We now see them as more vulnerable to environmental hazards.
    b. We understand their adherence to a biologically determined timetable.
    c. We realize their need for attachment to a single, full-time caretaker.
    d. We recognize their strengths in understanding their worlds.

7. Imagine that in 1992 you are a graduate student in psychology involved in studies of intelligence. You would be likely to base your work on the idea that

    a. an IQ test provides a valid measure of intelligence.
    b. intelligence is determined solely by environmental factors.
    c. there are actually multiple intelligences.
    d. cognitive bias keeps people from manifesting their true intelligence.

8. You would be most likely to rely on the research of Amos Tversky and Daniel Kahneman if you were investigating

    a. why people were suddenly worried about the greenhouse effect.
    b. how childhood abuse led to adult personality disorders.
    c. under what conditions bystanders would help a victim.
    d. at what age children developed the idea of object permanence.

9. What fundamental assumption of Western culture profoundly affects how we assign responsibility?

    a. Situations alter our perceptions.
    b. Each individual determines his or her own fate.
    c. Human nature is fundamentally aggressive.
    d. The mind controls the body.

10. Psychological research suggests that when a person is isolated, then he or she

    a. achieves greater mastery of the environment.
    b. becomes more actively involved in seeking personal fulfillment.
    c. is at risk of developing mental and physical disorders.
    d. ceases to function normally.

11. When William James published *Principles of Psychology* in 1890, his vision of the future of psychology was one in which

    a. only the observable would be investigated.
    b. a synthesis of knowledge would be investigated.
    c. therapy would be based on psychodynamic theory.
    d. the application of psychological knowledge would improve human lives.

12. Most psychologists seem ready to welcome cognitive studies as part of their discipline. Someone who actually deplores this development is

    a. F. W. Putman.
    b. B. F. Skinner.
    c. Dan Slobin.
    d. Richard Thompson.

13. Testing is likely to change over the next decade by becoming more concerned with

    a. ranking individuals for selection purposes.
    b. assessing individual strengths and weaknesses.
    c. comparing characteristics of different population groups.
    d. developing tests for college admission.

14. According to Martin Seligman, who has studied explanatory style, psychology can contribute greatly to human well-being by shifting to a model that emphasizes

    a. Freudian psychodynamics.
    b. behavioral management.
    c. social context rather than individual responsibility.
    d. prevention rather than therapy.

15. Psychologists today have very different approaches to what to study and how. When, in the history of psychology, did such differences first appear?

    a. They have been present since the beginning.
    b. They arose in the 1920s.
    c. They arose in the 1950s.
    d. They are a very recent development.

16. Why would an experimenter employ a double-blind procedure?

    a. To keep the placebo effect from occurring
    b. To check the accuracy of measurements
    c. To make results easier to replicate
    d. To avoid biasing the results

17. Imagine that you read about a survey of American plumbers which suggested that most had very negative attitudes toward children. What question should you ask about the research?

    a. Did the people surveyed understand the questions?
    b. Was the sample representative of the population?
    c. Was there a cause-effect relationship or just a correlation?
    d. Was the placebo effect at work?

18. The two hemispheres of the brain are connected by the

   a. cerebral cortex.
   b. hippocampus.
   c. pons.
   d. corpus callosum.

19. Runners and other athletes report experiencing a natural "high" that elevates mood and decreases perception of pain. This effect is caused by a category of neurotransmitters called

   a. corticosteroids.
   b. endorphins.
   c. androgens.
   d. stimulants.

20. The modern world is full of stress, and stress is known to harm health. Michael Meany has shown that young rats cope with stress better if they have

   a. been raised on a low-fat diet.
   b. mothers who were subjected to high stress levels in pregnancy.
   c. had regular handling as newborns.
   d. environments that are enriched.

21. Which of the following ways of studying the brain and behavior is most clearly a field study?

   a. Studies of brain wave patterns of people in different countries
   b. Studies of people in REM and non-REM sleep
   c. Studies of grafts of fetal brain tissue
   d. Studies relating social rank and health in baboon colonies

22. Imagine you are the parent of a shy young child. If you asked Jerome Kagan, who has done extensive work on shyness in children, he would probably tell you,

   a. "Children are born shy or bold, and nothing can change it."
   b. "Shyness is a stage most children go through, so don't worry about it."
   c. "Shyness is genetic, but it can be modified by sensitive parenting."
   d. "Children learn shyness from parents, so the parents must overcome it first themselves."

23. How is Piaget's theory of development most like Erikson's?

   a. Both theories cover the entire life span.
   b. Both theories set up a series of stages.
   c. Both theories concentrate on cognitive growth.
   d. Both theories were based mainly on research with male subjects.

24. If language development is considered in the light of the nature-nurture debate, then the evidence suggests that the growth of language competence depends

    a. mainly on the maturation of the brain and the muscles in the mouth and tongue.
    b. mainly on the language acquisition device that children are born with.
    c. primarily on the interaction with parents and other caregivers.
    d. on the interplay of biological and environmental factors.

25. What is the main reason that psychologists study perceptual illusions?

    a. To learn how normal perception works
    b. To help people correct the errors that they make
    c. To analyze the difference between "top-down" and "bottom-up" processing
    d. To study the relation between sensation and perception

26. What does the term *habituation* mean?

    a. The development of a behavior pattern that is applied in different situations
    b. A decrease in responding when a stimulus is presented repeatedly
    c. A false sensory perception produced by a variety of conditions, including mental disorders, brain diseases, and some drugs
    d. A cognitive strategy used as a shortcut in solving a complex inferential task

27. What is a fundamental tenet of the behaviorist approach in psychology?

    a. Cognition is the key causal factor in behavior.
    b. Unconscious drives provide the motivational energy for behavior.
    c. Behavior can be explained by understanding brain processes.
    d. Behavior is determined by conditions in the environment.

28. B. F. Skinner developed the Skinner box to study behavior that was based on

    a. classical conditioning.
    b. social learning.
    c. operant conditioning.
    d. trial-and-error learning.

29. Current ideas of memory are based on an analogy that compares the mind to

    a. a computer.
    b. an electromagnet.
    c. a hydraulic machine.
    d. a steam engine.

30. Robin is a subject in an experiment on short-term memory. If she wants to remember more items, what should she do?

    a. There is nothing she can do, since short-term memory can contain only seven items.
    b. She should visualize the name of each item.
    c. She should chunk items together in a way she finds meaningful.
    d. She should rely on procedural memory rather than semantic memory.

31. When we hear a word like "prom," we can easily imagine what people will wear and do. This cluster of knowledge is an example of

    a. an engram.
    b. an evoked potential.
    c. a heuristic.
    d. a schema.

32. Lorraine feels annoyed with herself for agreeing to go out with somebody she doesn't really like. But when she does go out, she finds she likes the person much better. This result might well be predicted by the theory of

    a. cognitive dissonance.
    b. the self-fulfilling prophecy.
    c. the availability heuristic.
    d. psychic numbing.

33. Carl Rogers and Abraham Maslow are thinkers in the humanistic tradition in psychology. What did they see as the motivation underlying human action?

    a. People seek pleasure and avoid pain.
    b. People are motivated by sexual and aggressive desires hidden from conscious awareness.
    c. People try to fulfill their potential.
    d. People follow fixed action patterns in response to environmental forces.

34. Your friend Carlotta tells you that she never dreams. Based on your knowledge of dream research, what would you tell her?

    a. She must be under so much stress that she doesn't dream.
    b. Everybody dreams several times a night, but not everybody remembers his or her dreams.
    c. The latent content in her dreams must be very threatening to make her forget her dreams.
    d. She is perfectly normal because a certain percentage of the population doesn't dream.

35. How is hypnosis like multiple personality disorder?
    a. Both involve dissociation.
    b. Both are caused by an outside agent acting on the individual.
    c. Both alter the perception of physical reality.
    d. Both are more likely to occur in introverted people.

36. Which theory of personality emphasizes the role of early experience and the importance of the unconscious?

    a. Freudian
    b. Cognitive
    c. Humanistic
    d. Behaviorist

37. Imagine that you are a school principal who wants to help students become more creative. What would tend to promote that goal?

    a. Having creativity contests where the best entries get prizes
    b. Emphasizing freedom in creative work
    c. Having students use models of great works to copy from
    d. Arranging students into "Jigsaw Classrooms"

38. A researcher is concerned about the reliability of one of the measurements she is using in her work. This means she is concerned that the instrument

    a. gives consistent scores.
    b. is not biased against certain population groups.
    c. measures what it is supposed to.
    d. has been standardized on an appropriate population.

39. How does the masculine gender role in the United States affect the health of American men?

    a. Positively, by encouraging good health practices
    b. Positively, by stressing the importance of physical well-being
    c. Negatively, by emphasizing feelings and thus leading to depression
    d. Negatively, by encouraging behaviors that put men at risk for diseases and accidents

40. What life crisis does Erikson see as occurring at the end of the life cycle?

    a. Initiative versus guilt
    b. Ego-integrity versus despair
    c. Intimacy versus isolation
    d. Generativity versus stagnation

41. Zelda has little patience with people who feel depressed. She believes the depression is their own fault for giving in to their feelings. This way of thinking can be termed

    a. the stereotype effect.
    b. reasoning by representativeness.
    c. the fundamental attribution error.
    d. cognitive appraisal.

42. In general, how does being anonymous change people's behavior?

   a. They behave in more antisocial ways.
   b. They are less likely to conform to group pressure.
   c. They act in ways that tend to individuate them.
   d. They are more likely to behave altruistically.

43. Models of mental disorder that emphasize an individual's perceptions and interpretations of experience are called

   a. biologically oriented models.
   b. psychodynamic models.
   c. behaviorist models.
   d. cognitive models.

44. Vincent Van Gogh's paintings reflect the fact that he suffered from manic-depressive disorder. How would he probably be treated for this disorder today?

   a. Through psychosurgery
   b. With lithium
   c. With psychoanalysis
   d. Through group therapy

45. What is the basic principle underlying biofeedback?

   a. The body's response to stress is to fight or flee.
   b. Medical problems can have psychological origins.
   c. The mind can learn to control biological functions.
   d. Optimism and pessimism influence the response to stress.

Questions to Consider

Note: These questions are designed to promote personal reflection and speculation. Because there are no right or wrong answers, an answer key has not been included in the Appendix.

1. Who will you be in the year 2000? Describe yourself. What personal, family, social, and cultural changes do you anticipate? How will the work of psychologists affect you?

2. If you had the power to distribute $10 million in research grants, what three areas of psychology would be highest on your list of possible recipients? Why?

3. Are human beings responsible for their behavior? Or are they victims of environment, their personal history, or biological determinants? Consider what psychologists and psychiatrists can contribute to our understanding of criminal behavior. Does the "psychologizing" of American culture complicate the judicial process? How might the "new psychology' influence the value of

expert testimony? What would B. F. Skinner say about the ability of psychologists to testify about what a defendant was thinking?

4. If Martin Seligman is correct, the future of psychology will increasingly include efforts to prevent psychological problems and enhance human potential. How will this work be carried out? Who should decide who needs preventive intervention?

5. Management consultant Peter Drucker has raised questions about the legal and ethical basis of requiring corporate employees to attend psychologically oriented seminars *(Wall Street Journal,* February 9, 1989). His concerns also apply to schools and other settings in which participants are involved in training and educational programs. How can students and employees be protected against involuntary participation? How would you feel if you were required to attend a personal growth group as a condition of passing this course?

Optional Activities

1. Observe children in a kindergarten classroom, shoppers in a store, students taking an examination, or people standing in line outside a theater. Make a list of questions that illustrate the different types of behavior of interest to psychologists. Compare your questions with those you generated for activities in previous units. Do they reflect a more sophisticated awareness of the internal and external determinants of behavior?

2. Choose one of your personal habits or typical behaviors. Speculate how psychologists from different areas of psychology might describe and explain it.

Additional Resources

Books and Articles

The following readings touch upon current issues in psychology or speculate about the future of the field.

Drexler, Madeline. (1988, October 3). The Couch and the Courtroom. *Boston Globe Magazine,* 72-73. Drexler looks at how psychiatrists are used to provide expert testimony in the courtroom.

Drucker, Peter F. (1989, February 9) New Age Sessions Are Same Old Brainwashing. *Wall Street Journal*, A22. Drucker describes potential abuses of preventive psychology and personal growth programs.

Gazzaniga, Michael.(1988). *Mind Matters: How Brain and Mind Interact to Create Our Conscious Lives.* Boston: Houghton Mifflin. Insights from the field of neuropsychology can help us better understand the nature of consciousness.

Hurley, Dan. (1988, January). Getting Help from Helping. *Psychology Today,* 62-67. Mutual-help groups such as Alcoholics Anonymous have been around for years, but mental health professionals have only recently recognized and studied their programs of therapy. More professionals are now contributing to these organizations, and the groups themselves are growing rapidly.

Miller, L. (1994, Spring). Biofeedback and Behavioral Medicine: Treating the Symptoms, the Syndrome, and the Person. *Psychotherapy,* 31, 1, 161-169.

Miller, L. (1993, Spring). Psychotherapeutic Approaches to Chronic Pain. *Psychotherapy,* 30, 1, 115-124.

Puckett, Sam B. (1988, January). When a Worker Gets AIDS. *Psychology Today,* 26-27. Misconceptions and anxiety about AIDS can lead to panic at the workplace when a worker is infected with the HIV virus. Although a cure for the disease has not yet been found, education can help managers and workers work together in preventing such fear and panic.

Roberts, M., and T. G. Harris.(1989, May). Wellness at Work: How Corporations Help Employees Fight Stress and Stay Healthy. *Psychology Today,* 54-58. In providing fitness plans and structuring other ways to reduce stress on the job, employers help workers stay healthy . . . and productive. This new trend may have been influenced by the insights of health psychology.

APPENDIX

ANSWER KEY: REVIEW QUESTIONS

Unit 1

1 c	6 d	11 d	16 d	21 a	26 c
2 b	7 b	12 c	17 a	22 c	27 d
3 a	8 b	13 c	18 a	23 c	28 d
4 c	9 b	14 c	19 a	24 b	29 a
5 b	10 a	15 b	20 b	25 d	30 b

Unit 2

1 a	6 b	11 b	16 c	21 c	26 d
2 c	7 a	12 c	17 c	22 c	27 a
3 b	8 d	13 c	18 c	23 b	28 b
4 b	9 a	14 c	19 b	24 a	29 a
5 d	10 c	15 b	20 d	25 c	30 a

Unit 3/4

1 d	6 c	11 a	16 d	21 b	26 b
2 a	7 b	12 d	17 a	22 b	27 d
3 b	8 b	13 a	18 c	23 b	28 a
4 c	9 a	14 b	19 b	24 b	29 b
5 c	10 c	15 c	20 b	25 a	30 b

31 d	36 d	41 b
32 a	37 b	42 d
33 a	38 d	43 b
34 a	39 b	44 c
35 d	40 a	45 d

Unit 5

1 b	6 d	11 d	16 d	21 b	26 c
2 a	7 b	12 a	17 d	22 c	27 d
3 c	8 a	13 b	18 b	23 c	28 d
4 d	9 d	14 d	19 d	24 a	29 b
5 c	10 c	15 c	20 b	25 a	30 a

Unit 6

1 c	6 b	11 b	16 a	21 b	26 c
2 d	7 c	12 a	17 c	22 d	
3 b	8 d	13 c	18 d	23 b	
4 a	9 a	14 d	19 b	24 d	
5 b	10 a	15 c	20 d	25 c	

Unit 7

1 d	6 a	11 b	16 d	21 b	26 a
2 c	7 a	12 c	17 a	22 d	27 c
3 c	8 a	13 d	18 b	23 d	28 a
4 a	9 c	14 a	19 a	24 d	29 c
5 d	10 c	15 a	20 d	25 b	30 d

31 a	36 a	41 d
32 c	37 c	42 b
33 b	38 d	
34 a	39 a	
35 a	40 b	

Unit 8

1 b	6 c	11 b	16 b	21 d	26 d
2 d	7 c	12 d	17 c	22 b	27 b
3 d	8 a	13 c	18 c	23 a	28 d
4 a	9 d	14 c	19 a	24 d	29 c
5 b	10 c	15 c	20 b	25 c	30 d

Unit 9

1 d	6 a	11 c	16 b	21 c	26 c
2 c	7 b	12 d	17 d	22 d	27 d
3 b	8 a	13 d	18 a	23 a	28 c
4 b	9 b	14 d	19 a	24 a	29 b
5 d	10 b	15 a	20 d	25 c	30 b

Unit 10/11

1 d	6 c	11 b	16 d	21 c	26 a
2 c	7 a	12 d	17 d	22 a	27 b
3 b	8 c	13 b	18 b	23 c	28 d
4 a	9 a	14 a	19 d	24 d	29 b
5 b	10 c	15 c	20 b	25 b	30 d

31 b	36 a	41 b
32 b	37 a	42 a
33 c	38 c	43 c
34 a	39 d	44 d
35 c	40 d	45 b

Unit 12

1 d	6 c	11 a	16 b	21 c	26 b
2 b	7 c	12 b	17 b	22 a	27 c
3 b	8 a	13 c	18 b	23 c	28 d
4 c	9 d	14 d	19 d	24 d	29 a
5 a	10 b	15 c	20 d	25 a	30 b

Unit 13/14

1 c	6 b	11 a	16 d	21 d	26 c
2 b	7 c	12 b	17 b	22 b	27 a
3 d	8 b	13 a	18 c	23 c	28 d
4 b	9 b	14 d	19 a	24 c	29 c
5 a	10 b	15 a	20 a	25 b	30 b

31 b	36 a	41 b
32 d	37 b	42 c
33 b	38 b	43 c
34 a	39 d	44 c
35 b	40 d	45 d

Unit 15

1 c	6 d	11 a	16 d	21 c	26 c
2 b	7 d	12 b	17 c	22 b	27 d
3 a	8 b	13 a	18 c	23 c	28 b
4 b	9 c	14 a	19 c	24 d	29 c
5 a	10 b	15 a	20 a	25 c	30 a

Unit 16

1 b	6 c	11 c	16 c	21 a	26 a
2 d	7 b	12 c	17 a	22 a	27 c
3 a	8 d	13 c	18 b	23 d	28 c
4 c	9 c	14 a	19 b	24 a	29 d
5 d	10 b	15 b	20 b	25 d	30 b

Unit 17

1 d	6 a	11 c	16 d	21 b
2 b	7 d	12 a	17 c	22 c
3 a	8 c	13 d	18 d	23 a
4 b	9 c	14 b	19 a	24 b
5 c	10 a	15 d	20 a	25 c

Unit 18

1 c	6 d	11 a	16 b	21 b
2 d	7 a	12 a	17 b	22 b
3 b	8 c	13 a	18 a	23 b
4 a	9 d	14 c	19 b	24 c
5 b	10 b	15 b	20 c	25 b

Units 19/20

1 a	6 a	11 b	16 b	21 a	26 c
2 c	7 c	12 c	17 c	22 a	27 d
3 d	8 d	13 c	18 b	23 d	28 c
4 a	9 c	14 d	19 a	24 a	29 a
5 b	10 a	15 a	20 d	25 d	30 d

31 b	36 d	41 d
32 d	37 c	42 b
33 a	38 b	43 c
34 b	39 b	44 d
35 c	40 b	45 b

Unit 21

1 d	6 b	11 d	16 a	21 c	26 d
2 b	7 c	12 b	17 a	22 a	27 b
3 b	8 a	13 c	18 b	23 d	28 a
4 d	9 d	14 c	19 a	24 a	29 a
5 a	10 b	15 b	20 d	25 a	30 a

Unit 22

1 c	6 b	11 a	16 b	21 c	26 d
2 a	7 d	12 c	17 d	22 a	27 c
3 d	8 c	13 b	18 b	23 b	28 a
4 b	9 c	14 d	19 b	24 a	29 d
5 a	10 d	15 d	20 c	25 d	30 c

Unit 23

1 c	6 c	11 b	16 c	21 d	26 c
2 b	7 a	12 d	17 d	22 c	27 a
3 d	8 b	13 a	18 b	23 c	28 b
4 b	9 c	14 c	19 b	24 a	29 d
5 d	10 d	15 a	20 d	25 a	30 a

Unit 24

1 b	6 d	11 a	16 b
2 d	7 c	12 d	17 d
3 c	8 d	13 a	
4 d	9 a	14 c	
5 a	10 b	15 a	

Units 25/26 — Course Review

1 d	6 d	11 b	16 d	21 d	26 b
2 b	7 c	12 b	17 b	22 c	27 d
3 a	8 a	13 b	18 d	23 b	28 c
4 d	9 b	14 d	19 b	24 d	29 a
5 a	10 c	15 a	20 c	25 a	30 c

31 d	36 a	41 c
32 a	37 b	42 a
33 c	38 a	43 d
34 b	39 d	44 b
35 a	40 b	45 c

ANSWER KEY: QUESTIONS TO CONSIDER

Note: There are not always clear-cut right or wrong answers to these questions, but it may be helpful for students to compare their ideas to the ideas provided in this Answer Key.

Unit 1. Past, Present, and Promise

1. The fundamental issues of psychology include the relationship of mind and body; the role of heredity and environment in determining personality and behavior; the role of the conscious and the unconscious in determining behavior; the influence of individual dispositional and external social and situational forces in behavior; the influence of early experience on later life; and the significance of individual differences and similarities.

2. Many people are not aware of the many different kinds of work that psychologists do. A popular stereotype is that of the slightly nutty Freudian-style analyst depicted in popular movies of the 1930s and 1940s. As you will learn, the treatment of mental illness is only one part of psychology. Psychologists are scientists who can also help people teach more effectively and learn more efficiently. They help people improve their physical and emotional well-being, enhance communication, find the right job, quit smoking, make decisions, improve social relations, understand child development, promote world peace, and fight poverty and prejudice.

3. The media are rifled with claims, myths, and biased conclusions. We need to be open-minded but skeptical of what we read or see on television. We need to learn how to evaluate the validity of claims and enhance our sensitivity to sources of bias. Our understanding of human behavior influences the decisions we make as learners, consumers, voters, policymakers, friends, and parents.

4. Observer bias influences our choices about what is relevant and what isn't. Our values, interests, and expectations can even influence our perceptions, leading us to see things that are not there and overlook things that are.

5. Thinking (perceiving, remembering, imagining) is now an accepted focus of psychological study. There have been various approaches to studying thinking behavior. Subjects are asked to think out loud while solving problems or to report their reactions to internal or external events. Mental processes can also be inferred from such measurable behaviors as reaction times in decision making, problem-solving strategies, changes in brain waves or eye movements, body language, and speech patterns.

Unit 2. Understanding Research

1. For every person who is supposedly healed, there are many more who are not. Faith healing is big business, and desperate people are purposely deceived in money-making scams. The sick not only lose money to faith healers for empty promises, but they may not follow proven medical treatments that might help them.

2. The results of being graded on a curve depend on how the test is constructed, what percentage of the students do well, and whether you perform at the top of the class or are an average student. The distribution of scores around the mean would have different impacts on the A student and the C student.

3. Objections to the study of mental processes (dreams, judgment, perceptions) include the claim that they rely on self-reports, are too personal, and cannot be verified. Because mental events cannot be observed directly, they are difficult to study scientifically. But psychologists believe that by defining terms carefully, they can draw inferences from measurable behaviors. Personal experiences such as sensations, emotions, and reactions to internal and external events can be inferred from changes in heart rate, brain waves, eye movements, speech patterns, and body language—all of which can be measured.

4. The subject matter, human beings and their behavior, is very complicated and variable. The behaviors change from day to day and from situation to situation. No two people are exactly alike. In addition, virtually every behavior has multiple causes.

5. A person's subjective experience of illness or pain is difficult to measure objectively. Not all drugs work for all patients. A person can still feel ill even when all measurable indicators of illness (fever, tumor, and so forth) are gone.

6. Scientists use animal subjects to conduct research that cannot be done with humans. When research includes harming animals, it creates ethical dilemmas. You might consider an experiment justified if its findings were of direct benefit to humans. The APA's guidelines represent an attempt to prevent mistreatment and to inform the public of its professional standards.

7. People who volunteer are a self-selected group; they are not representative of the general population. Volunteers may be less inhibited or more strongly opinionated about a particular topic. For example, the results of a magazine survey may depend on a group of readers with specific characteristics not represented in the general population.

Unit 3. The Behaving Brain

1. If we know what causes a problem, we can avoid spending a lot of time and money on useless treatments. Even though many conditions are not correctable, knowing the cause gives us a sense of control. For example, some drugs are used to treat depressed and schizophrenic patients.

Sometimes the doctors don't even know why the drugs have the desired effect. Nevertheless, these drugs clearly relieve the patient's symptoms.

2. Although early research by Delgado and others showed that electrical stimulation of the brain could produce certain results, such as initiating or inhibiting aggressive behavior, the explanation for its effects has been questioned by other research. Elliot Valenstein's analysis points out that repeated stimulation to the same spot may not predictably elicit the same feeling or action. Although electrical stimulation has been used to relieve cancer patients of pain by blocking messages in the spinal cord, most doctors consider electrode implants too radical a treatment for healthy patients with weight problems.

3. There are many unknowns in the complex chemical system in the body. And there are many side effects or long-term consequences of taking megadoses of vitamins, hormones, home remedies, folk medicines, and self-treatments. Many people believe that if a little is good, more is better. They do not understand the toxic properties of some substances. These claims are characteristic of overly simplistic approaches to complex problems and may do more harm than good. Consumers should be very skeptical about advertisements that promote these products or claim miracle cures.

4. Techniques such as the EEG, CAT, MRI, and PET provide information that can be used to help distinguish between normal and abnormal brain structures and functions. The process of mapping or imaging the brain promises to help identify the chemical or structural abnormalities underlying such problems as Alzheimer's disease, schizophrenia, learning disabilities, and depression.

Unit 4. The Responsive Brain

1. Does an athlete who takes steroids have an unfair advantage over his or her competitors? Most organizations and competitions prohibit competitors from taking drugs to enhance performance. In noncompetitive situations, the issue of taking drugs should involve consideration of the unintended side effects or the individual's long-term health effects.

2. For premature infants, sessions that included touching and movement stimulation caused significant weight gain and advances in organized behavior over the control group of premature infants. You might conclude that in general, infants receiving a lot of contact and stimulation would be more advanced physically, perhaps healthier, and more alert than low-touch infants. (However, there are many other factors that influence later development.) Observation studies of people in different cultures have suggested that some European cultures are more demonstrative and more expressive than that of Americans, for example. You might assume that high-touch families would create more expressive individuals.

3. You may be able to cite specific examples of how circumstances interact with biological variables to enhance or detract from a person's life. For example, research has shown that an attractive person is more likely to be hired for certain jobs. Tall people and first-borns tend to be more successful than shorter people and those in different birth positions. Healthy people may be more

active (which often leads to a healthier pattern of exercise) than people with chronic or serious health problems (which may lead to inactivity).

4. Federal and state governments sponsor many nutrition programs as well as drug and alcohol prevention, treatment, and education programs. In some states legislation has been proposed that would regulate a pregnant woman's behavior if it were judged dangerous to the fetus.

Unit 5. The Developing Child

1. The trait of boldness is expressed differently by each individual. Its advantages or disadvantages depend on the extent of the trait and the context in which it is expressed. In most situations, boldness is influenced by social expectations about appropriate gender-related behavior. For a girl, boldness may have a negative connotation, while the same behavior in a boy might be considered masculine or attractive.

2. Watson was devoted to behaviorism. He possessed a rather cold, objective view of the child, emphasized shaping and training, and discounted the importance of inherited traits and personality. Gesell emphasized that development depended on maturation. He contended that there was no point in training children or trying to speed up learning because they couldn't learn until they were biologically ready.

3. Lack of knowledge or inappropriate expectations can cause unnecessary frustration and misunderstanding. Some child abuse may be related to unrealistic expectations, especially in toilet training and bed-wetting. In the past, parents were warned not to spoil their children by handling them too much. This was followed by a period of attentive indulgence. Currently, childrearing advice falls somewhere between these two extremes.

4. "Body language" of an adult primarily refers to facial expressions, movements, and gestures. The body language of an infant includes these as well as physiological measures. A change in arousal level could be used in infants or adults to measure a response to a stimuli. These might include a change in temperature, heart rate, or brain wave activity. Adults also tend to look at what interests them. Tracking eye movements can reveal what a person notices, prefers, or recognizes.

5. Today, researchers and writers, such as Erik Erikson, believe that infants' needs for contact, comfort, and stimulation should be met as fully as possible within the constraints of the caregiver's schedule. Positive contact with a caregiver promotes trust and initiative in the baby.

Unit 6. Language Development

1. Whether gorillas or chimps are truly capable of language is still hotly debated. It really depends on your definition of language.   Your textbook definition may include such characteristics as specialization, arbitrariness, displacement, productivity and novelty, and iteration and recursion. Although animals do use symbols, no animal consistently and naturally organizes symbols according to specific rules. Human language seems to be unique, and humans appear to be uniquely "programmed" to acquire it.   Recent research studies have suggested that there is higher-level communication between gorillas and chimps, and mothers trained in signs and symbols can transfer their learning to their offspring. The debate goes on.

2. Language helps structure thought, and people use words to think, solve problems, and define and use concepts. But thinking also involves visual and sensory images. Certain cognitive operations, but not all, are dependent on language.

3. Nonverbal communication includes body movements, postures, gestures, eye contact, and use of physical space. Other important elements of communication include such verbal features as voice intonation, hesitation, and volume. Nonlinguistic and nonverbal elements account for a significant portion of the total message.

4. The pitch and intonations of baby talk elicit the same attention response in some pets as they do in infants. Some people anthropomorphize their animals and thus speak to them as they do to infants. "Baby talk" expresses the warm, nurturing feelings that people have for their pets. Animals may also be sensitive to simple cues in structured interactions, so their responsiveness may reinforce their owners for talking to them in a certain way.

5. Parentese is characterized by a responsiveness to the child's level of language development. A parent whose speech does not adapt to the infant might not provide the cues he or she needs to discriminate sounds, recognize important intonations of the language, or practice social interaction patterns. It might suggest the parent's inability to respond appropriately to the child. The child's language development might be somewhat delayed if there are no other sources of interaction.

6. By the age of six, most children have a skillful and functional command of their own language. However, people refine their use of language throughout their lives, including, but not limited to, expanding vocabulary and improving grammar.

Unit 7. Sensation and Perception

1. To improve the environment for individuals with visual deficits, one could print large labels on medicine bottles and other containers. For people with impaired balance, handrails in hallways and safety rails in bathrooms could be installed. To adjust for hearing loss, background noise could be reduced by better insulation, and blinking lights that indicate when the phone is ringing could be installed. For those with a loss of sensitivity to smells, smoke detectors or fire alarms could be

installed. And, if loss of smell is affecting appetite, special effort should go into planning a diet to enhance flavors and ensure adequate nutrition.

2. Some people assert that those who practice and promote ESP are abusing science, particularly at a time when public decisions depend on the application of good science. Others decry the spending of money on worthless books and gadgets. Admittedly, science cannot fully explain many phenomena, and people turn in frustration to miracle cures, often accepting irrational explanations that do not hold up under rigorous and repeated scientific testing. Yet people continue to support those who promote belief in the paranormal.

3. The eye is constantly organizing and interpreting visual information. Graphic artists use proximity, similarity, closure, and continuity to create associations and meaning. For example, a car ad may suggest dependability, safety, or excitement, depending on who is driving the car, its color, and where it is. A cereal ad may establish it as a fun food or health food. Notice the people who are eating the cereal, their age, and the way they are dressed. You should be able to use Gestalt principles in interpreting the purpose and effect of the ad.

4. By training yourself to pay close attention to visual and aural elements, you can become increasingly aware of the purposeful choices directors make and how they use and combine various techniques to influence your perceptions. For example, children's toys are frequently photographed in ads so that they appear larger or sturdier than they really are. In films and television programs, dim lighting, a low camera angle, and shadows are used to create suspense or danger. Music is often used in television and film to evoke certain emotions.

Unit 8. Learning

1. Compulsive gambling could be considered a disease and a learned behavior. There is an organization called Gamblers Anonymous that is based on the same principles as Alcoholics Anonymous. However, analyzing compulsive gambling in terms of antecedents and consequences might suggest ways to eliminate cues that lead to gambling, thereby leading to extinction. The best policy might be to avoid all settings where gambling takes place. Because any winning would serve to reinforce gambling, the best goal for a behavior change program is no gambling. Gambling is reinforced intermittently, and may be very resistant to extinction.

2. Some states are requiring companies to provide incentives such as free gasoline and choice parking spots for car pools, cash bonuses, free or discounted bus passes, and showers for bicyclists. Many communities are increasing parking fees and cracking down on parking violations. And in some major cities, tolls on bridges and in tunnels are reduced or eliminated during rush hours for vehicles carrying three or more passengers.

3. Intention is not always a prerequisite for learning. We learn many behaviors without setting out to do so. However, if intention can help us focus attention, learning is enhanced. To date, there is

little evidence that we can learn while sleeping. When the claims for sleep learning tapes have been investigated by independent researchers, they have not been substantiated.

Unit 9. Remembering and Forgetting

1. Helpful memory strategies include paying attention, minimizing distractions and interference, and encoding information in more than one way, such as reading out loud, outlining important points, or chunking information in some personally meaningful way. It is also helpful to add meaning by linking new facts and ideas to familiar information, to use visual imagery, to review material distributed in study sessions, to study before going to sleep, and to over learn material.

2. Recall of childhood memories is often difficult if not impossible. The schemas we used as children are very different from the ones we have developed as adults. Most people reconstruct memories from family stories or photographs. Language helps us label and organize memories. There is also evidence that early memories may be lost due to physiological maturation.

3. The ABC song offers many devices to aid retention. The letters are chunked or grouped in units that conform to the capacity of short-term memory. The letters at the end of each phrase rhyme, which is a mnemonic device. The song encodes the information in sounds as well as in movements. And the fun of it also motivates multiple rehearsals and performances.

4. Most of us are justifiably impressed with the capacity of our long-term memory. Society esteems and rewards people for good memories, starting in early childhood. Playing trivia games can set off a host of associations to events and ideas that we often don't even know we have in memory.

5. There is substantial controversy over what "leading" questions do to memories. The way a person perceives and recalls an event depends on perceptual and cognitive biases that even the eyewitness may not be aware of. Jury members are subject to their own biases when they hear and judge testimony. Jury members need to be especially alert to leading questions that might introduce details or prompt a witness to report an event in a particular way. The more informed a jury member is about how memory works, the better he or she may be able to weigh the value of testimony.

Unit 10. Cognitive Processes

1. To interpret the poem you need to consider language rules and underlying structure—word order, forms, endings, and sounds and language patterns. Although there are many strange and made-up words, some clearly echo familiar words—so that there are some built-in associations that imply meaning.

2. Scripts might include types of activities and dress, level of education, achievement, income, social status, family patterns, interests, vacation ideas, restaurant preferences, and health status.

3. Political cartoons juxtapose well-known people and well-known symbols to exaggerate, ridicule, or emphasize a specific quality. Cartoonists use a visual language. They depend on the reader's concepts and schemas, a shared knowledge of common symbols and their associations within a particular society or culture.

4. Definitions of common sense may include the ability to do multilevel processing, to generalize from experience, and to learn. Computers approach tasks in a logical, orderly way according to a specific routine. No computer is self-aware, curious, or interested in a topic. The computer cannot feel happy or good or care about anything. Therefore, it can only calculate; it cannot make the value judgments involved in common-sense decision making.

5. Children have scripts—expectations built on their knowledge of routine experiences. They are also able to learn procedural information and can store and manipulate visual information.

Unit 11. Judgment and Decision Making

1. Doctors might be basing their diagnosis on their experience with a biased sample of the population. They may also have a tendency to err on the side of caution, assuming a person has a strep throat and treating it rather than not treating a possibly seriously ill patient. In addition, doctors know that test results are not always 100 percent accurate, and they may have difficulty accepting a result that differs from their own opinion.

2. Pitfalls of problem solving include the inability to define the problem, to be illogical in situations in which emotions are involved, and reluctance to consider opposing points of view. People also depend on certain familiar approaches and strategies and often do not recognize when these are no longer useful. Cognitive bias and mental shortcuts also cause people to draw false conclusions or make bad decisions.

3. A child with these qualities might easily be considered precocious, disruptive, or difficult. Although most teachers respond positively to children with good verbal skills, schools typically put more emphasis on following the rules. This may be difficult for the creative, independent child.

4. The experimental method requires exploring alternate possibilities to the hypothesis. It also requires searching for other possible explanations for the conclusions and setting up double-blind situations. Good researchers are always interested in challenging their assumptions and replicating their findings.

Unit 12. Motivation and Emotion

1. An individual's sexual script is based on a unique combination of personal, social, and cultural beliefs and attitudes. Scripts are influenced by family role models, the media, and feedback from social experiences. Boys and girls are typically treated differently during development. Cultural stereotypes tend to reinforce some personal choices and not others. Sexual scripts are often not overtly expressed and may be a source of friction and disappointment in a relationship. If a couple can talk about mismatched role expectations and values, they may be able to negotiate a shared script. The threat of AIDS and other sexually transmitted diseases may change the norms governing sexual activity and thereby rewrite the social scripts that guide sexual behavior. Expect to see changes in what characterizes an acceptable mate, dating patterns, and other relationship issues.

2. The optimist tends to emphasize global, external, and changeable or unstable reasons for failure, while claiming all the credit for success. The pessimist attributes success to luck or other random events out of his or her control and tends to take personal blame for failure.

3. In general, position, movement, and gestures provide clues to emotional states. Some people are more controlled than others, and some are better at picking up body language or clues than others. Being able to infer meaning or spot a discrepancy between words and body language is easier if you know the person well. For example, a mother can read subtle signs in her child. One spouse can sometimes tell if something is bothering the other. Although generalizations can be made, it is very difficult to interpret gestures or other forms of nonverbal communication when you are not familiar with a person or his or her culture.

4. The principle of motivation states that, typically, people are motivated to approach those activities or goals that increase pleasure and to avoid those that cause pain. Although food is generally thought of as something pleasurable, even as a reward or incentive, people with eating disorders see food as something to avoid. They distort or inhibit their eating behavior in an attempt to achieve an idealized body shape.

5. Both extreme happiness and sadness create physiological changes. Stress occurs when the body attempts to adapt to these changes. If adaptation results in prolonged arousal, the body becomes exhausted and illness may even occur.

6. How you respond might be determined by your need for achievement. If you believed you could get an A, you probably would want a grade. Your motivation to study might be reduced by the less rewarding pass/fail option. If you thought you could only earn a C, a pass/fail option might be

more appealing. You would eliminate the potentially handicapping stress of working for a grade. Working for a grade might also interfere with your intrinsic motivation to learn. If you were very interested in the course but didn't want the pressure of working hard, you would not need the incentive of being graded, and a pass/fail option would be more appealing.

Unit 13. The Mind Awake and Asleep

1. Filter theory states that there are limits on early stages of perception. Other sensory information is held briefly but not processed. Although attention reduces confusion and sensory overload, it is not an all-or-nothing situation. There is some screening of the sensory input for meaningful information and some partial analysis below a level of conscious awareness.

2. Mindlessness enables us to deal with far more information than we could handle if sensory inputs had to go through conscious processing item by item. But mindlessness can be maladaptive if a situation requires new discriminations and new adaptations.

3. In the sense that perception is influenced by norms and expectations, our selective attention can be said to be determined by cultural context. We form concepts based on experience and language. Our perceptual habits are influenced by the environment and by the culture, which communicates what is important to notice and remember. Language helps to categorize elements of experience. But personal motivation and individual characteristics also create enormous variation within cultures.

Unit 14. The Mind Hidden and Divided

1. Illness, love, and grief can cause many changes in mental functioning typically associated with altered consciousness. Love and grief particularly can cause people to experience intense or extensive changes in consciousness and behavior.

2. Treatment should take into account the social and psychological factors as well as the chemical effects and physiological factors. Drug education programs must prepare students to evaluate the social and psychological components of drug use that lead to dependence and addiction. Some drug education programs aimed at children attempt to establish a certain mind-set that counteracts peer and cultural pressures and promotes critical thinking about prodrug messages.

3. Effects of extensive television viewing include heightened arousal and suggestibility, depression, and lowered motivation, as well as a distorted sense of time, disorientation, impulsivity, and hyperactivity, especially in children. Studies tend to be contradictory. Prolonged inactivity can lead to a kind of stimulus deprivation. Young children do not have the intellectual ability or sufficient experience and information to distinguish fantasy from reality, so they may be confused by the distortions of reality they see on television.

Unit 15. The Self

1. One interpretation of the poem is that the speaker has a poor self-image, is lonely, and feels unappreciated. However, the speaker seems to use the self-serving bias to suggest that people who are popular are always bragging and croaking about themselves. So being a nobody may be better than being a somebody.

2. Shy people tend to be pessimistic. They have more social anxieties than those who are not shy. Shy people also tend to anticipate rejection and social failure and to interpret social encounters negatively, thus confirming their sense of inadequacy and helplessness.

3. The id is the driving energy of our passion, curiosity, and excitement. According to Freud, it is the life force that operates on the pleasure principle. On the positive side, it is the drive for self-preservation. It is also the place where sexual urges arise, thus ensuring the survival of the species. The fantasies of the id are the basis for imagination and creative endeavors. The id also contains aggressive and destructive drives that can be turned against the self or against society.

4. Your answer is probably yes, that different experiences of success or failure can change your sense of efficacy and your level of self-esteem. But success and failure are relative. If a task is too easy, it doesn't help a person with a low self-esteem. Also, research has suggested that self-esteem is often affected by a social referent. An extremely attractive person sitting next to you before a job interview might make you feel dissatisfied with yourself, but a disheveled or unattractive person might make you feel better about yourself.

5. The information is so universal that anyone can see him- or herself in the description. The information is usually easy to accept because it is so general. Anyone can think of a time when he or she was generous or selfish, gregarious or shy.

Unit 16. Testing and Intelligence

1. No. Environment still has an important influence on the expression of any trait or ability. This is obvious from studies of development in enriched and impoverished environments. Impoverished environments lower a person's test performance. Both heredity and environment play a role.

2. Some might say that people already tend to sort and segregate themselves according to intelligence, even if judgments are based on informal, personal assessments. If IQs become public knowledge, this might have the largest effect on those at the top and bottom of the scale, leading to institutionalized forms of discrimination.

3. Educational systems tend to classify children, and the labels can last a lifetime. Some standardized tests determine whether a child has access to a particular school curriculum, training program, or college. For a student with a very high test score everything he or she does is cast in a favorable

light. On the other hand, there can be considerable pressure to perform well. Test results can also lead to a narrowing of expectations. People who do not perform well on intelligence tests may lose motivation as well as their sense of self-efficacy and self-esteem. The results become part of a self-fulfilling prophecy.

4. Projective tests use ambiguous images to elicit information thought to reveal inner feelings, concerns, values, needs, conflicts, and personality traits. This information is combined with data gathered in other ways to obtain a complete personality description. Intelligence test performance may be one of those additional assessments used to build a rounded picture of a person. Intelligence is usually considered to be independent of creativity. Studies show that people who score high on intelligence tests are not necessarily creative. Projective tests have been used to assess creativity. Both tests of intelligence and creativity may include measures of cognitive style.

5. Intelligence tests and psychological assessments attempt to avoid personal bias and to obtain an objective measure of a person's abilities. However, the tests can be used as a short-cut in place of a more thorough and personalized evaluation. Tests are often misunderstood and misapplied. People have an inappropriate reverence for scores. Few people question the authority of a computer printout. Objections to the tests include claims that they are not objective and that they do not measure what they are intended to measure. People often use tests to focus on what is wrong with the individual instead of considering what is wrong with the system. Test scores have been used to argue for the heritability of intelligence, which has important public policy implications for immigration, education, employment, and affirmative action.

Unit 17. Sex and Gender

1. A person's sexual script includes knowing which behaviors are acceptable and unacceptable. It includes personal and social norms that prescribe what to do, when, where, how, and with whom. This may include rules that dictate who opens doors and who picks up the check. Gender roles are an important part of the scripts that influence interpersonal and sexual behavior. When people share complementary scripts they may be more compatible than people whose expectations and preferences do not mesh.

2. Merely knowing if someone is male or female leads to an exaggeration of gender differences. From the beginning, infants are perceived to be female or male although differences in appearance and behavior are negligible. Research shows how the same behavior may be judged differently depending on whether it is done by a man or a woman. A man's protest, say, over a course grade, may be perceived as assertive, but the same behavior by a woman may be judged pushy. Judgments about the suitability of people for particular jobs and occupations sometimes ignore individual traits and are based solely on gender.

3. Children show different play and toy preferences. Research has shown that as early as four years of age children choose to play with members of their own sex and in same-sex play groups.

4. Male traits are often perceived as more desirable by both men and women. Being assertive, achieving, and independent seems related to a better self-concept for both men and women. In general, the labels used to describe male traits are more positive. However, in judging the relative merits of masculine and feminine traits for adjustment, it is important to specify exactly what that means. For example, one study suggests that feminine traits contribute to happier marriages.

5. Some people insist that it doesn't make a difference, but many past studies have shown that both men and women make different judgments based on the sex of the author. In general, articles are viewed more favorably when study participants believed they were written by a man. However, recent evidence suggests that this effect has diminished, and ratings of works by men and women are converging in the 1990s.

Unit 18. Maturing and Aging

1. Until recently, the study of aging was dominated by pathology, studies of the sick elderly. Now that there are large numbers of healthy, active older people, the focus of research has changed. Statistics show that most older people do not fit the stereotype of the frail elderly. Some of the psychological problems and memory loss can be attributed to drug interactions, lack of stimulation, or the feeling of a loss of control. Studies can show the effects of life-style and environment. Problems of depression, for example, might affect anyone who suffered the loss of loved ones, a job, intellectual stimulation, or control over his or her own life. Also, it shouldn't be considered an oddity that elderly people talk more about the past; they have more past than future. Comparing the status of the elderly in different cultures reveals the influence of cultural attitudes and social patterns.

2. The midlife crisis, an emotional upheaval or disorientation, is a process of self-assessment in which individuals confront such issues as the value of their lives, their social roles and relationships, the gap between their dreams and accomplishments, and the realities of aging and death. Of course, not everyone goes through a crisis. In fact, some experts believe that "crisis" is too strong a word.

3. Any changes in intelligence depend on how one defines and measures intelligence. Not all cognitive abilities change at the same rate. Some decline, some improve, and some stay the same. Data on IQs collected using the cross-sectional method show more decline than results obtained from longitudinal studies. There is also some evidence that shows that fluid intelligence primarily related to speed of CNS functioning tends to decline in adult years, while crystallized intelligence, primarily related to the application of knowledge, tends to increase.

4. The social conditions and economic constraints and opportunities of every generation shape the attitudes, expectations, and values characteristic of different age groups in society. For example, increasing the ethnic and cultural diversity of the cities, the growing number of women who delay marriage and childbearing, changing sexual attitudes and values, and the rise in the divorce rate will all affect the social characteristics of the adult and elderly population of the future. The increase in the numbers of healthy, active older adults will change the way young people view older people

and how older people view themselves. The need for older people to contribute to the economic system has already begun to change policies and attitudes about early retirement.

5. Social attitudes and economic conditions determine which changes and responsibilities are considered appropriate for adult roles. For example, the age at which marriage is acceptable or at which children are expected to become self-supporting is often set by economic and social conditions in the larger society.

6. Being a parent was once the norm. Taking on the responsibilities of parenthood was one of the major milestones in adult development and was considered the step that moved a person from a stage of selfishness to a stage in which nurturing and intimacy become a priority. However, not everyone accepts the idea that having children is the only way to be productive, creative, and nurturing.

Unit 19. The Power of the Situation

1. Milgram's subjects could avoid blaming themselves if they reasoned that the situation was influencing their behavior. They could rationalize that they were only following orders and did not have to accept responsibility for their behavior. Thus they could avoid guilt, much as the Nazis did when they claimed they were only following orders.

2. Many patients are intimidated by their doctor's expertise. They defer to the doctor's greater medical knowledge and stifle their doubts and fears. Because patients assume that doctors have the education and training to handle medical problems, many patients do not feel qualified to question the doctor's judgments. If patients disagree with their doctors they may not fill a prescription or take prescribed medication. They may change doctors without notice or explanation. Or they make seek out a second opinion. Today, movements to promote patients' rights and advances in patient education make questioning medical authority more acceptable.

3. Roles involve expectations about behavior. Roles and social obligations are sometimes perceived as social traps, especially when behavior is dictated by social expectations and norms rather than by personal feelings and individual taste. You may conform only to win approval or to avoid social rejection. For example, being respected in the community might require church attendance, even if you are not a believer. When social expectations conflict with feelings, alienation or resentment may result. When behavior coincides with role expectations, it reinforces a sense of true identity.

4. Everyone has had good and bad teachers and bosses. Choose specific situations and analyze the style of authority or leadership. Analyze your participation and performance. In which situation did you learn or accomplish the most? In which situation did people support and help each other the most? Which situations were most relaxed?

5. Although extreme examples of blind obedience, such as Nazi Germany or even Milgram's experiment, are easy to identify, there are many ambiguous situations in which the difference is not

so clear. In schools, churches, and the workplace, cooperation is highly esteemed and compliance is usually rewarded. Efforts to undermine authority are typically considered to be a threat by the leader of the group. Parents and teachers tend to reinforce compliant behavior in children. It may be useful to cite examples of people who buck authority and to help illustrate possibilities for legitimate dissent. However, most research on social influence shows that unquestioning obedience is the norm.

Unit 20. Constructing Social Reality

1. Individuals do not respond to situations identically. Some individuals have such strong personal values and self confidence that they do not seek social approval as much as others. Also, people usually choose what they hear and watch. They can turn off the television, ignore a program, or walk out of the movie theater. They can read selectively, actively looking for articles that support their ideas or challenge them. They can associate with people who share their beliefs and opinions or purposely expose themselves to new ideas and experiences.

2. Nationalism can be a source of pride and cohesiveness for a population. However, this is all too often gained at the expense of making certain classes of people into internal or external enemies. These out-groups are used to divert attention from national problems and often become a target for anger. Nationalism can encourage "us versus them" thinking and escalate conflicts. An "us versus them" mentality is simple to create. It depends only on drawing some distinction—meaningless and arbitrary, or meaningful—between groups of people.

3. Rosenthal's experiment would probably not meet today's ethical standards. Children cannot legally give their consent. Therefore, they would not be willing participants according to ethical guidelines. Also, there might be some harm done to a child's self-esteem by the arbitrary manipulation of the success of some of the children and not others.

4. Dissonance reduction, the self-serving bias, and defense mechanisms are very similar. They are all efforts to reduce anxiety or resolve an apparent conflict between desirable self-perceptions and unacceptable attitudes and actions.

5. Children who watch television tend to think that there is more violence in the streets than there really is. At the same time, they rarely experience the true impact of violence. They tend to see men and women in stereotyped roles and relationships. In most situation comedies, problems get resolved in 30 minutes.

Unit 21. Psychopathology

1. Courts differ on how they deal with the insanity defense. In order for a person to be excused from legal responsibility for criminal actions, the defense must demonstrate severely impaired judgment and lack of self-control. A person is not considered legally responsible if he or she is unable to distinguish right from wrong. The definition may vary from country to country, from state to state, even from court to court. It is a highly controversial issue.

2. The *Diagnostic and Statistical Manual* has been criticized for inflating disorders, basing some criteria on myth rather than on empirical evidence, and for stigmatizing people. It is also, clearly, a relative assessment guide subject to cultural forces. For example, homosexuality was once characterized as a disorder. Today, the self-defeating personality has been proposed as a disorder to be included. Women's groups and others are very concerned that such a label will lead to a blaming of the victim.

3. Statistically, homosexuality is unusual. However, cultural standards are relative. Psychological assessments show no differences in personality or adjustment between heterosexuals and homosexuals. Today, the DSM-III does not list homosexuality as a disorder. It is considered a problem only if it causes guilt or self-hate. However, at one time homosexuality was considered a disorder.

4. Women may be more willing to talk about distress and emotional problems. They are more often denied opportunities for independence and achievement and may feel angry, hopeless, or helpless, justifiably. There is a male bias toward traditional concepts of mental health.

5. Many psychological problems are just extreme instances of behavior that most of us exhibit at one time or another. If you are extremely worried about a certain behavior, if the behavior is disruptive to relationships, or if it has become a persistent problem, you might consider getting a professional evaluation.

6. Split personality, which is a dissociative disorder, is commonly confused with schizophrenia, a term that was often used as a grab-bag definition for any condition that did not fit neatly into other classifications. Today, psychologists define schizophrenia as the breakdown of integrated personality functioning, withdrawal from reality, emotional distortions, and a disturbed thought process.

Unit 22. Psychotherapy

1. It is difficult to determine the success of a particular therapy because faith in the effectiveness of any treatment may be enough to bring about changes in a patient's feelings or behavior. Also, some problems resolve themselves over time without professional intervention.

2. Comparison of therapies is difficult. There is enormous variation among patients and the intensity and duration of their problems, so that therapies are very individualized. There are also differences in the training, expertise, and personality of individual therapists. Criteria for successful outcomes will vary with the specific problem and type of therapy.

3. Finding the right match between a problem and an approach to therapy starts with how you define the problem and your attitude or beliefs about the kind of help you need. A person might seek assistance in making the decision from a physician or person in the community who is familiar with available resources and services.

4. Unit 22 describes therapies that focus on illness and problem solving, as well as on those designed to address life management issues, self-esteem, relationships, and potential. Most people, at some time, could benefit from professional intervention.

5. In American culture, there is typically a stigma associated with seeking help of any kind. Our culture emphasizes individuality, self-sufficiency, and strength, especially for men. That makes it harder to admit weakness or the need for support.

Unit 23. Health, Mind, and Behavior

1. Friends can help reduce stress in several ways. They can offer practical help. For example, when there is illness or a crisis in a family, friends can relieve temporary concerns about money, child care, food, or transportation needs. They can also offer emotional support, being there to listen and empathize with you about what you are going through and reassuring you that you are not going crazy even when you feel most vulnerable and confused. Friends may also offer advice in an unfamiliar situation, helping you to think through decisions. Social support makes people less vulnerable to stress-related problems. Social networks counteract a sense of isolation by providing a sense of belonging. In support groups, individuals help each other by providing a social reference group. They share advice, feelings, and information specific to the situation.

2. Victims of a curse may feel such intense or prolonged fear that it wears down the body's ability to cope. One theory suggests that the body's attempt to counteract an extreme emotional reaction may go too far, slowing down important systems and processes to the point of death.

3. Most people use defense mechanisms at times. Some defenses help us gain time to adjust to a trauma or other type of problem. Rationalization may be a stress-reducing strategy in the face of frustration or failure. Any defense mechanism can be part of a coping approach, but it may prevent us from confronting and solving our real problems if it becomes habitual.

4. Self-defeating thoughts undermine a person's sense of self-esteem, optimism, efficacy, and control—all necessary for adequate coping.

5. Perfectionists unnecessarily stress themselves by setting impossible goals and standards. They may compare themselves with inappropriate models of achievement, never being satisfied with their own accomplishments. They may feel they have inadequate resources to measure up to their unreasonably high standards. These attitudes can create stress and can undermine their ability to perform.

Unit 24. In Space, Toward Peace

1. Basic or pure research is done for the sake of knowledge, while applied research is designed to solve concrete problems. For example, investigators doing basic research that focuses on the genetic influences on brain chemistry may simply be interested in defining, understanding, and predicting the effects of chemical reactions in the brain. Eventually the information may be applied. It may be used to plan treatment to correct abnormal brain conditions or to alter brain chemistry in an attempt to cure certain diseases.

2. When we call a machine "user friendly" we mean that it is easy to use. Its controls and displays are designed with human comfort and sensory and motor abilities in mind. The design of the machine minimizes mistakes and may even anticipate and correct mistakes. Organizational psychologists also address practical concerns and quality-of-life issues in the workplace. They influence organization effectiveness by applying their skills and insights to solving problems of human relations, communication, mediation, employee selection and training, leadership, job satisfaction, and stress.

3. Yes. People can use principles of persuasion and coercion to influence the behavior of others. For example, cults use carefully structured methods to recruit and convert new members. Advertisers might design campaigns to persuade people to buy things they don't need. Con artists use principles and techniques to sell products and to enlist cooperation from people.

CUMULATIVE GLOSSARY OF PROGRAM TERMS

agonist—a chemical or drug that mimics the action of a neurotransmitter

amnesia—partial or complete loss of memory of information or past events

androgynous—having both masculine and feminine traits

antagonist—a chemical or drug that blocks the action of a neurotransmitter

applied psychology—the practical application of psychological knowledge and principles to concrete problems

arousal—a heightened level of excitation or activation

autocratic—governed by one person with unlimited power

behavioral confirmation—a form of social feedback in which our self-beliefs determine how we are perceived and evaluated by others

beta-endorphin—a type of opioid which, under conditions of maternal deprivation, can block the action of the early regulators of insulin and growth hormone

biological biasing—a genetic predisposition that increases the likelihood of getting a disorder if exposed to prolonged or intense stress

biological senescing—growing older physically, or biological aging

cognitive control—the power of beliefs to give meaning to a situation

cognitive developmental theory—the theory stating that children use male and female as fundamental categories and actively sex-type themselves to achieve cognitive consistency

democratic—practicing social equality

developmental strategies—behaviors that have evolved to conform to the sex roles typical of the adult members of a species

disposition—a person's internal or personal characteristics

double-blind procedure—an experimental procedure in which neither the researcher nor the subject knows which subjects are receiving the real treatment and which are getting the placebo

dread factor—the fear of unfamiliar or potentially catastrophic events which makes us judge them to be riskier than familiar events

enzymes—protein molecules that act as catalysts in body chemistry by facilitating chemical reactions

ERP (event-related potentials)—variations in brain waves as recorded by the electroencephalogram (EEG) which are triggered by specific internal or external events

field study—research carried on outside the laboratory where naturally occurring, ongoing behavior can be observed

framing—the way information is presented which tends to bias how it is interpreted

genetic counseling—counseling that advises a person about the probability of passing on defective genes to offspring

glucocorticoids—substances produced by the adrenal cortex that act on the hippocampus to alter the stress response

Heisenberg indeterminacy principle—principle stating that our impressions of other people are distorted by how we observe and assess them

hypnagogic state—a period of reveries at the onset of the sleeping state

hypnotic analgesia—lack of pain perception while under hypnosis

invariance—the principle stating that preferences between options should be independent of different representations

jet lag—a sense of disorientation caused by disruption of internal circadian rhythms

laissez-faire—allowing complete freedom, with little or no interference or guidance

language acquisition device—the innate ability to acquire language; a hypothesis put forth by Noam Chomsky

legitimate authority—a form of power exercised by someone in a superior role such as a teacher or president

life-span development—developmental changes continuing throughout the life cycle

LSD—lysergic acid diethylamide, a hallucinogen

lucid dreaming—the awareness of dreaming without awakening, and sometimes the ability to control the content of a dream

maternal deprivation—the lack of adequate affection and stimulation from the mother or mother substitute

micro level—the smallest unit of analysis in psychology; for example, studying P-300 brain waves or other neural or biochemical changes

molar level—the analysis of larger units of behavior of the whole person in complex situations, taking into account cultural background and social experiences

molecular level—the analysis of discrete, observable behaviors such as body language, crying, or laughing

morpheme—the smallest unit of language that has meaning

optimism—the tendency to attribute failure to external, unstable, or changeable factors and to attribute success to stable factors

parentese—modified speech that parallels children's level of language development

pessimism—the tendency to attribute failure to stable or internal factors and to attribute success to global variables

phoneme—the smallest unit of sound that affects the meaning of speech

posthypnotic amnesia—forgetting selected events by suggestion

prejudice—a bias for or against someone formed without sufficient information

psychic numbing—being emotionally unaffected by an upsetting or alarming event

psychogenic—organic malfunction or tissue damage caused by anxiety, tension, or depression

psycholinguists—scientists who study how the structure of language is related to speaking and listening

psychological adolescing—developing psychologically to full potential

Pygmalion effect—the effect of positive and negative expectations on behavior

random sample—an unbiased population selected at random

receptor—a specialized nerve cell sensitive to particular kinds of stimulus energy

reference standard—a norm or model of behavior that is used to decide how to behave in a particular situation

selective optimization—making the most of what you have

self-handicapping—a process by which we try to explain away potential failures by blaming them on something other than our lack of ability

senile dementia—biochemical and neuronal changes in the brain that lead to a gradual reduction in mental efficiency

sex typing—the psychological process by which boys and girls become masculine or feminine

shyness—a form of social anxiety caused by the expectation of negative social evaluation

similarity heuristic—an error based on the tendency to see a connection between belonging to a certain category and having the characteristics considered typical of members of that category

social learning theory—the theory stating that children are socialized by observing role models and are rewarded or punished for behaving appropriately

stage theory—a theory that describes development as a fixed sequence of distinct periods of life

status transaction—a form of interpersonal communication in which we establish relative degrees of social status and power

stereotype—the belief that all members of a group share common traits

subjective reality—the perceptions and beliefs that we accept without question

syntax—a set of rules for combining words into phrases and sentences

time-limited dynamic psychotherapy—a form of short-term therapy